W9-CJN-512

ELIZABETH CADY STANTON

ELIZABETH CADY STANTON

Pamela Loos

CHELSEA HOUSE PUBLISHERS
PHILADELPHIA

Frontispiece: Elizabeth Cady Stanton—women's rights leader, social critic, and reformer. Stanton was one of the organizers of the 1848 women's rights convention in the United States, where for the first time women publicly requested the right to vote.

Chelsea House Publishers
EDITOR IN CHIEF Stephen Reginald
PRODUCTION MANAGER Pamela Loos
ART DIRECTOR Sara Davis
DIRECTOR OF PHOTOGRAPHY Judy L. Hasday
MANAGING EDITOR James D. Gallagher
SENIOR PRODUCTION EDITOR J. Christopher Higgins

Staff for **Elizabeth Cady Stanton**
SENIOR EDITOR Lee Anne Gelletly
ASSISTANT EDITOR Rob Quinn
ASSOCIATE ART DIRECTOR/DESIGNER Takeshi Takahashi
PICTURE RESEARCHER Patricia Burns
COVER ILLUSTRATOR Cliff Spohn
COVER DESIGNER Keith Trego

The Chelsea House World Wide Web address is
http://www.chelseahouse.com

3 5 7 9 8 6 4 2

Library of Congress Cataloging-in-Publication Data

Loos, Pamela.
Elizabeth Cady Stanton / Pamela Loos.
   p. cm. — (Women of achievement)
Includes bibliographical references and index.
ISBN 0-7910-5293-1 — ISBN 0-7910-5286-9 (pbk.)
1. Stanton, Elizabeth Cady, 1815–1902—Juvenile literature. 2.
Suffragists—United States—Biography—Juvenile literature. 3. Women—
Suffrage—United States—Juvenile literature. [1. Stanton, Elizabeth Cady,
1815–1902. 2. Suffragists. 3. Women's rights. 4. Women—Suffrage. 5.
Women—Biography.] I. Title. II. Series.

HQ1413.S67 L66 2000
324.6'23'092—dc21
[B]
                                                    00-031536

CONTENTS

WOMEN of ACHIEVEMENT

Jane Addams
SOCIAL WORKER

Madeleine Albright
STATESWOMAN

Marian Anderson
SINGER

Susan B. Anthony
WOMAN SUFFRAGIST

Clara Barton
AMERICAN RED CROSS FOUNDER

Margaret Bourke-White
PHOTOGRAPHER

Rachel Carson
BIOLOGIST AND AUTHOR

Cher
SINGER AND ACTRESS

Hillary Rodham Clinton
FIRST LADY AND ATTORNEY

Katie Couric
JOURNALIST

Diana, Princess of Wales
HUMANITARIAN

Emily Dickinson
POET

Elizabeth Dole
POLITICIAN

Amelia Earhart
AVIATOR

Gloria Estefan
SINGER

Jodie Foster
ACTRESS AND DIRECTOR

Betty Friedan
FEMINIST

Althea Gibson
TENNIS CHAMPION

Ruth Bader Ginsburg
SUPREME COURT JUSTICE

Helen Hayes
ACTRESS

Katharine Hepburn
ACTRESS

Mahalia Jackson
GOSPEL SINGER

Helen Keller
HUMANITARIAN

**Ann Landers/
Abigail Van Buren**
COLUMNISTS

Barbara McClintock
BIOLOGIST

Margaret Mead
ANTHROPOLOGIST

Edna St. Vincent Millay
POET

Julia Morgan
ARCHITECT

Toni Morrison
AUTHOR

Grandma Moses
PAINTER

Lucretia Mott
WOMAN SUFFRAGIST

Sandra Day O'Connor
SUPREME COURT JUSTICE

Rosie O'Donnell
ENTERTAINER AND COMEDIAN

Georgia O'Keeffe
PAINTER

Eleanor Roosevelt
DIPLOMAT AND HUMANITARIAN

Wilma Rudolph
CHAMPION ATHLETE

Elizabeth Cady Stanton
WOMAN SUFFRAGIST

Harriet Beecher Stowe
AUTHOR AND ABOLITIONIST

Barbra Streisand
ENTERTAINER

Elizabeth Taylor
ACTRESS AND ACTIVIST

Mother Teresa
HUMANITARIAN AND
RELIGIOUS LEADER

Barbara Walters
JOURNALIST

Edith Wharton
AUTHOR

Phillis Wheatley
POET

Oprah Winfrey
ENTERTAINER

Babe Didrikson Zaharias
CHAMPION ATHLETE

"REMEMBER THE LADIES"

MATINA S. HORNER

"Remember the Ladies." That is what Abigail Adams wrote to her husband John, then a delegate to the Continental Congress, as the Founding Fathers met in Philadelphia to form a new nation in March of 1776. "Be more generous and favorable to them than your ancestors. Do not put such unlimited power in the hands of the Husbands. If particular care and attention is not paid to the Ladies," Abigail Adams warned, "we are determined to foment a Rebellion, and will not hold ourselves bound by any Laws in which we have no voice, or Representation."

The words of Abigail Adams, one of the earliest American advocates of women's rights, were prophetic. Because when we have not "remembered the ladies," they have, by their words and deeds, reminded us so forcefully of the omission that we cannot fail to remember them. For the history of American women is as interesting and varied as the history of our nation as a whole. American women have played an integral part in founding, settling, and building our country. Some we remember as remarkable women who—against great odds—achieved distinction in the public arena: Anne Hutchinson, who in the 17th century became a charismatic religious leader; Phillis Wheatley, an 18th-century black slave who became a poet; Susan B. Anthony, whose name is synonymous with the 19th-century women's rights movement, and who led the struggle to enfranchise women; and in the 20th century, Amelia Earhart, the first woman to cross the Atlantic Ocean by air.

These extraordinary women certainly merit our admiration, but other women, "common women," many of them all but forgotten, should also be recognized for their contributions to American thought and culture. Women have been community builders; they have founded schools and formed voluntary associations to help those in need; they have assumed the major responsibility for rearing children, passing on from one generation to the next the values that keep a culture alive. These and innumerable other contributions, once ignored, are now being recognized by scholars, students, and the public. It is exciting and gratifying that a part of our history that was hardly acknowledged a few generations ago is now being studied and brought to light.

In recent decades, the field of women's history has grown from obscurity to a politically controversial splinter movement to academic respectability, in many cases mainstreamed into such traditional disciplines as history, economics, and psychology. Scholars of women, both female and male, have organized research centers at such prestigious institutions as Wellesley College, Stanford University, and the University of California. Other notable centers for women's studies are the Center for the American Woman and Politics at the Eagleton Institute of Politics at Rutgers University; the Henry A. Murray Research Center for the Study of Lives, at Radcliffe College; and the Women's Research and Education Institute, the research arm of the Congressional Caucus on Women's Issues. Other scholars and public figures have established archives and libraries, such as the Schlesinger Library on the History of Women in America, at Radcliffe College, and the Sophia Smith Collection, at Smith College, to collect and preserve the written and tangible legacies of women.

From the initial donation of the Women's Rights Collection in 1943, the Schlesinger Library grew to encompass vast collections documenting the manifold accomplishments of American women. Simultaneously, the women's movement in general and the academic discipline of women's studies in particular also began with a narrow definition and gradually expanded their mandate. Early causes, such as woman suffrage and social reform, abolition, and organized labor were joined by newer concerns, such as the history of women in business and the professions and in politics and government; the study of the family; and social issues such as health policy and education.

Women, as historian Arthur M. Schlesinger, jr., once pointed out, "have constituted the most spectacular casualty of traditional history. They have made up at least half the human race, but you could never tell that by looking at the books historians write." The new breed of historians is remedying that omission. They have written books about immigrant women and about working-class women who struggled for survival in cities and about black women who met the challenges of life in rural areas. They are telling the stories of women who, despite the barriers of tradition and economics, became lawyers and doctors and public figures.

The women's studies movement has also led scholars to question traditional interpretations of their respective disciplines. For example, the study of war has traditionally been an exercise in military and political analysis, an examination of strategies planned and executed by men. But scholars of women's history have pointed out that wars have also been periods of tremendous change and even opportunity for women, because the very absence of men on the home front enabled them to expand their educational, economic, and professional activities and to assume leadership in their homes.

The early scholars of women's history showed a unique brand of courage in choosing to investigate new subjects and take new approaches to old ones. Often, like their subjects, they endured criticism and even ostracism by their academic colleagues. But their efforts have unquestionably been worthwhile, because with the publication of each new study and book another piece of the historical patchwork is sewn into place, revealing an increasingly comprehensive picture of the role of women in our rich and varied history.

Such books on groups of women are essential, but books that focus on the lives of individuals are equally indispensable. Biographies can be inspirational, offering their readers the example of people with vision who have looked outside themselves for their goals and have often struggled against great obstacles to achieve them. Marian Anderson, for instance, had to overcome racial bigotry in order to perfect her art and perform as a concert singer. Isadora Duncan defied the rules of classical dance to find true artistic freedom. Jane Addams had to break down society's notions of the proper role for women in order to create new social situations, notably the settlement house. All of these women had to come to terms both with themselves and with the world in which they lived. Only then could they move ahead as pioneers in their chosen callings.

Biography can inspire not only by adulation but also by realism. It helps us to see not only the qualities in others that we hope to emulate, but also, perhaps, the weaknesses that made them "human." By helping us identify with the subject on a more personal level they help us feel that we, too, can achieve such goals. We read about Eleanor Roosevelt, for instance, who occupied a unique and seemingly enviable position as the wife of the president. Yet we can sympathize with her inner dilemma; an inherently shy woman, she had to force herself to live a most public life in order to use her position to benefit others. We may not be able to imagine ourselves having the immense poetic talent of Emily Dickinson, but from her story we can understand the challenges faced by a creative woman who was expected to fulfill many family responsibilities. And though few of us will ever reach the level of athletic accomplishment displayed by Wilma Rudolph or Babe Zaharias, we can still appreciate their spirit, their overwhelming will to excel.

A biography is a multifaceted lens. It is first of all a magnification, the intimate examination of one particular life. But at the same time, it is a wide-angle lens, informing us about the world in which the subject lived. We come away from reading about one life knowing more about the social, political, and economic fabric of the time. It is for this reason, perhaps, that the great New England essayist Ralph Waldo Emerson wrote in 1841, "There is properly no history: only biography." And it is also why biography, and particularly women's biography, will continue to fascinate writers and readers alike.

At the July 1848 women's rights convention, Elizabeth Cady Stanton listed the grievances of 19th century women. Among other things, they could not enter most professions; their earnings belonged to their husbands; and they were not allowed to vote.

1

THE STRUGGLE
BEGINS

"We hold these truths to be self-evident: that all men and women are created equal."

—Declaration of Sentiments

On a warm July day in 1848, a small group met in a friend's parlor and did just what many might do: they lamented their situation. But what made this discussion so different from any other was that while it certainly started with laments, it grew into a plan for action, and that action, in turn, would trigger a historic movement for women's rights that would persist through the next century and beyond.

The dynamic discussion was led by Elizabeth Cady Stanton, then 33 years old. An intelligent, witty, and self-reliant individual, she was in a "tempest-tossed condition of mind" before she even arrived, as she would later write in her autobiography, *Eighty Years and More*. The group had been invited to the Waterloo, New York, home of Mrs. Richard Hunt, an acquaintance of Elizabeth's friend Lucretia Mott. Elizabeth had met Lucretia, a Quaker minister,

Elizabeth Cady Stanton in an 1848 photograph with two of her sons, Henry (left) and Neil. As the mother of three young sons at that time, Elizabeth felt overwhelmed by household and child-care demands. She shared her concerns with a group of like-minded women, inspiring them "to do and dare anything" about the position of women in society.

eight years before in London, at the World Anti-Slavery Convention.

"It seemed as if all the elements had conspired to impel me to some onward step," Elizabeth later wrote about that July meeting. Recently in her own life, she had come to understand the difficulties of being a mother with many children who were often sick, and a wife whose husband was frequently not at home. She was living in a somewhat remote location where few good servants were available, and away from intellectual enticements and other interesting adults. At the same time, she had come to deeply empathize with the struggling poor women in her neighborhood.

Years ago, Elizabeth had learned of the injustices toward women that existed in early 19th-century America. From her visits to her father's law office and the courtroom itself, she knew of women's limited legal status. Additionally, she remembered the agreement made with Lucretia Mott eight years earlier when the two first met. There at the World Anti-Slavery Convention, amidst a group of the world's most enlightened and open-minded reformers of the time, women were refused participation. Despite the tireless work so many of them had already done for the antislavery movement, they were seated in a sectioned-off gallery. At that convention in 1840, Elizabeth had proposed to Lucretia that they hold their own convention on women's rights in the United States. But after the London meeting, Elizabeth's life had been busy with giving birth to and caring for three young children, which had prevented her from moving ahead with the idea—until now.

While it had taken eight years for the plan to crystallize, Elizabeth was now well prepared. Aside from her own personal frustrations as a young mother and her observations of other struggling women in her neighborhood, Elizabeth had learned of other inequities while corresponding with Lucretia by letter during these interim years. The Quaker minister, who was 20 years Elizabeth's senior, had expansive liberal views on politics, religion, and overall reform. She had groomed Elizabeth in women's issues, recommending that she read works of Mary Wollstonecraft, Frances Wright, and the sisters Angelina and Sarah Grimké.

Aside from what was taking place personally with Elizabeth and the women gathered in the parlor, there were greater reasons for holding a convention now. Revolutionary upheavals were breaking out on the European continent, focusing on equality and political rights. Locally, just a few months before, the state legislature of New York had passed the Married Woman's Property Act. While it contained reforms related only to married women's property rights, with its passage wives gained control over their dowries and inheritances. Previously, a woman's property was solely in the

Eight years before the Seneca Falls convention, Elizabeth Cady Stanton had become close friends with Lucretia Mott when the two met at the World Anti-Slavery Convention in London. Long active in the abolitionist movement, the liberal Quaker minister wrote often to Stanton after meeting her in London, recommending books and offering her views on politics, religion, and reform.

charge of her husband, and in the event of his death, the oldest son assumed that authority. Other states had also modified statutes relating to women's rights. It appeared that the public was ready for change.

"I poured out, that day, the torrent of my long-accumulating discontent, with such vehemence and indignation that I stirred myself, as well as the rest of the party, to do and dare anything," Elizabeth later wrote about that July day in 1848. The five women—Lucretia Mott, her sister Martha C. Wright, Mary Ann McClintock, Jane Hunt, and Elizabeth—started planning a women's rights convention. They published a brief announcement in the local newspaper, the *Seneca County Courier,* the next day. It stated that a women's rights convention would take place in five days at the local Wesleyan Chapel, which was Seneca Falls' Methodist church. Then they quickly prepared.

The women created an agenda, deciding who would speak on the first day of the convention and determining that the second day would be spent reading their list of grievances and demands, and then voting on them. Elizabeth sparked the idea of using the format of their country's Declaration of Independence to state the case for women. Doing so would signify that the convention organizers respected their country and its ideals; it allowed them to protest within a context of tradition.

Elizabeth did most of the writing of the Declaration of Sentiments and its resolutions. The document asserted that women deserved the same freedoms that men had gained as a result of the American Revolution. Just like the original Declaration of Independence, the Declaration of Sentiments listed 18 grievances. Included on the list were the following: only one liberal arts college, Oberlin College, admitted women; women were allowed into few professions, and in the nonprofessional jobs they could hold, they were paid far less than their male counterparts; women had no legal rights with regard to their own children; their earnings belonged to their husbands; and they couldn't vote.

The organizers were not expecting many attendees because the meeting had been announced only locally, without much advance notice, and many farm workers would be busy because it was harvest time. Yet when July 19, the first day of the convention, arrived, the women were elated by the strong turnout. The attendees included reformers, curious townspeople, and Quakers who had broken away from their more conservative communities. Some participants had traveled from as far as Rochester, New York, which was 50 miles away. Despite the intense heat, by the second day of the convention, at least 300 men and women had gathered.

While the convention organizers had previously agreed that men should not be a part of the proceedings, 40 men had come and were allowed to participate. Curiously, the rebellious women succumbed to the tradition of the day that women not lead a meeting where men were present. Although several women did give speeches before the group, James Mott, Lucretia's husband, was enlisted to serve as chairman.

One attendee was Amelia Bloomer, the comanager of the Seneca Falls post office who would later edit and publish a women's publication advocating temperance (restraint in, or abstinence from, drinking alcohol). According to Bloomer, Elizabeth spoke so softly on the first day that she could hardly be heard. Yet while Elizabeth's voice might have been soft, her words were anything but demure. She reprimanded both men and women, criticizing the current belief that men were superior, as well as another popular notion that men and women each had strengths, but only in their respective spheres. She chastised women who had spoken out against, or were indifferent to, women's rights, chiding that too many were wooed into complacency.

Elizabeth warned the gathering that

> [m]en like to call [woman] an angel—to feed her on what they think sweet food—nourishing her vanity; to make her believe that her organization is so much finer than theirs, that she is not fitted to struggle with the tempests of public life, but needs their care and protection!! Care and protection—such as the wolf gives the lamb—such as the eagle the hare he carries to his eyrie!! Most cunningly he entraps her, and then takes from her all those rights which are dearer to him than life itself.

Elizabeth acknowledged that the struggle to obtain equal rights would be difficult: "We do not expect our path will be strewn with the flowers of popular applause, but over the thorns of bigotry and prejudice will be our way." Yet she ended her speech with hope, explaining that reforms would benefit all, not just women:

> The world has never yet seen a truly great and virtuous nation, because in the degradation of woman the very fountains of life are poisoned at their source. . . . God, in his wisdom, has so linked the whole human family together that any violence done at one end of the chain is felt throughout its length, and here, too, is the law of restoration, as in woman all have fallen, so in her elevation shall the race be re-created.

On the second day of the convention, when the Declaration of Sentiments' resolutions were presented, the assembly voted unanimously to pass them all—except one. Rather at the last minute and against Lucretia's advice, Elizabeth had decided to add a resolution for woman suffrage—for women to have the right to vote. While this had been in the list of women's grievances, it hadn't been included in their resolutions, yet Elizabeth had come to believe it imperative. Previously, Elizabeth had talked with the well-known abolitionist (antislavery activist) Frederick Douglass, who was once a slave himself. Douglass had explained that he believed the only way for blacks to achieve true equality was by empowering them with the right to vote. After listening to Douglass, Elizabeth realized the same was true for women.

But at the time of the Seneca Falls meeting, even the abolitionists, who were then much more organized than the women and who had their own radical members, hadn't yet dared request that blacks receive the right to vote. Similarly, publicly asking for women's right to vote was a most drastic move. While women's rights had been publicly debated before, the vote had never been requested. There were many reasons why:

At the Seneca Falls convention, only one of the resolutions initially did not pass—the call for a woman's right to vote. However, the abolitionist Frederick Douglass (above) convinced the assembly that the controversial resolution was necessary, and it just squeaked through.

- For many Quakers, the right to vote in the United States meant participation in a government that believed in war. But all Quakers opposed war and any involvement in it, so votes for such a resolution would not be easily garnered from them at Seneca Falls.
- More generally, the country was going through its own adjustments with democracy and an open economic system—one's name or wealth no longer secured one's status. This uncertainty helped renew more conservative attitudes toward women, since men did not want to feel threatened by them as well.

- Religious revivals and temperance organizations were very popular at the time, and women had major roles in these movements. Many saw women as a calm, secure base for moral reformation that began in the home. Politics, on the other hand, had come to be seen by many as an aggressive, masculine world in which women had no place. Voting polls were frequently set up in barbershops and bars, and heavy drinking and fistfights were not uncommon on election days.

Even Lucretia, known for standing up for what she believed in, felt that requesting that women be allowed the vote was too extreme for the time. Henry Stanton, who had helped his wife create the women's list of resolutions, was extremely upset upon hearing of the added demand for the right to vote. Among other things, he feared that it would seriously jeopardize his role in forming the new abolitionist Free-Soil Party, whose leaders were to meet in just a few weeks. As a result, Henry did not attend the convention. (By November of that year, as it turned out, he would be elected to the New York State legislature as a Free-Soil representative.) Only after an eloquent speech given by Frederick Douglass, the only black at the Seneca Falls convention, did the resolution for women's right to vote finally pass.

Indeed, attendees' fears proved warranted. Although in their Declaration of Sentiments, the women had admitted they expected to be ridiculed and misrepresented because of their requests, none had expected the intensity of the onslaught that occurred after the convention. While the abolitionist newspapers stood by the activists, as did other papers such as the *Factory Girl's Voice* and Frederick Douglass's the *North Star,* the mainstream press, from Maine to Texas, invoked caustic ridicule.

"[S]o pronounced was the popular voice against us,

in the parlor, press, and pulpit," Elizabeth later wrote in *Eighty Years*, "that most of the ladies who had attended the convention and signed the declaration, one by one, withdrew their names and influence and joined our persecutors." Daniel Cady, Elizabeth's father, traveled to Seneca Falls along with Daniel Eaton, the husband of Elizabeth's sister Harriet, to convince Harriet to remove her signature from the declaration. She did and returned home. Daniel Cady tried to convince Elizabeth, too, to remove her name, but she refused. Seemingly the most daring of all the attendees, even she admitted that if she had had any idea of the vehement responses their declaration would provoke, "I fear I should not have had the courage to risk it."

As a young girl growing up in a male-oriented society, Elizabeth Cady yearned for her father's approval, as she tried to prove she was equal to her brother.

2

"I WISH YOU WERE A BOY"

"How well I remember my joy in winning that prize."

—Elizabeth Cady Stanton, in *Eighty Years and More*

Elizabeth Cady actually had learned about courage and determination years before the women's rights convention she spearheaded in 1848. As she points out in her autobiography, even before she reached age 11, she was questioning the strict rules of the Cady household: "I was wondering why it was that everything we like to do is a sin, and that everything we dislike is commanded by God or someone on earth. I am so tired of that everlasting no! no! no! At school, at home, everywhere it is no! Even at church all the commandments begin 'Thou shalt not.' I suppose God will say 'no' to all we like in the next world, just as you do here," she complained to her nurse as a young girl.

Elizabeth's nurse was dismayed by the outburst. But Margaret Cady, who was two years younger, listened attentively to her sister's complaint and then devised a new approach for happier survival in their strict Presbyterian home. She proposed a few days later to

Elizabeth was particularly close to her father, Daniel Cady, who pursued a distinguished career in law and politics. Elizabeth had more difficulty relating to her mother, Margaret Livingston Cady, who maintained a cold and reserved attitude toward her lively and inquisitive daughter.

Elizabeth and their older sister, Harriet, that from then on the girls would do as they thought fit, without asking for permission first; they might be punished for their actions later, but at least they would have had their fun. While Elizabeth had been the one to voice the initial protest, she hesitated in accepting the proposal because she was a worrier. Nevertheless she gave in to the idea, although sometimes Margaret had to literally pull her to their next adventure.

As it turned out, the girls' exploits were relatively harmless. On summer nights after they had been sent to bed, they would squeeze through the bars outside their bedroom windows and enjoy the moon and stars. At other times they and their other siblings would sneak into the attic or cellar. There they would crack open barrels of hickory nuts, nibble on large cakes of maple sugar, whirl retired spinning wheels, dress up in long-gone relatives' clothes, and play hide-and-seek and other games.

"Our parents were as kind, indulgent, and considerate as the Puritan ideas of those days permitted, but fear, rather than love, of God and parents alike, predominated," Elizabeth wrote in her autobiography.

The year that Elizabeth was born, 1815, in Johnstown, New York, was the same year that her father, Daniel Cady, a distinguished lawyer who had served several sessions in the New York Assembly, was elected to the U.S. House of Representatives. In 1847 he would become a New York State supreme court judge.

The son of a humble farmer, Daniel Cady was a self-made man of impeccable integrity. He was sensitive, modest, and had a playful side, yet he frequently was so reserved that his children feared him. Although Elizabeth was distant from her mother, thinking her overly harsh, the young girl was to become her father's favorite daughter. Daniel would allow Elizabeth to sit and read his law books, which she loved, whenever she was sent by her mother to his office as "punishment." Still, his conservative perspective affected her very much, and until he died his influence persisted into her adult life.

Elizabeth's mother, Margaret Livingston Cady, was from one of the oldest and wealthiest families of New York. The Livingstons were leaders in the state's political, social, and business arenas. Margaret's father, James, had been a member of the state assembly and on the first board of regents of the state university. Like many in the Livingston family, he had served with distinction in the Revolutionary War.

Margaret Livingston was nearly six feet tall. A self-reliant woman, she was at ease in all situations. In 1801, at the age of just 16, she married the 28-year-old Daniel Cady.

With the birth of Elizabeth on November 12, 1815, Margaret Cady had had seven children, three of whom had died when still young. While the death of young

Elizabeth was born and raised in one of the finest homes in Johnstown, New York, where her father practiced and taught law. Adjoining the house was Daniel Cady's office, where young Elizabeth soon became familiar with his many law books.

children was not an uncommon circumstance at the time, Daniel and Margaret were very disturbed by the loss because two of the three who died had been boys. At that time in the United States, men could maintain family reputations and distinguish themselves in a number of professions, whereas women were forced into subordinate positions—not allowed to enter college or train for professions. In 1814, one year before Elizabeth was born, her father suffered intensely when his namesake, at the age of seven, became the second boy to die. This then left the family with one boy—Eleazer—and two girls—Tryphena and Harriet. After Elizabeth was born, two more girls—Margaret and Katherine—followed.

During Elizabeth's childhood, Johnstown was a hotbed of intellectual thought and a magnet for many famous lawyers. Aside from her early introduction to law in her father's office, Elizabeth as a young girl gained further perspective on the legal system. At her grammar school, Johnstown Academy, she and her sisters became fast friends with the daughters of the county sheriff and the hotel keeper, whose inn was frequented by lawyers and judges. She and the other girls would visit the jail; they became friendly and sympathetic with the prisoners there, who appreciated their concern and treats of candy and cakes.

The girls also became close to a family servant named Peter Teabout, who enjoyed attending trials. "His love for us was unbounded and fully returned," Elizabeth wrote years later in her autobiography. The girls and the tall black man would sit and listen to proceedings in the courthouse, and their parents felt their youngsters were safe with him.

While there had already been tragedy in the Cady household, more would follow in 1826. Elizabeth's only brother, Eleazer, smart and full of promise, died just after graduating from Union College. His death sent Daniel Cady into a deep, inconsolable episode of grieving. "We early felt that this son filled a larger place in our father's affections and future plans than the five daughters together," wrote Elizabeth later. On the day of the funeral, she sat with her father in a darkened room with her brother's still body:

> As he took no notice of me, after standing a long while, I climbed upon his knee, when he mechanically put his arm about me and, with my head resting against his beating heart, we both sat in silence, he thinking of the wreck of all his hopes in the loss of a dear son, and I wondering what could be said or done to fill the void in his breast. At length he heaved a deep sigh and said: "Oh, my daughter, I wish you were a boy!" Throwing my arms about his neck, I replied: "I will try to be all my brother was."

With those words, Elizabeth determined that being boyish would require more courage and intelligence.

She vowed to spend less time playing and more time studying, until she could move to the head of the class and help heal her father's heart. She also decided she could become equal to a boy by learning Greek and horseback riding. The very next day she hurried to the family's neighbor, Reverend Simon Hosack, who was also the Cady's pastor. It was early morning and he had been working in his garden as he listened to Elizabeth's story. When she finished, he let loose his hoe, ushered her into his library, and immediately began her instruction in Greek.

Elizabeth was committed to her plan and hopeful of alleviating her father's anguish. For months, each evening she watched him suffer at her brother's grave, literally throwing himself on the still-fresh dirt "with outstretched arms, as if to embrace his child." Only the cold of November finally put an end to his graveside visits.

The young girl persisted in her studies and surprised even her teacher, "who thought me capable of doing anything," she wrote in *Eighty Years and More*. When the reverend would visit their home, he would lavishly praise his new student, yet her father seemingly remained unmoved, causing Elizabeth to "hide [her] tears of vexation on the doctor's shoulder." Still undaunted, she pressed on, studying Latin, Greek, and math with boys in the academy, many of whom were much older than she was. After three years of work, she received a second-place prize in Greek. She could only think of how impressed, finally, her father would be:

> So, as soon as we were dismissed, I ran down the hill, rushed breathless into his office, laid the new Greek Testament, which was my prize, on his table and exclaimed: "There, I got it!" He took up the book, asked me some questions about the class, the teachers, the spectators, and, evidently pleased, handed it back to me. Then, while I stood looking and waiting for him to say something which would show that he recognized the equality of the daughter with

In Troy, New York, Emma Willard founded the Troy Female Seminary, the first school for women that claimed to provide an education equal to that found at men's colleges. Elizabeth Cady attended Mrs. Willard's seminary from 1830 to 1833.

the son, he kissed me on the forehead and exclaimed, with a sigh, "Ah, you should have been a boy!"

My joy was turned to sadness. I ran to my good doctor. He chased my bitter tears away, and soothed me with unbounded praises and visions of future success.

While Elizabeth was soothed by the reverend and her sisters as well, years later she would also look back on the experience and realize it had a beneficial twist. It was one of the first times that she decided to take action and shape her own self, a behavior that many at the time thought reserved only for men. "I became a very extraordinary woman," she wrote, according to biographer Lois W. Banner. In her future speeches and writings, Elizabeth would repeatedly encourage other women to be self-reliant, just as she had become.

Although Elizabeth wrote of Eleazer's death in her autobiography, she made no mention of further grief that came to her family not long after. In the year following Eleazer's death, 1827, Margaret Cady had another son, even though she had had no children during the previous seven years. She and her husband also named the newborn Eleazer, yet the child lived only until 1829. While Margaret had remained strong with the deaths of her other children, with this loss she was shaken. Soon she and her husband, himself distressed and also burdened with responsibilities from his legal career, began to turn over household responsibilities to their oldest daughter, Tryphena, and her husband, Edward Bayard, who after their marriage had been living with the Cadys.

With this change and the addition of Edward to their Johnstown home, Elizabeth felt a new freedom. Edward brought his brother, Henry, to study law with Daniel Cady in Johnstown. Just out of college, the two young men could readily help the girls with their studies, and as a result they had more time for fun—picnics, parties, games, and frequent jaunts on horseback. Since her father's office adjoined the house, it was easy for Elizabeth to continue to listen in on his meetings with clients and his teachings to the Bayards and other students who, because of her father's reputation, had gravitated there. At his office she could also learn more about the laws regarding women.

In 1830 Elizabeth graduated from Johnstown Academy, and as she later wrote, her "vexation and mortification knew no bounds" when she couldn't go on to Union College in Schenectady, New York, like all of her other male classmates. Young women weren't allowed, neither at that college nor at any other college in the country.

Instead Elizabeth enrolled in Troy Female Seminary

in Troy, New York, an all-female boarding school that was different from the other women's schools. Its founder, Emma Willard, accepted the prevailing perspective that young women needed to learn social skills and other domestic responsibilities. Yet she also insisted on providing an education that she considered equal to that at men's colleges. The school offered a teacher-training program and numerous free scholarships. Elizabeth was impressed at the beginning of the year when she saw the excitement of the teachers and of classmates who knew Mrs.Willard well from previous years of study.

While Elizabeth would later comment that the education she received at Mrs. Willard's was not much more than the one she had obtained in Johnstown, at Troy Seminary she devoted herself to subjects new to her—French and music—and, in her words, "took great delight" in dancing. She embraced the novelty of living with a variety of girls in a new city. Later, Elizabeth reflected that the tough training in writing skills that she received at Troy equipped her with the tools to develop her own literary style. She also praised the school's founder, Mrs.Willard, saying she "was one of the remarkable women of that period, and did a great educational work for her sex."

However, it was at Troy that the still-impressionable teenaged Elizabeth became, as she later described it, "one of the first victims" of Reverend Charles G. Finney, ex-president of Oberlin College and a "terrifier of human souls." Finney held a series of revivals at Troy for six weeks and then throughout upstate New York. While he discussed issues such as social and personal reform, his preaching on religion distressed Elizabeth, as well as many of her classmates attending the revivals. His powerful presentation vividly emphasized the negative: In his lectures, she later explained, "we learned the total depravity of human nature and the sinner's awful danger of everlasting punishment. . . .[T]he most innocent girl believed herself a monster of iniquity and felt

As a young girl, Elizabeth became apprehensive about religion and the fate of her soul. Her discussions with her father, sister Tryphena, and brother-in-law Edward Bayard during their stay at the resort town of Niagara Falls, New York, eventually helped Elizabeth overcome her obsessive fears.

certain of eternal damnation." His intent was to use fear to motivate his audience.

But Elizabeth was overwhelmed. She was reminded of many childhood fears she had suffered as part of her strict religious upbringing. Extremely disturbed, Elizabeth could not be helped by her school friends. She became obsessed with fears of judgment day. When visiting at home, she was driven to wake her father at night, requesting that he pray for her in case she died in her sleep and ended up in hell.

Finally, her father, along with Tryphena and Edward, took her to Niagara Falls, after making a pact not to speak at all about religion during the trip. As it turned out, however, during this vacation it proved beneficial for Elizabeth to discuss that very topic. She had many discussions about religion, especially with Edward, who questioned the Cady family's conservatism. She rested and read the writings of more liberal philosophers and theologians, and finally she returned to her old self.

In her autobiography Elizabeth would later write that nothing in her long life could compare to what she suffered as a result of harsh religious ideology. As with other significant events in her life, this awareness would eventually inspire her to action.

When newly married Elizabeth Cady Stanton attended the 1840 World Anti-Slavery Convention in London, England, she was disturbed to see that women delegates to the meeting were not allowed to participate. The event made her question women's roles in society and helped inspire a lifelong interest in women's rights.

3

SILENCED

"It was really pitiful to hear narrow-minded bigots, pretending to be teachers and leaders of men."

—Elizabeth's description of speakers at the World Anti-Slavery Convention, from *Eighty Years and More*

Renewed from the Niagara Falls vacation and returned to her old self, Elizabeth graduated in 1833 from Mrs. Willard's academy. As a young woman of the upper class, Elizabeth reveled in her newfound freedom: no school, no great responsibilities, the chance to decide—nearly on her own—where and when to come and go, what to eat, drink, and wear. She would describe this time as "indeed like a birth into a new world of happiness and freedom." While she was responsible for cleaning her room, making and mending her clothes, and ironing, most of her time was spent horseback riding, reading, and visiting with friends and relatives in New York.

As Elizabeth and her sisters matured and their father's reputation expanded, many young men from Union College, as well as

As a young man Edward Bayard, the husband of Elizabeth's sister Tryphena, fell in love with Elizabeth and begged her to run away with him. Knowing she could not destroy her sister's marriage, Elizabeth rejected his suit.

numerous friends they had made at Mrs. Willard's school, visited their home. While there was always time for fun, practical jokes, music, games, long walks (no matter what the weather), and dancing, the young people also filled their time with intellectual jousting, often led by Elizabeth's brother-in-law, Edward Bayard. They listened to and discussed his instruction on law, philosophy, politics, history, and poetry. Together they read aloud the weekly installments of pieces by contemporary authors like James Fenimore Cooper and Charles Dickens.

Unsuspecting first-time male visitors who arrived at the Cady home ready to try their powers of debate on the women found they were formidably matched. Elizabeth's relished long discussions with them about women's equality. "I confess," she later wrote, "that I did not study so much for a love of the truth or my own development, in these days, as to make those young men recognize my equality. I soon noticed that, after losing a few games of chess, my opponent talked less of masculine superiority."

When Elizabeth was in her midtwenties, a gentleman revealed that he loved her and wanted to elope. Unfortunately, that man was Edward, her sister Tryphena's husband. Ten years older than Elizabeth, he was frustrated in his own childless marriage, and more romantic and idealistic than his down-to-earth wife. While Elizabeth was attracted to Edward, she knew she could not upset her sister, and the distressed young woman told Edward that an elopement was out of the question. She kept the incident a secret from her family, and even years later did not mention it in her autobiography.

However, she would remain on good terms with Tryphena and Edward throughout her long life, although Edward would never allow himself to be alone with her again.

During the 1830s, Elizabeth would sometimes visit her cousin Gerrit Smith, who lived in Peterboro, New York. The journey there took several days by horse and carriage. The Smiths' home was always filled with a mixture of fascinating guests—reformers, philosophers, statesmen, aristocrats, and the Southern relatives of Gerrit Smith's wife, Ann Fitzhugh Smith. All of them would participate in debates, especially on topics such as reform and the abolition of slavery. The home also was a part of the Underground Railroad, a network of houses whose owners would hide, feed, and clothe runaway slaves who were traveling north to Canada to gain their freedom.

Curiously, while Ann Smith dared to openly speak her mind, which was rather uncommon for women at the time, women's rights reform was not wholeheartedly embraced in the Smith household. Curiously, too, while the Smiths had many radical beliefs, they still attracted numerous people who held rather conservative opinions. The family had one child, Elizabeth, who, although seven years younger than Elizabeth Cady, became a lifelong friend. "There never was such an atmosphere of love and peace, of freedom and good cheer, in any other home I visited," Elizabeth Cady wrote in her autobiography. "And this was the universal testimony of those who were guests at Peterboro."

During a visit to the Smiths' in 1839, Elizabeth met a man she would later describe as "one who was then considered the most eloquent and impassioned orator on the anti-slavery platform"—Henry Brewster Stanton. The young woman was among the guests at Peterboro attending a monthlong series of antislavery conventions being held in nearby Madison County. Two carriages full of guests from the Smith home would venture over the color-drenched autumn hills each morning to the conventions, and they would not return until late each night. "The enthusiasm of the people in these great meetings, the thrilling oratory, and lucid arguments of the speakers, all conspired to make these days memorable as among the most charming in my life," Elizabeth wrote in her autobiography. "I felt a new inspiration in life and was enthused with new ideas of individual rights and the basic principles of government."

While Elizabeth was revitalized by the conventions, she also became personally intrigued with the renowned speaker, Henry Stanton, for his eloquence, skill, and power were apparent not only on the platform but in the Smiths' parlor as well. Ten years older than Elizabeth, Henry was a "fine-looking, affable young man" who enjoyed her company on horseback rides in the crisp country air. For her part, Elizabeth's sense of fun and her warm smile, energy, and wit made her very attractive. Within a month of meeting, she and Henry were engaged.

Henry had had a dramatic past—he belonged to a famed group of radical abolitionists that had frequently been attacked by proslavery mobs. At times, he said, he had narrowly escaped death during these tramplings, mostly because he managed to subdue the crowds with his verbal agility. He could guide a crowd not only into peace but also into laughter or tears. When he first met Elizabeth, Henry was an executive of the American Anti-Slavery Society, working as an abolitionist lecturer and organizer in his native New England. Previously, he had been a newspaper reporter and minor government official in the Rochester, New York, area.

When Gerrit Smith heard of the engagement that had taken place on his own property, he had a long talk with his cousin Elizabeth. He knew that her conservative family would vehemently object to her engagement to an abolitionist, and he warned her of the difficult life she would have. From his words, Elizabeth took to heart one piece of advice: to let her family know of the engagement by letter, so she need not experience their initial ire in person. She sent off her note, believing that Gerrit could help her determine what was best to do or say next. However, Daniel Cady wasted little wrath on them, knowing his response would be much more potent when he delivered it in person.

Finally, recognizing that she had put off the return to her agitated homestead long enough, Elizabeth headed back to Johnstown. There Daniel lectured her at great length on the mistake of her engagement, focusing on its financial ramifications. Curiously, he was criticizing Henry Stanton for being a self-made man, just like himself. After months of increasing anxieties, Elizabeth eventually broke off the engagement.

At the Peterboro, New York, home of her cousin Gerrit Smith, Elizabeth Cady enjoyed the company and intellectual conversation of many reformers involved in the antislavery movement.

Henry Stanton actually had much to be proud of in his past. His ancestors dated from the colonial and Revolutionary War era, and his father was a successful merchant who had held public office in Connecticut. But when Henry was a teenager, his father's business had gone bankrupt, and from then on Henry not only supported himself but also helped his two brothers pay for their education. Henry had no money of his own and no prospect of inheriting any. Additionally, as an abolitionist, he and his future wife would forever be outside the elite society that the Cadys belonged to because of their connection to the Livingston family.

But Elizabeth had come to view the aristocracy as

Twenty-three-year-old Elizabeth met her future husband, Henry B. Stanton, at her cousin Gerrit Smith's home. Intrigued by the renowned antislavery activist, who was 10 years older than she, Elizabeth accepted Henry's offer of marriage just one month after their introduction.

offensive. She had begun to blame the Livingston family for her mother's harshness and inflexibility that had so distressed Elizabeth as a child. Then Stanton wrote to tell her that he had been chosen as a delegate to the World Anti-Slavery Convention, which was to take place in London, England, that June. When he proposed that she come with him so they could honeymoon abroad, the young woman determined to push aside her worries and quickly agreed.

Their marriage took place on May 11, 1840. Only her sister Margaret, or "Madge," and a few close friends attended the ceremony, which was performed by Reverend Hugh Maire. He conceded to Elizabeth's urging to delete from the vows the woman's standard promise to obey her husband. From Elizabeth's perspective, she was entering into a relationship of equality, and the word *obey* had no place in wedding vows. Additionally, as would be the case for many feminists in the later 19th century, she did not give up her name. She called herself Elizabeth Cady Stanton, rather than what would have been traditionally expected—Mrs. Henry Stanton.

Not long after, the newlyweds headed for the New York port to board their ship, the *Montreal*, for England. There they received a fond but somewhat sad send-off from Elizabeth's two sisters Madge and Harriet, as well as Harriet's husband, Daniel Eaton, who was a merchant in New York City.

At the ship the couple met a close friend of Henry's, James Birney, who was the nominee from the abolitionists' Liberty Party for the upcoming U.S. presidential election. Birney was also a delegate on his way to the World Anti-Slavery Convention. During the 18-day voyage, he and Henry taught Elizabeth as much as they could about abolitionism through conversation and books, and she was a ready student.

Upon finally arriving in London, Elizabeth was both in awe of the beautiful city gardens and excited to learn more about the antislavery movement. Yet she quickly become disillusioned at the convention because of the delegates' treatment of women. Representatives from countries around the world were supposed to participate in the World Convention. However, because the reform associations in England excluded women from sharing authority with men, the English delegates believed that women should not be admitted as equal members to the World Convention.

Antislavery societies in the United States had also been divided over the inclusion of women. Because many of the U.S. delegates were staying in the same lodgings as Elizabeth and her husband, the newlyweds had the opportunity to clearly hear both sides of the issue. Members led by the New York delegates, who were called political abolitionists, had decided that women should organize separately from the men in establishing antislavery societies, fearing that the combination of men and women would undermine abolitionist reforms. Henry Stanton and James Birney supported the New Yorkers' position, and Elizabeth had heard some convincing arguments for this view while en route from New York to the convention.

But the Boston and Philadelphia members of the antislavery societies and their followers believed differently. Called the Garrisonian contingent (after the famed abolitionist William Lloyd Garrison), they believed that women should participate equally in the

The marriage proposal of abolitionist Henry B. Stanton (right) to Elizabeth concerned her father, who complained about his prospective son-in-law's limited job prospects: "Mr. Stanton's present business cannot be regarded as a business for life. If the object of the Abolitionists be soon accomplished he must be thrown out of business."

societies, since they had fought alongside men in so many ways and for so many years in the antislavery conflict. While the Garrisonians held power in the national antislavery society, both the Garrisonians and the political abolitionists had sent delegates to London. However, only the Garrisonians included women among their delegates.

When the convention began on June 12 in Freemasons' Hall in London, the divergent views collided. On the first day of the meeting, delegates fought over whether women should be acknowledged as delegates. Since the conservatives had the majority, women were excluded from speaking and from sitting on the convention floor. They were relegated to a curtained-off gallery at one end of the hall. Although Henry Stanton had previously sided with the New Yorkers, he now made an eloquent plea for the female delegates to be admitted.

The clergy delegates delivered the most violent arguments against including the women, and, as Elizabeth later wrote, "were in agony lest the women should do or say something to shock the heavenly hosts." Clergymen held their Bibles and declared that the Book's words supported the view that women were subservient, and had always been so, starting with the creation of Eve. Elizabeth described how in response George Bradburn "with a voice like thunder . . . swept all their arguments aside by declaring with tremendous emphasis that, if they could prove to him that the Bible taught the entire subjection of one-half the race to the other, he should consider that the best thing he could do for humanity would be to bring together every Bible in the universe and make a grand bonfire of them."

To protest the women's exclusion, William Lloyd Garrison joined them in their gallery, thus giving up his right to speak for the full 12 days of meetings, "[a]fter coming three thousand miles to speak on the subject nearest his heart," Elizabeth noted. "It was a great act of self-sacrifice that should never be forgotten by women," Elizabeth wrote. Garrison was joined by one other man, an antislavery newspaper editor named Nathaniel P. Rogers.

Ironically, events at the convention inspired a new activism among women, both in England and the United States, and were discussed for some time afterward. Elizabeth, who as a young girl had taken action to console her father upon the death of her brother, once again became determined to bring about change. She proposed to her new friend, Philadelphia delegate Lucretia Mott, that they hold a women's rights convention upon their return to the United States. Lucretia

Newlywed Elizabeth Cady Stanton was impressed by abolitionist William Lloyd Garrison (right), whom she first met at the World Anti-Slavery Convention. When the women delegates were excluded from the conference, Garrison protested the unfair treatment by sitting with the female delegates and refusing to speak before the assembly. "It was a great act of self-sacrifice that should never be forgotten by women," Elizabeth noted.

was a Quaker minister, a role that the Religious Society of Friends allowed women to attain, unlike many other religious faiths of the time. With her experience as a speaker, Mott was self-confident when challenging others, yet also gentle and serene. In light of Elizabeth's own struggles with religion in the past, she was interested in further conversation with Lucretia and frequently made time for it.

For six weeks following the convention, many delegates stayed in London, where they attended numerous breakfasts, teas, and dinners—both public and private—as well as large meetings. Henry Stanton, who had been elected secretary of the convention; James Birney;

William Lloyd Garrison; and others were repeatedly invited to speak. All were guests of leading English families, many of whom were Quakers. The American delegates also heard famous English preachers and statesmen, and toured Westminster Abbey, the Houses of Parliament, law courts, art galleries, and castles, and as many other famous sites as they could manage.

Many antislavery convention delegates continued traveling with the Stantons when they spent a month in Paris, France, then returned to England. Traveling further to Ireland and Scotland, the Stantons were finally left alone to enjoy the early days of their marriage, taking frequent, long walks through the hills. During their travels, Henry wrote articles about the sights for New York newspapers, whose editors urged the couple to visit many lesser-known areas.

But all was not pleasant. Both Elizabeth and Henry were struck by the poverty found throughout much of Ireland and by England's rigid class system. After spending so many months overseas, Elizabeth was relieved to board their steamship, still a relatively new mode of travel, for the return home. The Stantons arrived in New York City just one day before Christmas of 1840.

Motherhood would occupy a great deal of time in the life of Elizabeth Cady Stanton, who gave birth to seven children in 17 years. Her attitudes about child care, like many of her other beliefs, often ran counter to those of the rest of society, and she enjoyed challenging traditional methods.

4

A MOTHER IS
BORN

"I was ambitious to absorb all the wisdom I could."

—Elizabeth Cady Stanton, in *Eighty Years and More*

Still excited by their trip overseas, the newlyweds stayed in New York City with Elizabeth's sister Harriet for the 1840–41 holidays. Yet even amid the celebrating, Henry and Elizabeth knew that a decision had to be made relatively quickly about his career, for while he was an executive of the American Anti-Slavery Society, its treasury was nearly empty. Luckily an offer soon came, although from a somewhat unexpected source. Elizabeth's father, Daniel Cady, proposed that the couple come and live with the Cady family while he taught Henry law in his office. It was a most generous offer. So despite the anxieties and trouble that had surrounded Elizabeth's engagement and quick wedding, she and her new husband headed to the Johnstown homestead.

Elizabeth once again delighted in her sisters' company. Madge and Katherine still lived at home, and Elizabeth now saw their time together as quite precious, knowing it would be relatively short-lived. The Cady sisters pursued familiar pastimes of taking long walks and going horseback riding together. When Elizabeth was on her own, she would read books on law, history, and politics, and she occasionally became involved in abolitionist and temperance activities. Yet Elizabeth could not completely revert to her girlhood, for she was not only a new wife but also soon became a mother, giving birth to Daniel Cady Stanton on March 2, 1842.

Elizabeth's self-reliance, questioning of the norms, and pursuit of knowledge now had a new outlet. She watched how the hired nurse cared for the new baby. While she never doubted that the nurse's best intentions were always in the forefront, she wondered about some of the child-care practices followed not only by this nurse but also by other parents and doctors. She was distressed that her new son cried so much. During the early 19th century many infants died during the first year of life; the Stanton's nurse had taken care of ten children, five of whom had died. Elizabeth was determined that her son would not only live but also be happy and well. She refused to accept the popular thought that children were destined to be afflicted with many illnesses.

The new mother read all that she could about child-rearing. But she found most of the works were confusing and seemed to advocate the opposite of good common sense. She finally found a book called *Infancy*, by Scottish physician Andrew Combe, that supported her belief in logic and homeopathy, a popular type of treatment that focused on accelerating the body's own self-cure. Elizabeth decided that a whole new approach to child care was necessary for her son.

One of the first issues the new mother wrestled over with the nurse was bandaging. At the time, most people believed that a newborn had to be kept tightly bandaged to prevent its bones, which were believed to be as soft as cartilage, from becoming malformed. Yet

Elizabeth would not give in to old wives' tales just because these recommendations had been followed for generations. "It is very remarkable that kittens and puppies should be so well put together that they need no artificial bracing, and the human family be left wholly to the mercy of a bandage," she told the baby's nurse. "Suppose a child was born where you could not get a bandage, what then? Now I think this child will remain intact without a bandage, and, if I am willing to take the risk, why should you complain?"

The nurse, however, was concerned about her reputation if something were to happen to yet another child in her care. So, for the time being, she would bandage the child in the morning, and Elizabeth, just as regularly, would shortly thereafter unbandage him.

The nurse stayed in the Johnstown home for six weeks and eventually came to agree with many of Elizabeth's seemingly newfangled ideas. Elizabeth opened

Poet and essayist Ralph Waldo Emerson, seen here addressing an audience in the summer school of philosophy that he helped establish in Concord, Massachusetts. Elizabeth reveled in the opportunities to attend lectures such as Emerson's, as well as reform meetings, plays, and concerts. Such events were easily accessible when the Stantons lived in Boston.

windows frequently to let in fresh air and sunshine, rather than keeping the house warm and stuffy; she uncovered the child's head so he could breathe easily, rather than keeping his face under a blanket so he was forced to keep breathing the same air. She fed him regularly and allowed him none of the many potions of the day that were forced down children's throats at the slightest indication of illness. Soon after the baby's mother had taken matters under her control, he stopped his ceaseless crying. The second nurse Elizabeth hired readily followed the new mother's directions.

Inspired by her happy baby, Elizabeth persisted in learning as much as she could about child care. As she came to study more and have more children of her own, she would frequently offer to help other parents she came upon in her travels. In her autobiography, she wrote: "Tom Moore tells us 'the heart from love to one, grows bountiful to all.' I know the care of one child made me thoughtful of all. I never hear a child cry, now, that I do not feel that I am bound to find out the reason."

It was fortunate that Elizabeth so readily became an adept mother, for by the fall of 1843 Henry had passed the bar exam, and he and Elizabeth left the Cady Johnstown home so he could begin practice in Boston, Massachusetts, with another lawyer. Boston was now a center for reformers, and here the couple met with many activists and thinkers of the day, including poet and essayist Ralph Waldo Emerson, author Nathaniel Hawthorne, and abolitionists Frederick Douglass, Wendell Phillips, and William Lloyd Garrison, the latter of whom had made such an impression on Elizabeth when they first met at the London antislavery convention.

For two years, the Stantons boarded in the Chelsea section of Boston with Elizabeth's cousin Mary Livingston and her husband, Reverend John Wesley Olmstead, a Baptist minister. Within the Olmstead home the Stantons met and often engaged in heated debates with

many leading Baptist ministers. In the city of Boston, Elizabeth also attended many plays, concerts, and lectures, as well as conventions on temperance, religion, peace, prison reform, and abolitionism. The antislavery meetings surpassed "any meetings I had ever attended," she wrote in her autobiography. "[T]he speeches were eloquent and the debates earnest and forcible." Those who led the Garrisonian meetings also allowed participants to speak from the floor, which made the assemblies more interesting but, at the same time, more prone to trouble.

Indeed, Elizabeth had to be careful of having a very public association with the radical Garrisonian antislavery groups, since her husband was still intent on building a political career. Yet she began to spend time in the state capital of New York, Albany, where her parents and two of her sisters and their husbands had moved to establish the men's legal careers, and her activism began. She and others circulated petitions and met with many members of the New York State senate

When they first moved to the Chelsea section of Boston in 1843, the Stantons lived with Elizabeth's cousin Mary Livingston and her husband Reverend John Wesley Olmstead. Later they set up housekeeping in their own home, which had scenic views of nearby Boston Bay.

After four years in Boston, the Stantons moved to this house in west central New York, just outside the village of Seneca Falls. However, Elizabeth soon found that the rural community did not provide the intellectual excitement and energy she had experienced in Boston.

and assembly to promote passage of the then-pending Married Woman's Property Act. Its primary provision gave a married woman the right to keep all of her family's money upon her husband's death, rather than turn it over to her oldest son. Elizabeth spent so much time in Albany, in fact, that her next son, Henry, was born there in March 1844.

In 1845 the Stantons moved from the Olmstead house into their own home, which had beautiful views of Boston Bay, the city, and the surrounding countryside. Here Elizabeth took charge of the entire housekeeping, since her husband was so busy with his business. She reveled in being able to "reign supreme," and with two hired servants became an expert in housekeeping, money management, cooking, preserving, and pickling—benefiting from her natural inclinations toward order and cleanliness. "I put my soul into everything," she proclaimed in her autobiography. Shortly after the move, her third son was born in September and named Gerrit Smith, after Elizabeth's cousin.

But in the spring of 1847, the Stantons moved back to New York State, this time to the small town of Seneca Falls, where they hoped the weather, which was less damp and harsh than in Boston, would be better for the elder Henry's chronic lung congestion. Additionally, change seemed in order. Henry had failed to win any elections despite repeated tries, and he was disheartened as well with the unethical practices of his law partner. Once again, Daniel Cady helped the couple by offering them the Seneca Falls house in which Tryphena and her husband Edward had lived earlier.

A small manufacturing town in a growing area, Seneca Falls was not far from the reform centers of Rochester and Buffalo and a large Quaker community in Waterloo. It was in a region of the state known as the "burned-over" district, because it had often been a hotbed for "fires" of evangelical revivals and reform movements. Elizabeth thought she would feel comfortable in the town, having made acquaintances during frequent visits to her sister when she lived there.

While Henry was still tying things up in Boston, Elizabeth headed off to see her parents, now back in Johnstown. She left her three sons in their care, and then happily set out for her new home. Because the house had been closed for a number of years, it needed many repairs and work on its land. Elizabeth had been given a check by her father, who, with a smile, challenged her to set to work. She readily bargained with and hired carpenters, painters, paperhangers, and yardmen, and oversaw the building of a new kitchen and woodshed. For some diversion and advice, she met with Ansel Bascom, a former classmate of hers from Johnstown Academy who was now a member of the constitutional convention in session in Albany. Elizabeth pressed him to propose an amendment that would

Seneca Falls, New York, would gain fame as the site of the first public meeting on women's rights. At the end of the convention, 68 women and 32 men signed the Declaration of Senti-ments, which included the controversial resolution call-ing for woman's suffrage.

eliminate the word *male* from the section of the state constitution that allowed suffrage for men only.

Within a month, the house was ready and the Stan-tons moved in. However, running a household quickly began to lose its appeal for Elizabeth and instead became "irksome" at best. While Seneca Falls was in a good location, their home was on the outskirts of town, and as the area was still developing, roads were frequently muddy and sidewalks rather infrequent. Additionally, Elizabeth now had three small children in her care and could not find servants as good as the ones she had had in Boston. In Seneca Falls, she felt intel-lectually stifled and soon became depressed.

As if Elizabeth were not overwhelmed enough, all of her children, as well as her servants, were struck down with malaria. The symptoms of chills and fever, given the remedies at that time, didn't subside for three months. The Stanton home was no longer the haven of order and cleanliness it had been in the Chelsea neighborhood. Now Elizabeth could accomplish only what was absolutely necessary in a given day, and for the first time she understood how a woman could sit down for a rest in the midst of complete chaos.

It was in this state of mind that Elizabeth met Lucretia Mott and together planned the first female suffrage convention, held in Seneca Falls in 1848. While her children had recovered from their illness by the time she saw Lucretia, Elizabeth's frustration had not abated, and action was necessary.

No one could have predicted the success of the women's rights convention nor the intense backlash it would create, yet by participating in it, Elizabeth felt revitalized. "[E]xpressing myself fully and freely on a subject I felt so deeply about was a great relief," she later wrote in her autobiography. Within a month of the Seneca Falls meeting, she attended another women's rights convention, held in Rochester, New York. But almost two years would pass before other meetings were held—in the states of Ohio, Indiana, Massachusetts, and Pennsylvania, and in the city of New York. None of those conventions produced such a provocative declaration as did the Seneca Falls meeting, yet the Massachusetts meeting garnered attendees from nine states, featured well-known reform speakers, and attracted much attention in the press.

While Elizabeth was encouraged that these meetings were being held, her own problems were still keeping her from completely participating in the women's movement: her husband was frequently away, her Johnstown family pressured her to stay home, and she herself felt uncomfortable about leaving her children in another's care. Yet despite these and other obstacles that had initially seemed overwhelming, Elizabeth overcame her depression and frustration. Once again, she worked around her situation and took action.

Elizabeth was invited to speak on various issues at

several homes and churches right in her own neighbor-hood, an opportunity she thoroughly enjoyed. She began to write persuasive articles and letters, first to the county newspapers and then to the *New York Tribune*, whose editor, Horace Greeley, was at the time a sup-porter of women's rights. She wrote compelling letters to be read at other conventions and to friends as well. With the help of fellow reformers, she wrote thorough replies to all attacks, citing examples from sources as diverse as the Bible, government constitutions, and books on civil law, science, philosophy, and history.

"Now my mind, as well as my hands, was fully occu-pied, and instead of mourning, as I had done, over what I had lost in leaving Boston, I tried in every way to make the most of life in Seneca Falls," Elizabeth wrote in her autobiography. When distressing moods threatened, she put herself to work on a task—whether mental or physical—often cleaning every corner of her house in defense. Because as a child she would force herself to sleep whenever upset or angry, now she could fall asleep at will—not with the intention of avoiding a bad mood but to have more energy for later. Naps could readily be had in the noisy playroom with her young children, on a bumpy wagon ride, or in a bustling train station. She considered this recently real-ized skill a major contributor to her ceaseless energy. On February 10, 1851, Elizabeth gave birth to her fourth son, Theodore, and the next day was out of bed and writing—behavior that was unheard of at the time.

Indeed, Elizabeth was not just a good speaker with a keen intellect. She also attracted many people with her attentive listening, compassion, and enthusiasm. She would invite reformers to stay at her home on their way to and from meetings, opening her doors to such famed activists as Lucy Stone and Antoinette Brown. These reformers were two of the very few college-educated women of the time, having graduated from Oberlin College (which in 1833 had become the first college to

open its doors to women).
Elizabeth also organized a
weekly Conversation Club.
Interested participants would
gather in each other's homes,
where a previously appointed
essayist would read a short
piece on a particular topic,
and a lively discussion would
follow. According to Elizabeth, these evenings "brought
together the best minds in the
community."

Besides these organized
gatherings, frequent visits
from friends and neighbors
filled Elizabeth's time. They
sought her advice on financial
and legal matters, as well as
on health issues. Elizabeth's
interest in learning about
medical issues and homeopathy, inspired when her first
son was born, remained
strong, and she equipped her-

self with a homeopathic manual and herbs, and even
delivered a few babies. Believing in the benefits of physical fitness, she set up a gymnasium in her barn for
neighborhood children to use, and she persuaded town
officials to provide athletic opportunities for girls, who
otherwise would have been excluded.

But aside from finding enrichment from these
acquaintances and friends in her immediate neighborhood, in 1851 Elizabeth met a woman who would be
close to her, publicly as well as personally, for the rest of
her life.

*Elizabeth Cady Stanton did
not follow the "acceptable"
practices of her day. Instead
of remaining bedridden for
several days after giving
birth, she proudly noted that
when Theodore (right) was
born in 1851, she was out of
bed the next day and writing. Daughter Margaret
was born the following year.*

*After being introduced in 1851, Elizabeth Cady Stanton and Susan B. Anthony
began what would be a lifelong collaborative effort in activism, particularly for the
women's rights movement. Stanton, who often remained at home when her children
were young, would craft many of the speeches that Anthony would deliver.*

5

"LARGE BRAINS AND GREAT HEARTS"

"When your children are a little more grown, you will surely be heard, for it cannot be possible to repress what is in you."

—Lucy Stone, in a letter to Elizabeth Cady Stanton, from *The Elizabeth Cady Stanton–Susan B. Anthony Reader*

After attending an antislavery meeting in Seneca Falls in 1851, Elizabeth escorted speakers George Thompson and William Lloyd Garrison back to her home to be her guests. Along the way they were stopped by Elizabeth's friend, Amelia Bloomer, who was the local assistant postmistress and editor of the reform paper, the *Lily*. Elizabeth had been educating Amelia in women's rights issues, and she had become a staunch supporter. Amelia introduced the group to her friend and fellow reformer Susan B. Anthony, a former schoolteacher who, although from a very wealthy Quaker family, had been taught to support herself.

Susan had given up her 15-year career as a schoolteacher to work on her father's farm and to further the antislavery and temperance movements. She was disciplined, earnest, moral, and introspective.

She and her family had just attended the women's rights convention in Rochester, and upon hearing reports about the Seneca Falls women's rights meetings had determined to become involved.

Elizabeth and Susan connected immediately. Shortly after meeting they began collaborating for reform—writing addresses for conventions on not only women's rights but also temperance, abolitionism, and education. "Every energy of her soul is centered upon the needs of this world. To her, work is worship," Elizabeth would write of her friend years later. Susan and Elizabeth were an effective team—one would watch the Stanton children while the other would write or research, and then they would switch responsibilities.

Even though Susan had been an excellent teacher, she found that watching the Stanton boys was no easy task. Elizabeth's approach to bringing up her children was to explain and teach, rather than demand, threaten, or invoke the fear she had experienced while growing up. Although she believed in her approach, her children were difficult to keep out of trouble: small children had to be rescued from the roof; a young baby placed by his brothers in an inventive life preserver (that luckily floated) was found in the Seneca River; and a pistol even ended up in a youngster's grip.

Still, the two women worked feverishly, developing resolutions, protests, appeals, and petitions. "In thought and sympathy we were one, and in the division of labor we exactly complemented each other," Elizabeth wrote. "I am the better writer, she the better critic. She supplied the facts and statistics, I the philosophy and rhetoric, and, together, we have made arguments that have stood unshaken through the storms of long years; arguments that no one has answered."

Elizabeth wrote many speeches that Susan delivered, since Elizabeth could do little traveling. "I forged the thunderbolts and she fired them," Elizabeth wrote in *Eighty Years*. Additionally, each kept the other from losing hope, no matter what the circumstance. And each continued to have admiring words for the other throughout their friendship that would last until death. A mutual friend, Theodore Tilton would later describe Elizabeth Cady Stanton and Susan B. Anthony: "Both have large brains and great hearts."

In the early 1850s some women in Seneca Falls had begun to make a statement not just with their words but with their dress as well. Elizabeth Smith Miller, Gerrit Smith's now-married daughter, came to visit Elizabeth Cady Stanton in 1850 dressed in attire that other women's rights advocates quickly adopted. Rather than wear the traditional long, heavy skirt that dragged through mud and dust, with its tightly laced waist and accompanying high shoes, Miller wore a comfortable shorter skirt with full trousers underneath. Elizabeth and other women soon began wearing the new outfit, too.

The pants became known as bloomers. Even though Elizabeth Smith Miller had designed them, they were named after Amelia Bloomer, Elizabeth's friend who first espoused the outfit's merits in her reform newspaper, the *Lily*. Local women frequently met in a small room at the post office where Amelia worked, and they read and discussed her publication and others that she received as well.

While many people agreed that a change in women's dress was a good idea, those who wore the bloomer dress were ridiculed continuously, not only in Seneca Falls but also in the press and in other towns and cities where women donned the attire. They were followed by obnoxious crowds of boys on the streets and assailed with rude remarks from grown men and women. In 1853 Elizabeth Cady Stanton was one of the first to reluctantly give up the outfit. "What incredible freedom I enjoyed for two years!" she wrote.

One of the few who persisted in wearing bloomers— for almost seven years—was Elizabeth Smith Miller. She

THE LILY.

DEVOTED TO THE INTERESTS OF WOMAN.

AMELIA BLOOMER, EDITOR AND PUBLISHER.—ISSUED SEMI-MONTHLY AT FIFTY CENTS A YEAR IN ADVANCE.

VOL. 5. SENECA FALLS, N Y., JUNE 15, 1853. NO.

AL MEETING—WOMEN'S N. Y. STATE TEMPERANCE SOCIETY.

Society met in Corinthian Hall, Rochester, ednesday, June 1st, 1853, at 10 o'clock A. The following officers were present: The lent, Mrs. E. C. Stanton, in the Chair; Vice lents, Mrs. D. C. Alling, Mrs. Lydia F. r, Mrs. H. Attilia Albro and Miss Emily . Recording Secretaries, S. B. Anthony, C. Vaughan; Corresponding Secretary, Amelia Bloomer; Treasurer, Mrs. C. E. . The meeting was opened by prayer by C. C. Foote, of Michigan The President read the following address;

MRS. STANTON'S ADDRESS.

tle more than one year ago, in this same hall we the first Woman's State Temperance Society.— lieved that the time had come for woman to out on this question, and to insist on her right to rd in the councils of the church and state. It oposed at that time that we, instead of forming a , should go en masse into the State Temperance . We were assured that in becoming members ing the sum of $1, we should thereby secure the speak and vote in their meetings. who had watched the jealousy with which man er eyed the slow aggressions of woman, warned ainst the insidious proposition made by agents at society. We told you they would no doubt receive *the dollar*, but that you would never be d to speak or vote in their meetings. Many of ought us suspicious and unjust towards the tem- e men of the Empire State. The fact that Abby had been permitted to speak in one of their public gs, was brought up as an argument by some agent

It has been objected to our society that we do not confine ourselves to the subject of temperance, but talk too much about woman's rights, divorce, and the church. It could be easily shown how the consideration of this great question carries us legitimately into the discussion of these various subjects. One class of minds would deal with effects alone; another would inquire into causes,—the work of the former is easily perceived and quickly done; that of the latter requires deep thought, great patience, much time, and a wise self-denial. Our physicians of the present day are a good type of the mass of our reformers. They take out cancers, cut off toncils, drive the posion which nature has wisely thrown to the surface, back again,—quiet unsteady nerves with valerian, and by means of ether infuse an artificial courage into a patient that he may bravely endure some painful operation. It requires but little thought to feel that the wise physician who shall trace out the true causes of suffering—who shall teach us the great immutable laws of life and health,—who shall show us how and where in our every day life, we are violating these laws, and the true point to begin the reform, is doing a much higher, broader, and deeper work, than h who shall bend all his energies to the temporary relief of suffering. Those temperance men or women whose whole work consists in denouncing rum-sellers, appealing to legislatures, eulogizing Neal Dow, and shouting Maine Law, are superficial reformers, mere surface workers. True, this outside work is well and must be done,—let those who see no other do this,—but let them lay no hindrances in the way of that class of mind, who seeing in our present false social relations, the causes of the moral deformities of the race, would fain declare the immutable laws that govern mind as well as matter, and point out the true causes of the evils we see about us, whether lurking under the shadow of the altar—the sacredness of the marriage institution, or the assumed superiority of man.

1st. We have been obliged to preach woman's rights because many instead of listening to what we had to say on temperance, have questioned the rights of a woman to speak on any subject. In all courts of justice

more importance than a stern faith. Their Bible permits war, slavery, capital punishment, and makes salvation depend on faith and ordinances. In their creed it is a sin to dance, to pick up sticks on the sabbath day, to go to the theatre, or large parties during lent, to read a notice of any reform meeting from the altar, or permit a woman to speak in the church. In our creed it is a sin to hold a slave,—to hang a man on the gallows,—to make war on defenceless nations, or to sell rum to a weak brother, and rob the widow and the orphan of a protector, and a home. Thus may we write out some of our differences, but from the similarity in the conduct of the human family, it is fair to infer that our differences are more intellectual than spiritual, and the great truths we hear so clearly uttered on all sides, have been incorporated as vital principles into the inner life of but few indeed.

We must not expect the Church to leap en masse to a higher position. She sends forth her missionaries of truth, one by one. All of our reformers have, in a measure, been developed in the Church, and all our Reforms have been started there. The advocates and opposers of the Reforms of our day, have grown up side by side, partaking of the same ordinances, and officiating at the same altars; but one by applying more fully his christian principles to life, and pursuing an admitted truth to its legitimate results, has unwittingly found himself in antagonism with his brother.

Belief is not voluntary, and change is the natural result of growth and development We would fain have all Church members Sons and Daughters of Temperance, but if the Church in her wisdom has made her platform so broad that wine bibbers and rumsellers may repose in ease thereon, we who are always preaching liberality, ought to be the last to complain. Having thus briefly noticed some of the objections to our movement I will not detain the audience longer at this time.

The Annual Report of the Executive Committee was then read by Mary C. Vaughan, one of the Recording Secretaries, as follows:

have poured .. regenerate fallen natures and quicken moral growths into more vigorous life.— And yet when the cause thus languished, firm, earnest hearts have rallied round its altars, consecrating to its service toil, and thought, and wealth, and ease. And still when the sacrificial fires have wavered and grown dim, new fuel has been found to feed them.

While true-hearted men have labored zealously and consistently in New York for the promotion of the cause, their efforts have been nobly seconded and sustained by women. The year has been one of toil and sacrifice to many of these, but the prospect which the future unrolls before them banishes all uneasiness, and kindling anew the enthusiasm which first animated their efforts beckons them on towards the goal of their hopes and labors. In city, village and hamlet, in the rural districts, in the little schoolhouse nestled away among green hills, or in the pretending hall, or modern church along our crowded thoroughfares has the voice of woman been heard through all this year, pleading for aid against the serpent evil which invades the paradise of homes and breathes its venom on the fairest hopes and brightest joys her hand has tended there. It supplicating tones have been heard even in ou halls of legislation, and 28,000 wives, mother and daughters of our State have asked protectio at the hands of power. The pleadings of woma and the powerful arguments of men by word an at the ballot box have not been fruitless. Me are fast learning the lesson of consistency in thi reform; and he whose actions are not the faithfu exponent of his words must henceforth bear upo his brow the brand of one recreant to his highes moral duties, false to his professions, and a cow

The Lily, *a temperance journal first published by Amelia Bloomer in 1849, later became a voice for Stanton and other women's rights advocates.*

went so far as to wear the outfit to fine dinners and receptions in Washington, D.C., where her father was a member of Congress.

Within a few years women's rights activists came to believe that it was better to avoid wearing the bloomers. By appearing more conservative in their dress, they would not be immediately categorized and feared as revolutionaries. Still, the experiment did get people in both England and the United States to look further at alternatives for women's dress, such as tighter, more flattering leggings (instead of the puffy bloomer), a split skirt, or boots with a lower heel and broader sole.

In January 1852, Susan B. Anthony, who for many years had been active in the women's temperance movement, was invited along with several other women to the New York Men's State Temperance Society's annual

Amelia Bloomer, publisher of the Lily, *became best known for the less restrictire dress that she publicized, although did not invent. Bloomers were actually designed by Elizabeth Smith Miller, the daughter of Stanton's cousin Gerrit Smith.*

meeting in Albany. There she and the others realized that their hosts intended to gain control over the local women's temperance groups. During the Albany meeting, women were not allowed to participate. Susan was angry, and her natural lack of temerity, as well as her experience with fellow Quakers who freely spoke their minds, drew her to object. Yet, the men quickly ruled that she was out of order and shouted her down. Vehement, she and some of the other female attendees left the hall, and under Susan's guidance they made plans to form their own women's state temperance organization.

When Elizabeth heard what had happened at the men's temperance meeting, she became hopeful—having been treated so poorly, the women were ready to act. After the Seneca Falls convention of 1848 and its subsequent backlash, Elizabeth hadn't even tried to form a women's rights organization. Even though she lived in Seneca Falls, where so many reform movements had flourished, she had felt she would garner few supporters. Now she saw an opportunity. She could convince these agitated women that fundamental changes, not just in temperance reform, were necessary to dissolve man's tyranny over woman.

In April 1852 the New York Woman's Temperance Society was established in Rochester, New York. Elizabeth attended, as did Lucy Stone, Ernestine Rose, and sisters Lucretia Mott and Martha Wright. Susan garnered support to elect Elizabeth president of the new organization, and Susan became secretary. Elizabeth wore her bloomers to the meeting but toned down her acceptance speech, to appeal to her somewhat conservative audience.

In her speech, Elizabeth advocated liberalizing divorce laws in New York State to allow for divorce in cases where the husband was chronically drunk, believing this appeal would work with temperance advocates. However, she went even further, saying she would continue to speak out on other problems resulting from current beliefs on marriage, prostitution, and female education.

Unfortunately, the listeners were even more conservative than Elizabeth had anticipated. Criticism of her speech was heated. Attendees lashed back that the marriage contract was a pact that should not be broken, and that a woman with a drunken husband was duty bound to reform him and not leave him. While a number of western states at the time allowed divorce in instances of extreme cruelty or desertion, New York

LOVE · PURITY · AND · FIDELITY

Division No. State of

This is to Certify

That Brother was regularly
initiated and invested with the badge of the Order of the

Sons of Temperance

on the day of in the year of our Lord
One Thousand Eight Hundred and In
witness whereof we hereunto annex our names.

18   W. P.
                                                   R. S.

*Because the Sons of
Temperance (later renamed
the Mens' State Temperance
Society) did not allow
female members, Susan B.
Anthony decided to found a
woman's temperance orga-
nization, with Elizabeth
Cady Stanton as president.
However, members of the
newly formed Woman's
State Temperance Society
soon found Elizabeth's ideas
too radical; after 1853 the
two friends focused on
women's rights activities
instead.*

permitted divorce only in cases of adultery. For the
most part, divorce was still considered detestable to
many. Even many radical reformers believed such laws
shouldn't be liberalized. Others believed it was the
wrong time to tackle the issue. Then the meeting continued in another direction that the more radical
women never anticipated: attendees voted to allow men
to be members.

But the radicals would not be deterred. In January
1853 Stanton wrote a speech for Anthony to deliver to
a hearing of the New York State legislature. It requested
that laws be passed either to license liquor outlets, and

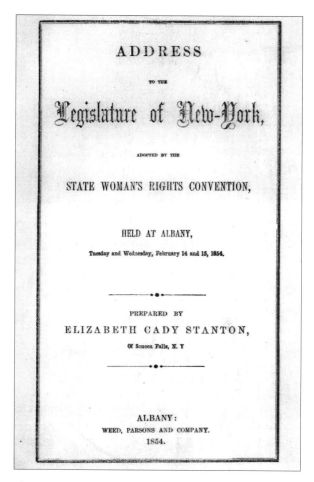

ADDRESS

TO THE

Legislature of New-York,

ADOPTED BY THE

STATE WOMAN'S RIGHTS CONVENTION,

HELD AT ALBANY,

Tuesday and Wednesday, February 14 and 15, 1854.

PREPARED BY

ELIZABETH CADY STANTON,

Of Seneca Falls, N. Y

ALBANY:
WEED, PARSONS AND COMPANY.
1854.

Stanton presented this speech at the 1854 women's rights convention in Albany, New York, although its ideas were intended for the state legislators who were meeting nearby. Printed copies were distributed across the state and placed on the desk of each New York legislator.

thereby limit them, or to let women vote on such proposals. Again, more conservative temperance reformers were appalled. Not so surprisingly, by June 1853, when the first annual meeting of the women's state organization was held, Stanton was not reelected. The conservative women rose against her, along with the male members, who by then had come to dominate the group.

From this experience, Elizabeth decided to depend on fellow agitators, and not try to transform those who weren't ready to listen. Elizabeth, Susan, and their core supporters promptly formed their own state women's rights convention, first held in 1854 in Albany and scheduled specifically when the New York State legislature was in session so the women could lobby their representatives. Susan organized members to cover the state, speaking and gathering signatures on petitions, while she traveled and spoke extensively herself. Elizabeth still was not traveling very far, having given birth to her first daughter, Margaret, in 1852. Her second daughter, Harriot, was born in 1856. Still, Elizabeth was gaining a reputation in public speaking. Twenty thousand copies were distributed of a speech she gave before the joint judiciary committee in the New York Senate, and in 1860 she spoke before a joint session of the legislature.

Without the support of powerhouse activists like Stanton and Anthony, the women's state temperance movement in New York fell apart. Similarly, the *Lily,* read by many women temperance advocates, stopped publication in 1856. Although Stanton had written some articles for the publication earlier, its editor, Amelia Bloomer, had sided with the more conservative temperance movement after the 1853 meeting.

In 1860 the radical women's rights activists were victorious. One day after Elizabeth spoke before the joint session of the New York legislature, it voted to pass the Married Woman's Property Act. Among other provisions, the act gave married women the right to their income and equal custody of their children with their husbands. According to biographer Lois W. Banner, this accomplishment for women's rights reminded Elizabeth of her experiences with the failed women's temperance movement in the early 1850s: "A multitude of timid, undeveloped men and women . . . are a hindrance rather than a help in any reform."

The victory was welcomed not just publicly. It provided Elizabeth with some optimism that helped her through the aftermath of a number of personal problems she experienced in 1859. She was 44 years old that year, and pregnant once more. Whereas her previous pregnancies had progressed smoothly, this time she had difficulties. Then, when her last child, Robert, was born in 1859, she suffered postpartum depression. That same year her dear friend and cousin, Gerrit Smith, spent some time in a mental institution. He was distraught over the failed radical abolitionist raid led by John Brown at Harpers Ferry, Virginia. Smith had given financial support to the attack, which ended miserably with Brown's execution for treason. And in 1859 there was yet another sorrow for Elizabeth. Her father, who although strict with his children had always had a soft spot for Elizabeth (just as she for him), passed away.

The passage of the Married Woman's Property Act in 1860 helped Elizabeth cope. And by the winter of 1861, just after Lincoln was elected president of the United States, Elizabeth's energies were pulled in

In 1859 John Brown heads for the gallows after being sentenced to death for treason—for attempting to bring about a slave revolt in Harpers Ferry, Virginia. The radical abolitionist's actions had been funded by Elizabeth's cousin Gerrit Smith, who suffered a mental breakdown upon hearing of its failure.

another direction. Fearing that Lincoln, a moderate on slavery, might compromise with the South, Garrisonian abolitionists planned a series of antislavery conventions in big cities throughout the North. Elizabeth Cady Stanton, Susan B. Anthony, and Beriah Green were invited to speak in the central New York area, while nearly every other available speaker was called upon for other parts of the North. By this time Elizabeth had found a Quaker housekeeper, Amelia Willard, who became a second mother for the family, ultimately staying with the Stantons for 30 years. By committing to speak at the antislavery conventions, Elizabeth would have to leave her children for several weeks, the longest she had ever done so.

Yet little did the Garrisonians realize the furor their meetings would provoke. Only one year after the John Brown raid, Republicans and Democrats alike felt the antislavery discussion should wait. However, the Republican party, because it opposed allowing slavery in the new western states that were now entering the Union, included political abolitionists within its ranks. The abolitionists' message was antagonistic to the South and seen as implicitly favoring war. The possibility of a civil war created intense fear among many Americans.

At each antislavery meeting, from Buffalo to Albany, hecklers filled the meeting halls and kept Elizabeth and her fellow speakers from being heard. Protesters disrupted speeches with laughs, groans, claps, cheers, and other disturbances. Eventually, speakers stopped trying to address the crowd and spoke, instead, among themselves on various issues. At times they were joined by interested attendees who crowded the platform to join the discussion.

In Buffalo, the police chief and his men stood by and did nothing, rather than follow their orders to protect the abolitionists' right to free speech. Determined mobs stopped the proceedings not only in central New York but also throughout that state and in other northern states. Elizabeth described a New York State legislative meeting held during this time: "a radical member sarcastically moved '[t]hat as Mrs. Stanton and Miss Anthony were about to move on Albany, the militia be ordered out for the protection of the city.'"

It was only a few months later that the Civil War began. In April 1861, President Lincoln called out 75,000 troops, and shortly thereafter in July, 400,000 more. By the end of the Civil War, 3 million men would be called to serve. The nation could concentrate only on this, and "all hands were busy in solemn preparations for the awful tragedies to come," Elizabeth wrote.

Further change came for Elizabeth in 1862, when her husband gained a position as deputy collector of the New York Customs House, a political appointment that acknowledged his hard work for the Republican Party. Elizabeth welcomed the opportunity to move to New York City, not only because her sisters Tryphena and Harriet and their husbands lived there but also because she would once again have ready access to cultural and reform events.

As the war progressed, everyone worked to aid in whatever way they could. In May 1863 Elizabeth met with fellow abolitionist supporters, among them Horace Greeley, William Lloyd Garrison, Robert Dale Owen, and Susan Anthony. Together they formed the National Women's Loyal League, whose goal was to convince Congress, by petition, to free all Southern slaves. Among the resolutions adopted at the League's first meeting was the establishment of all rights for women and for those of African descent when the war was over. Yet ending slavery quickly became the first concern, in order to weaken the South and win the war. Many people did not realize that Lincoln's Emancipation Proclamation, issued in January 1863, had freed only slaves living in the Southern territories occupied by Union armies.

Petitions demanding immediate freedom for slaves were circulated for months throughout the Northern states and signed by a staggering number of people. By some accounts 300,000 people signed the appeals; these same reports indicate this was the most names ever garnered in a single petition campaign. According to other sources, as many as 400,000 may have signed. From their headquarters at the Cooper Institute in New York City, Elizabeth and her fellow Loyal League organizers sent appeals to the president, House of Representatives, the Senate, and the people at large.

Those involved in women's rights organizations suspended their meetings. All attention focused on ending slavery. Unfortunately, as a result, women actually lost some of their rights at this time, as conservative legislators, left nearly unchecked, slipped new laws through.

By this time, many people had changed their perspectives about slavery and abolitionists. Lectures given at the Cooper Institute were well received and reaffirming letters arrived from many parts of the country. Elizabeth noted how the press, too, became advocates: "The leading journals vied with each other in praising the patience and prudence, the executive ability, the loyalty, and the patriotism of the women of the League, and yet these were the same women who, when demanding civil and political rights, privileges, and immunities for themselves, had been uniformly denounced as 'unwise,' 'imprudent,' 'fanatical,' and 'impracticable.'"

In the spring of 1864, Massachusetts senator Charles

During the Civil War, the women's rights effort lost momentum as suffragists devoted their time to helping the Union cause. Here members of one relief association work at their office at the Cooper Institute, in New York City.

Sumner presented the League's petitions to the U.S. Senate. The following year, in January 1865, Congress passed the Thirteenth Amendment, which, once signed by the president and ratified (approved by three-fourths of the states), would abolish slavery. In April, the Civil War was over.

Once the Civil War ended, Stanton counted on Republican leaders to support the women's right to vote, just as they had supported black suffrage. She and other suffragists would be disappointed.

6

"WHOM COULD WE TRUST?"

"[We] had been deceived once and could not be again."

—Elizabeth Cady Stanton, in *Eighty Years and More*

With the end of the war, the liberation of the slaves, and a South in need of rebuilding, the United States set to looking at itself once again and reconsidering its ideals. Elizabeth, many radical Republicans, and many abolitionists saw the end of the Civil War as a triumph over the South's belief in a society in which the rich were a privileged class. Reconstruction was seen as a chance for the country to reclaim its virtue and to become stronger by reinstating its democratic ideal of equal rights for all.

Unfortunately for women's rights activists, the Republicans believed that some ideals had to be temporarily compromised. To end abuses that persisted in the South, the black man's rights had to be secured first, Republicans thought. Yet they also believed that equal rights as a natural right could not be stated in a constitutional amendment, for this would mean that all of the outcast, including women, should have equal rights. Since most people were not

Abolitionists fully supported ensuring the black man's right to vote through ratification of the Fourteenth and Fifteenth Amendments, but many did not believe woman's suffrage should be demanded at the same time. Because Stanton and Anthony believed that one amendment should grant the right to vote for blacks and women, the two reformers opposed the passage and ratification of any suffrage amendment that did not include women.

ready to treat women equally, the Republicans believed that an amendment requesting rights for both blacks and women would never pass. At the time, many people in the United States still believed that women were not oppressed, that politics was no place for refined women, and that allowing women to vote would no longer make marriage an institution in which the husband and wife were as one.

In the spring of 1865, the Republicans apologized extensively to their feminist friends for their party's support of the Fourteenth Amendment, which was then being considered in Congress. The amendment guaranteed rights to freed slaves, but not to women. Susan, Elizabeth, and fellow supporters opposed the amendment and wrote letters, appeals, and petitions to women's rights advocates across the country. Yet Congress rejected their petitions and refused any discussion of women's rights.

Similarly, when in late 1866 Congress was considering a bill to allow blacks in the District of Columbia to vote, women could get no Republicans to support female suffrage there. While the suffragists did manage to convince a few Democratic senators to open discussion on the floor, the women received almost no other support. Many politicians believed that their parties would be crippled if they supported rights for blacks and women at the same time.

Undaunted, Stanton and Anthony presented many petitions to the New York State constitutional convention, asking that their own state support women's rights by including in its new constitution a provision giving women the right to vote in New York elections. Yet once again they were refused access.

As was now to be expected, the women received no assistance from their abolitionist friends, who were supporting a concurrent bill to allow black men to vote. Additionally, newspaper editors pressured the women, threatening that if they did not support the black vote now, the papers would work against women to defeat any future propositions.

Increasingly angry, Stanton lashed out even at Horace Greeley—a friend, member of the New York House of Representatives, and editor of the *New York Tribune*, to which Elizabeth and her husband had contributed articles. Although Greeley's paper had continuously been sympathetic to women's rights up until then, in legislative debates in 1867 he supported black suffrage and opposed woman's suffrage. After Elizabeth embarrassed him publicly, she was never again allowed to write for his paper and was always referred to in its columns as "Mrs. Henry B. Stanton," rather than her usual, more liberal version, "Elizabeth Cady Stanton."

Finally, in the spring of 1867, women were given a chance. The Kansas legislature became the first state legislature to pass two suffrage amendments that were to be voted on by its constituents. One amendment would give black men the right to vote, and the other would grant women that same right.

While the passage of these amendments in the Kansas State congress appeared promising, Stanton and Anthony knew there was still much work to be done. Because they were busy lobbying the New York constitutional convention, they convinced Lucy Stone and her husband, Henry Blackwell, to start campaigning for woman suffrage votes in Kansas. Stone, Blackwell, and fellow reformer Olympia Brown were well received when they arrived in the state. They held large meetings in the major cities and gained so much support from Republican speakers and newspapers that when they left the state in May, they believed the women's amendment would pass.

Just three months later, though, the situation had deteriorated. That was when Stanton and Anthony arrived in Kansas to continue campaigning. They found that Republicans not only had withdrawn support for the women's amendment but were now opposing it, again on the grounds that supporting the vote for both women and blacks would result in a win for neither. Even the reform and Republican newspapers from the East, it was later learned, were pressuring Republicans and abolitionists in Kansas not to support the women's amendment. As Elizabeth later reflected, "If the leaders in the Republican and abolition camps could deceive us, whom could we trust?"

No other eastern supporters were campaigning for woman's suffrage in Kansas when Stanton and Anthony arrived. Even Wendell Phillips and his fellow abolitionists withheld financial help, despite having received a large donation from a Boston merchant that was specifically to be used to support both black's and women's rights.

In spite of nearly overwhelming impediments, Elizabeth and Susan set to work. Instead of campaigning together, they split up and teamed with local support-

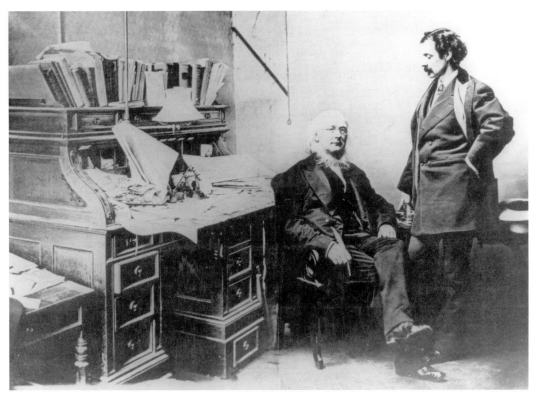

ers, thus extending the crusade even further throughout the state. Traveling in horse-drawn wagons to remote areas where no trains could reach, they frequently became lost and had to contend with poor roads and meager accommodations.

Elizabeth noted that she empathized with, and found it "a great privilege" to meet, many "noble" pioneers who readily welcomed them, sometimes despite difficulties such as serious illness, unfinished homes, mice nests in their beds, or difficult access to fresh drinking water. At times she spoke to as few as two dozen voters who had gathered in a log cabin, a schoolhouse, a barn, or an open field. Since the regular state elections were also to take place in November, "the interest increased from week to week, until the excitement of the people knew no bounds," Elizabeth wrote.

Still, as the Kansas election neared, the campaigners

New York Tribune *editor Horace Greeley (seated), who was also a member of the New York House of Representatives, supported the women's rights movement. But in 1867 he backed away from woman's suffrage and supported black suffrage only.*

knew they were in desperate need of more support. They turned to George Francis Train, a millionaire who had made his money in worldwide ventures and then returned to the United States to become an investor and politician. Train supported the issues of Irish independence from Britain and women's rights, although some believed he did the latter only to garner support for his planned presidential bid. He was a gifted, popular speaker who attracted large audiences, and when called into Kansas his dramatic speeches succeeded in securing more votes for female suffrage.

Despite the continuous, untiring efforts, when election day arrived in Kansas, both amendments were defeated. Frustrated, Elizabeth realized then that Susan had been right all along. Susan had persisted in the fight for women's rights throughout the Civil War, while nearly all other suffragists had succumbed to the Republicans' request that they fight solely for black rights. "[E]ver since, I have taken my beloved Susan's judgment against the world. . . . After we discuss any point together and fully agree, our faith in our united judgement is immovable and no amount of ridicule and opposition has the slightest influence," Elizabeth wrote in her autobiography.

Indeed, Elizabeth was not always strong in political strategizing. For example, the previous year, in 1866, she had become the first woman in the United States to run for Congress. Yet she did so with little planning and limited campaigning; running for a seat in the House of Representatives as a delegate from New York City, she received only 24 votes out of approximately 20,000.

After the defeat in Kansas, the women's long train ride home to New York could have been depressing; however, it proved to be just the opposite. After some discussion, they agreed to George Train's proposal to hold a series of woman-suffrage meetings at several stops along the return trip, for which he would foot the bill and see that they received attention in journals and

newspapers. The meetings proved to be a great success, and the newspapers gave them much coverage, yet many still believed the alliance with Train "a grave blunder," Elizabeth wrote. "To be sure our friends, on all sides, fell off."

Train had an eccentric style, speaking in full-dress clothing and wearing purple gloves. Additionally, many eastern reformers thought he was a racist, although Elizabeth and Susan did not. Eastern reformers also disagreed with Train's leanings toward the Democratic party's politics and his idea of forming a new national reform party to address problems of gender and class. Yet the women felt betrayed by Republicans and abolitionists; Elizabeth personally had been angered when in 1864 her husband had been accused of taking bribes at his job at the New York Customs House, and she blamed Republicans for the attack. The experience in Kansas had fed that anger.

Stanton and Anthony headed west in 1867 in an unsuccessful attempt to convince Kansas voters to approve a state amendment granting women the right to vote.

As it turned out, Elizabeth and Susan benefited from Train even more than they had anticipated, for he offered to finance their own radical journal. The two were especially grateful for this opportunity because much of the reform press had turned against them. When they had previously tried to start a publication on their own, they hadn't found the necessary financial support. Upon their return to New York, Elizabeth and Susan characteristically began working hard on this new journal, which they named the *Revolution* and launched in January 1868. Susan B. Anthony was its business manager, and the coeditors were Elizabeth Cady Stanton and Parker Pillsbury, who had quit his job as an antislavery editor when abolitionists refused to support the women's right to vote.

In the *Revolution,* nothing was held back. Within its pages, Stanton, Anthony, and Pillsbury continually argued against ratification of the Fourteenth Amendment and passage of the Fifteenth Amendment because woman's suffrage was omitted from their contents. Besides discussing marriage and divorce—from a radical perspective already known to upset readers—the new publication also spoke of rape, infanticide, prostitution, and wife beating—subjects almost never discussed in private at the time, let alone in a public forum. The journal received considerable negative reaction, but, as usual, the women persisted. As Elizabeth would later explain, "Considering the pressure brought to bear on Miss Anthony and myself, I feel now that our patience and forbearance with our enemies in their malignant attacks on our good name, which we never answered, were indeed marvelous."

With Train's financial backing, the *Revolution* editors could turn down any advertisements for products or companies that they considered inappropriate or disreputable. Similarly, financial freedom allowed them to keep the price of the journal low, so that any interested working woman could easily afford it. Elizabeth

The gifted speaker and millionaire George Francis Train provided financial support that allowed Stanton and Anthony to hold women's rights meetings and produce a women's rights journal. Feeling betrayed by the Republican Party, Stanton and Anthony accepted the Democrat's support, although other reformers considered him racist.

described the time working on the journal as "one of the happiest of my life, and I may add the most useful." Several months after starting the publication, she and her family moved to a large Victorian home in Tenafly, New Jersey, an hour's commute from New York City by train. Here the Stantons could be closer to nature and no longer have to contend with New York's extravagant property taxes or its violence.

Yet in 1869, Train ceased to support the *Revolution*. He left the United States and took his energies to England to fight for Irish independence. Despite a determined effort by Elizabeth and Susan, they could find no willing replacement supporters for the publication, and in the spring of 1870 the journal was sold. Elizabeth did not help repay the remaining $10,000 debt; Susan paid it off herself over the next five years, mostly with money received for lecturing and writing. The *Revolution*'s circulation had reached only 3,000 (there were 30,000 working women in New York City alone), having appealed to few outside the radical activist realm.

But meanwhile Susan and Elizabeth had made many plans for the suffrage movement and now started working toward them. They petitioned both the Republican and Democratic presidential nominating conventions to include woman's suffrage in their platforms. Neither party agreed, although the Democrats continued to support the women's efforts in both the state and federal legislatures. Next, Elizabeth and Susan moved their lobbying from the New York State legislature to the U.S. Congress, holding women's rights conventions in Washington, D.C., in January of each year, while Congress was in session. Susan would devote herself primarily to woman's suffrage from then on, although she would support Elizabeth's other causes periodically. In 1869 Susan moved to her own residence in Washington, D.C.

Additionally, rather than trying to spend time changing other federal amendments, the women worked on writing their own. In March 1869 their congressional allies actually introduced it in the House—a sixteenth amendment for woman's suffrage. Yet it was never discussed or brought to a vote.

After the Kansas debacle, alliances would prove untrustworthy for Elizabeth and Susan yet again. In May 1869 attendees were most embittered at the annual meeting of the American Equal Rights Association in New York City. Elizabeth and Susan had formed the group in 1866 to join the forces of the abolitionists and women's rights supporters. Up until then it had served mostly as a forum for debate and not been an active organization. Elizabeth chaired the 1869 meeting, and when discussion turned to the Fifteenth Amendment, which would give blacks the right to vote, she and Susan spoke against it. The crowd became increasingly agitated, directing their vehemence at the two women. They were harangued, booed, and accused of being racist.

Additionally, rancor grew because free-love advocates were attending the meeting. It was not uncommon for women's rights groups to open their platforms to free-love supporters, who believed in social and sexual communal groups. Yet the presence of free-love advocates further angered the attendees, who believed that Stanton, known for speaking out on divorce and sexual issues, was not just providing the free lovers with a forum but also supporting their views.

Animosity reached such proportions that a resolution was introduced requiring that Stanton and Anthony withdraw from the American Equal Rights Association. While the resolution was defeated, the group did vote to support the Fifteenth Amendment, a resolution introduced by Elizabeth's previous ally, Frederick Douglass. At this point no rebuttals from Stanton and Anthony were allowed. Nor would anyone listen when Lucy Stone and her husband Henry Blackwell tried to introduce a compromise.

Immediately after the meeting, Stanton and Anthony formed the National Woman Suffrage Association (NWSA), whose sole purpose would be garnering support for passage of a sixteenth amendment allowing women to vote. One hundred women joined the organization, mostly from New York and the West. Again, the two comrades would not be deterred.

Parker Pillsbury, who quit his job as editor for an antislavery paper when it refused to support woman's suffrage, was hired to coedit the Revolution. *Susan B. Anthony served as business manager and Elizabeth Cady Stanton as coeditor for the women's rights publication.*

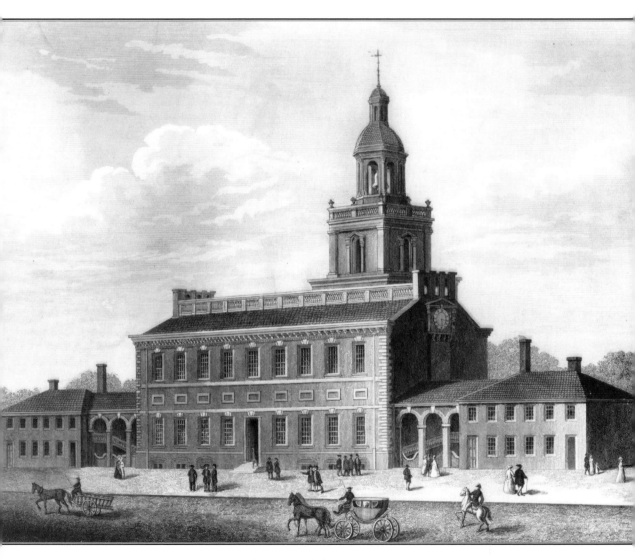

Independence Hall, Philadelphia, seemed the proper forum for suffragists to present their own declaration of women's rights during the Centennial Exposition held in 1876. Despite being denied permission to speak at Independence Hall, several suffragists disrupted the July 4th meeting with their bid for equal rights.

7

"ORDER, ORDER!"

"But the history of the world shows that the vast majority, in every generation, passively accept the conditions into which they are born, while those who demanded larger liberties are ever a small, ostracized minority, whose claims are ridiculed and ignored."

—Elizabeth Cady Stanton, in *Eighty Years and More*

At 54 years old, Elizabeth had tired of confrontations with New York reformers and unfair criticism from so many others, yet she still had much energy. In October 1869, only a few months after the uprising at the American Equal Rights Association meeting, she adopted a new occupation. She became a speaker for a New York bureau, which, as she described in her autobiography, arranged speaking engagements "on all the vital questions of the hour," wherever there was a ready crowd.

Lecturing on women's issues and reform by appealing to the nation's consciousness would certainly be easier than arranging administrative details and organizing reform strategies, Stanton thought. Across the country, since the 1820s, people had been

Lucy Stone (above) and her husband Henry Blackwell considered Stanton too radical. The women's movement was split when Stone and Blackwell formed their own organization, the American Woman Suffrage Association (AWSA), which worked to win the woman's right to vote by changing state laws and constitutions.

forming lyceums—associations that presented public lectures by notable speakers. The lyceums used booking agencies for help in finding the best orators. The three leading speakers' bureaus were located in New York, Chicago, and Boston.

Elizabeth said she became a lyceum speaker because her family needed more money (speakers would get from $100 to $200 a night), since her husband had resigned from his position with the customs house and now received a relatively low income from newspaper reporting and legal work. That explanation is questionable, however, because by that time her three oldest sons had finished college; her sister Harriet had paid for most of Elizabeth's two daughters' educations at Vassar College; and Elizabeth had inherited a sizable $50,000 from her father.

But regardless of her motivations, Elizabeth started on the speakers' circuit in October, leaving her husband and housekeeper at home with four children ranging in age from 10 to 18 years old. She would remain on tour until the following June, traveling from Maine to Texas, eventually receiving such an enthusiastic response from newspapers and local lyceums that she would become one of the most popular speakers.

Even the pains of traveling on a very tight schedule could not subdue Elizabeth's enthusiasm or sense of humor. She worked around unreliable public transportation, floods, snow blockades, poor sleeping accommodations, and lecture hall ceilings that leaked rainwater right onto the speaker's platform. Lectures organized through the speakers' bureau were held at night, and during the day Elizabeth would talk with many interesting people. When not at a regular engagement, she would often speak wherever anyone would listen, frequently talking about marriage, maternity, and health with groups of women, and even using her time spent traveling on trains to discuss reform or help a wailing baby and its distressed parents.

While Elizabeth's early commentary on liberalized divorce, equality for women, and sexuality had caused a furor, people were slowly changing and becoming more willing to listen to what she had to say. Now there were many more books on sex and contraception, and women were starting to have fewer children. Women's groups were growing both in membership and in number, although most espoused moderate views. In contrast to the negative reactions she had received when she first proclaimed her radical ideas, Stanton's reviews while on the speaking circuit were mostly positive. People saw her as gracious, witty, and firm, yet not overly so. Newspapers compared her to such well-respected women as Queen Victoria and Martha Washington, and people seemed comforted by her grandmotherly white curls and her now heavyset frame. Such experiences inspired her to continue to work as a speaker from October until June each year for the next 12 years.

Indeed, the escape of lecturing came at just the right time for Stanton. Only one month after she started on the speakers' circuit, a further division occurred in the suffrage movement. Lucy Stone and her husband Henry Blackwell formed their own organization—the American Woman Suffrage Association (AWSA), which splintered the NWSA that Stanton and Anthony had just formed. Lucy Stone had been retired from the women's movement, but at 51 years old she resented the power that Stanton and Anthony had gained. Increasingly conservative, Stone saw Stanton as an unfocused zealot who concentrated too much on women's social burdens and marital difficulties.

The goal of the National Woman Suffrage Association (NWSA) was to pass a sixteenth amendment granting women the right to vote. The NWSA worked for change at the federal level, circulating petitions, lobbying congressmen, and testifying at hearings, as well as holding conventions.

Additionally, Stone did not want to be associated with Stanton because so many believed her an advocate of free love. While Stanton never publicly declared the views of free lovers as wrong, privately she opposed sexual promiscuity. She did believe, however, that the voices of the free lovers encouraged more people to reconsider traditional views on sexuality, marriage, and divorce that were harmful.

By forming the AWSA in Cleveland, Ohio, Stone and Blackwell hoped to gain more western support. Blackwell had become a rich businessman and was ready with financing for the new organization.

While the division between the activists caused much animosity, the new group formed by Lucy Stone was actually not so very different from that of Stanton and Anthony. Stone's organization differed by requiring that its membership equally represent all the states, and its delegates concentrated on lobbying state, rather than federal, legislatures. But the AWSA focused on woman's suffrage, just as the NWSA did. And despite the minimal differences between the two groups, the formation of the new organization created a rancor that would persist for 21 years.

Elizabeth Cady Stanton was disgusted by this division in the women's movement, but she avoided public confrontation with her former friends. She had already been growing somewhat distant from the movement, and the creation of the AWSA intensified that. In years to come, Susan Anthony would have a difficult time getting Elizabeth to attend conventions. Stanton mostly watched from a distance as Anthony built relationships with the younger women who joined the NWSA. Elizabeth questioned whether these younger women appreciated what older women such as herself had gone through. Younger women now had access to more professions and colleges (by 1870, of the 582 colleges and universities in the United States, 169 were open to women). Elizabeth thought these women were hungry for more opportunity rather than attuned to problems of female subordination.

Despite the ill will of Elizabeth and others, in the spring of 1870 Theodore Tilton and Henry Ward Beecher, the first president of the AWSA, tried to combine the NWSA and AWSA. Against Stanton's protests, Theodore Tilton, who had recently created the Union Suffrage Association, convinced the NWSA to merge with his organization. Tilton then hoped to merge the NWSA with the AWSA. But AWSA founders Lucy Stone and Henry Blackwell nixed the merger with their group, and again the result was more anger among suffragists. Anthony immediately reorganized the NWSA, making Elizabeth Cady Stanton president.

From 1869 to 1873, Anthony took breaks from reform activities from time to time and accompanied Stanton on various trips west through Iowa, Missouri, Illinois, and Nebraska. In 1871, needing a rest after the

Henry Ward Beecher (above), a renowned abolitionist preacher, served as the first president of the AWSA. Along with Theodore Tilton, the head of another organization that had merged with the NWSA, Beecher made a failed attempt in 1870 to unite the two woman's suffrage organizations. The two groups would not unite for another 20 years.

attempted NWSA–AWSA merger, the two women relaxed on a trip to California. Although much of their time there was still spent making speeches and meeting new people, they took the opportunity to leisurely enjoy their surroundings.

In the fall of 1871 Elizabeth's mother died, and the following spring, further trouble ensued with the NWSA. One of the most controversial and daring free-love advocates, Victoria Woodhull, asked Stanton for the NWSA's support of her newly formed Equal Rights Party, whose intent was to promote Woodhull's bid for the U.S. presidency. While Stanton was hesitant about aligning herself with yet another notorious figure, she finally agreed to help Woodhull.

But as soon as Anthony heard of the alliance, she rushed back from her lastest speaking tour to Stanton's home in Tenafly, New Jersey. It is unclear how the discussion progressed between Anthony and Stanton the night before the NWSA meeting in New York. But once at the meeting, Susan was distressed to find that many other NWSA delegates also supported the controversial Woodhull. Fearing that Woodhull's plan was to take control of the association, Anthony refused to allow the Equal Rights Party advocate to speak, and finally turned out the lights to get her to leave. Stanton was furious and resigned as NWSA president. The incident strained her friendship with Anthony.

But as unpleasant as the NWSA meeting had been, afterward Stanton realized that Anthony was right and never again supported Woodhull publicly. Bruised relationships healed, and the activists set to planning their activities for the centennial celebration of the signing of the Declaration of Independence.

The enormous centennial exposition took place in Philadelphia, Pennsylvania, from May through November, 1876. Covering more than 200 acres, the fair contained international exhibitions of arts, manufactures, and agricultural products displayed in approximately 200 buildings constructed for the occasion. Almost 10 million visitors eventually attended the exposition, which Elizabeth later described as an event that "stirred the patriotism of the people to the highest point of enthusiasm."

When NWSA leaders first arrived for the Fourth of July celebration at the exposition, they saw that the women's building created for the event omitted any display of the women's activist movement. The leaders scoured the crammed downtown district and found a place to create and display their own exhibit at 1431 Chestnut Street.

Because Elizabeth Cady Stanton was still the movement's most talented writer, she was the primary author of a declaration of women's rights that was to be read at various places and times throughout the Fourth of July festivities, and especially during the celebration in Independence Hall. "Thousands were ordered to be printed, and were folded, put in envelopes, stamped, directed, and scattered. Miss Anthony, Mrs. Gage, and I worked sixteen hours, day and night . . . carrying immense bundles to be mailed," Elizabeth later recalled.

While nowhere near as impassioned as the Seneca Falls Declaration of Sentiments, this piece stated a complex, reasoned argument for why women should have the right to vote. The declaration also spoke out against inequitable laws, the lack of women on juries, the unfair taxation of women who had no voice in the government, and the dangers of denying women their independence and their right to an equal education.

Stanton framed her work as articles of impeachment against the U.S. government.

Yet, General Joseph Hawley, who was in charge of the Fourth of July celebration, refused to give the women a chance to speak at the Independence Hall gathering, saying the program was booked. He did, however, grant them six invitations to sit in the audience.

Not to be deterred, five of the suffragists used those invitations to gain seats in the mostly male-filled hall. After the Declaration of Independence was read, the women made their way through the listeners and up to the surprised speakers on the platform. The five presented the presiding officer, now pale and speechless, with a copy of their declaration of women's rights, then proceeded back down the platform, scattering printed copies as they headed toward the door. Elizabeth later recounted the scene: "On every side eager hands were outstretched, men stood on seats and asked for them, while General Hawley, thus defied and beaten in his audacious denial to women of the right to present their Declaration, shouted, 'Order, order!'"

Once outside, Susan B. Anthony read the pronouncement to an applauding crowd, while behind them sat the Liberty Bell, Elizabeth ironically noted— the "old bell that proclaimed 'liberty to all the land and all the inhabitants thereof.'" From there the women hurried to their own convention at the crowded First Unitarian Church. Many attendees had no seats, but they were reluctant to leave, even after five hours of standing on the oppressively hot July day.

Still somewhat distanced from the NWSA, Stanton did not take part in the radical demonstration inside Independence Hall. She was impressed and rejuvenated, though, from both the demonstration and the meetings taking place at the NWSA building at the centennial. There many members worked diligently, developing strategies and writing and distributing their message. Thus inspired, once again Elizabeth agreed to

The controversial feminist Victoria Woodhull asked Stanton to support her newly formed Equal Rights Party. However, Susan B. Anthony was so opposed to this idea that she prevented Woodhull from speaking before the NWSA—by turning out the lights.

serve as president of the organization, and she would remain so until 1890.

After the centennial celebration, the NWSA needed a new approach in its quest for woman's suffrage. Previously, the group had been supporting the view that the lack of specificity in the Fourteenth Amendment actually allowed women the right to vote. The amendment said that no state could "abridge the privileges . . . of citizens," and the interpretation followed that because women are citizens, they should be allowed to vote. Yet,

Spectators crowd around the main building at the Philadelphia Centennial Exposition, which celebrated the 100th anniversary of the signing of the Declaration of Independence. At the event, NWSA suffragists showcased the progress they had made in the women's rights movement and outlined the goals they still needed to accomplish.

in 1875 the Supreme Court had ruled against this interpretation, and suffragists realized they needed to petition Congress for a new amendment that would unequivocally provide women the right to vote.

Elizabeth Cady Stanton was probably the author of the draft of the new woman's suffrage amendment, although it became known as the Susan B. Anthony Amendment. After meeting with Stanton, California senator Aaron Sargent agreed to introduce the Anthony Amendment to Congress in early 1878. The amendment failed to reach the Senate for debate, but it would continue to be reintroduced at each subsequent session of Congress.

The NWSA, although small, stuck with its plan of devoting its energies to congressional lobbying. Their suffrage speeches were published in the *Congressional Record* and in materials distributed by various congressmen and senators. Congressional committees began to take more interest in suffrage testimony, and congressmen started attending NWSA conventions and receptions.

With renewed resolve, the NWSA grew in size, until by the mid-1880s it surpassed its rival AWSA. The AWSA's finances were great and it sponsored the successful periodical *The Woman's Journal,* while the NWSA had limited funds and only sporadic results with its own publication. Yet the NWSA's concentrated focus on Washington, D.C., as well as Anthony's superior organizational skills and energy, pulled the organization through.

Finally, in December 1886 the Anthony Amendment was debated on the Senate floor. But it was voted down in the Senate on January 25, 1887, by a vote of 16 to 34—far short of the two-thirds majority needed to pass. Nearly 40 years of lobbying had not been enough.

The two leaders of the early women's rights movement, Elizabeth Cady Stanton and Susan B. Anthony pose in front of Anthony's home in Rochester, New York. Susan moved from Washington, D.C., in 1891, making the Rochester residence her permanent home until her death in 1906.

8

871 PAGES AND MORE

"We cannot bring about a moral revolution in a day or year."

—Elizabeth Cady Stanton, in a letter to Susan B. Anthony

While working for passage of the amendment for woman's suffrage, Elizabeth found her attention also becoming more focused on her family life in Tenafly, New Jersey, with its accompanying picnics, dinners, teas, and dances. In October 1880 her daughter Margaret was married at home in a beautiful backyard ceremony. That same year, Elizabeth quit her lyceum tours and in November started writing her diary. She began it, as she had promised herself, on her 65th birthday, which turned out to be a quiet day because most of her family was away. Already in a somewhat somber mood, Elizabeth learned the following day of the death of her old friend Lucretia Mott, at the age of 87. One of Elizabeth's earliest mentors was gone.

Yet as usual, Elizabeth would have little time for quiet contemplation. Only one week later she was visited by Susan Anthony and Matilda Jocelyn Gage, past president of the NWSA. The three

In her Tenafly, New Jersey, home, Elizabeth Cady Stanton worked with Susan B. Anthony and Matilda Gage to compile and edit the first volume of the History of Woman's Suffrage, *which consisted of 871 pages.*

women were about to embark on what would become yet another historic undertaking—compiling and publishing a history of the woman's suffrage movement. Elizabeth and Susan had been discussing the project for years, and for equally as long Susan, the adept researcher, had been gathering every important document she could, as well as personal accounts from numerous sources. Once again, Susan moved in with Elizabeth's family, and the women set to work.

"We stood appalled before the mass of material, growing higher and higher with every mail," Elizabeth wrote in *Eighty Years and More.* "Six weeks of steady labor all day, and often until midnight, made no visible decrease in the pile of documents." The women edited the documents and commentary, and then Elizabeth wrote short narratives to pull the material together. Lucy Stone refused to contribute material on the AWSA, but Elizabeth's daughter, Harriot Stanton Blatch, wrote a chapter on the organization, convincing the annoyed Elizabeth and Susan that their text would appear biased without it.

After working for seven months with almost no interruptions, the women completed the first volume of *History of Woman Suffrage*. It came to 871 pages and covered the movement only from 1848 to 1861, but the authors felt that every piece was necessary. The book was published in May 1881. "I welcomed it with the same feeling of love and tenderness as I did my first-born," Elizabeth wrote in her autobiography. "I took the same pleasure in hearing it praised and felt the same mortification in hearing it criticised."

While they were in the throes of creating their book, Elizabeth and Susan had received a mixture of good and bad comments about compiling such a history. Now, upon its publication, they were happily surprised to receive many more positive commentaries than they had anticipated. One of its strongest reviews, published in a London newspaper, came from Reverend William Henry Channing, an American clergyman and reformer.

Most pleased with their published piece, only one month later, Elizabeth and Susan started volume 2. By May 1882 it was complete, and Elizabeth and her daughter Harriot set off for Bordeaux, France. They wished they could bring Henry Stanton along, but at the age of 77 he was now in poor health.

The travelers were warmly greeted in France by Elizabeth's son Theodore. He and Harriot were the two children to whom Elizabeth felt closest and who had the most interest in the women's rights movement. Though the aging activist had wanted a break from writing on this trip, it was not to be. While staying in France with Theodore, his wife, Marguerite Berry, and their baby, Nora, Elizabeth helped her son edit his own book on female rights, *The Woman Question in Europe*. She hadn't expected to work on her vacation, but as she explained, "it was labor in the cause of my sex . . . and so my pen did not grow slack nor my hand weary."

Elizabeth's daughter Harriot Stanton Blatch supported her mother's efforts in the women's rights movement by contributing to the History of Woman's Suffrage, *as well as accompanying Elizabeth in her travels abroad.*

Elizabeth would later comment on her fourth son's involvement in women's issues: "To have a son interested in the question to which I have devoted my life, is a source of intense satisfaction . . . I have realized in him all I could desire."

While living abroad, Elizabeth could not escape attention from other European feminists who sought her company, and she spoke with many on numerous issues. She also presented her idea of forming an international women's organization; however, it was not until much later that agreement on this new organization was reached. Susan Anthony had arrived that October to vacation and then to join Elizabeth Cady Stanton at the Liberal Conference being held in Leeds, England. It was not until their farewell reception in 1883 that fellow activists agreed to form an international association.

Upon returning to the United States, Elizabeth visited many friends to catch up on news and then traveled to her childhood home in Johnstown, New York. In the summer of 1884, Susan "arrived armed and equipped with bushels of documents" to create volume 3 of *History of Woman Suffrage*, believing that in Johnstown she and Elizabeth could take refuge from other distractions.

In the spring of 1886, the third volume of *History of Woman Suffrage* was complete. At this point Elizabeth declared that her age prevented her from continuing any further on the project. Privately, she maintained that she was exhausted from the tedious editing, but she also had been growing disaffected with the suffrage movement for some time. Susan continued on, working with Ida Husted Harper to complete volume 4, and eventually published two more long volumes by 1906. Freeing up more time for herself proved important for Elizabeth, as it would turn out, for not long after ending her part on the *History of Woman Suffrage* project, she was confronted with the death of her husband in 1887.

In March of 1888 the international women's meeting that Susan and Elizabeth had envisioned more than five years earlier finally took place over a one-week period in Washington, D.C. The convention was spearheaded by the National Woman Suffrage Association, and Susan did most of the organizing and fund-raising. Elizabeth urged many of her overseas friends to attend and gave the opening and closing speeches to large, diverse crowds.

During the meeting, two new women's rights groups formed—the International Council of Women and the National Council of Women for the United States—in an effort to unite as many women's rights forces as possible. Yet over time neither of the new groups would prove itself very effective. In fact, the International Council refused to make woman's suffrage one of its goals, and only years later, in 1904, was an international woman's suffrage organization formed.

From 1888 to 1889 Elizabeth traveled, visiting her children, who lived in Nebraska, Iowa, and New York. Then she returned to England, visiting from 1890 to 1891. Back in the United States in August 1891, Elizabeth started looking for a new place to live, having sold her large home in Tenafly shortly after her husband's death. She turned down Susan Anthony's invitation to live with her in Rochester, deciding instead to live with two of her children—her youngest son, Robert Stanton, now a lawyer, and her widowed

Representatives from Canada, Norway, England, Ireland, Scotland, France, and Finland join Anthony and Stanton (seated, second and fourth from the left) at the first International Council of Women, held in Washington, D.C., in 1888, nearly 40 years after the Seneca Falls convention.

daughter, Margaret Stanton Lawrence, a professor of physical education at Columbia Teacher's College in New York. After a few weeks of searching, the three decided on an apartment in New York City. "To be transported from the street to your apartment in an elevator in half a minute . . . to have your rooms all warmed with no effort of your own, seemed like a realization of some fairy dream," Elizabeth enthused about the new arrangement.

Only three of Elizabeth's six children—Margaret, Harriot, and Theodore—chose to become involved in the women's reform movement. All her sons were lawyers, like her father and husband. Her eldest son, Daniel, died in 1891, the same year she moved into the New York City apartment; he had become very wealthy from unscrupulous business transactions with the

Louisiana government during Reconstruction. Her son Henry was a corporate lawyer, and Gerrit was a real estate broker on Long Island, having switched careers after gaining some renown as a naturalist.

The now 76-year-old activist received many requests to speak and had much correspondence to keep up with. She also continued to write articles for newspapers and magazines on an array of topics as diverse as Cuba, prison reform, coeducation, and marriage and divorce, and she discussed less serious social issues such as why the World's Fair should stay open on Sundays, and why humanity need not fret over women riding bicycles.

Then in 1895 Elizabeth began work again on a dream of hers that had persisted for years—publication of *The Woman's Bible*, a book that would contain every Biblical reference to women (which, she would find, was less than one-tenth of the whole Bible), followed by commentary; the goal was to determine the true status of women according to the Christian and Jewish religions. Elizabeth believed that only the Universalist, Unitarian, and liberal Quaker faiths truly allowed women equal status. She felt that to a large extent it was the Protestant clergy that excluded women, as had occurred at the London antislavery convention she attended in 1840. She considered religious prejudice as one of the basic causes of the oppression of women.

For years at the NWSA conventions, Elizabeth and others had presented resolutions against religious bias, "but they were either suppressed or so amended as to be meaningless," Elizabeth noted. Yet by the 1890s in many religious faiths, women had begun demanding to be ordained as ministers, elders, and deacons, and to be admitted as delegates to church-governing bodies. One of the changes that had occurred during the Civil War was that women had gained control of many of the new missionary boards and now dominated the missionary fields.

While Elizabeth had thought about creating *The*

Woman's Bible for many years, she had first moved the project to the forefront in the mid-1880s as she became aware of the increasing momentum of religious conservatives. They introduced religious topics at suffrage conventions, rallied for teaching Protestantism in the public schools, and went so far as to lobby Congress to declare Christianity the official religion of the United States. In response, Elizabeth had started working on *The Woman's Bible*, with the help of her daughter Harriot Stanton Blatch and their friend Frances Lord. Hoping to garner aid from some Latin, Greek, and Hebrew scholars, Elizabeth had written to everyone she could think of to contribute to the book. While waiting for their responses, the threesome set to work.

Elizabeth wrote in her autobiography about the Pentateuch, the first five books in the Bible:

> I know no other books that so fully teach the subjection and degradation of woman. Miriam, the eldest sister of Moses and Aaron, a genius, a prophetess, with the family aptitude for diplomacy and government, is continually set aside because of her sex—permitted to lead the women in singing and dancing, nothing more. No woman could offer sacrifices nor eat the holy meats because, according to the Jews, she was too unclean and unholy.
>
> But what is the use, say some, of attaching any importance to the customs and teachings of a barbarous people? None whatever. But when our bishops, archbishops, and ordained clergymen stand up in their pulpits and read selections from the Pentateuch with reverential voice, they make the women of their congregation believe that there really is some divine authority for their subjection.

The women worked on the project for several weeks, even though they had been receiving numerous discouraging responses to Elizabeth's requests for help. Even Elizabeth's usual cohort in such undertakings, Susan Anthony, believed they were on the wrong track. Susan thought that when women were finally recognized as full-fledged citizens, then religious institutions

Although Susan B. Anthony had worked with Elizabeth Cady Stanton in many other areas, she did not agree with Elizabeth's desire to write The Woman's Bible. *Susan feared that a book that attacked organized religion would alienate women from the suffrage movement.*

would alter their publications and practices. She told Elizabeth that an anticlerical message would make it harder to convince religious women to become involved in the women's movement. Lacking the necessary help, Elizabeth stopped working on the book.

But nearly ten years later, in early 1895, Elizabeth resurrected the project. She now had more time, and several women were willing to help her. Part 1 of *The Woman's Bible* made it into print relatively quickly, by November of 1895. The book received great attention, with extracts and criticisms printed in newspapers throughout the United States, Great Britain, and

Europe. Some New York City newspapers gave the publication a full-page review, including pictures of its cover, its commentators, and its critics. Some clergy members called it the work of Satan himself, while other religious leaders viewed it as undeserving of any serious attention. Undeterred, Elizabeth and her committee, which had grown to about 25 members, completed part 2 by January 1898. That same year Elizabeth's autobiography, *Eighty Years and More,* was published.

Few suffragists supported the aging activist in her campaign against organized religion. Despite the recognition they gave her as one of the founders of the women's rights movement, tension between these active reformers and Elizabeth had persisted through the years. In 1890 Elizabeth had had little involvement when the NWSA and AWSA had finally merged, becoming the National American Woman Suffrage Association (NAWSA). Although she had become president of the new organization at Susan's insistence, she had resigned two years later and had never again attended an NAWSA meeting.

When *The Woman's Bible* was published in 1895, the NAWSA officially announced it had no connection with the publication. Even though most NAWSA members who were critical of the book hadn't even read it, they feared that supporting it would drive away the group's more conservative followers and potential members. NAWSA leaders would no longer read Elizabeth's resolutions and letters at the group's meetings.

Despite her differences with fellow suffragists, Elizabeth is not bitter toward them in her autobiography. Suffering from failing eyesight and health, she spent much time happily playing with her grandchildren, whom she adored, but also continued to read and write. She searched for financial backing to compile an edition of her speeches and writings, and published an article on divorce just one week before her death.

As Elizabeth's health continued to deteriorate, she

In 1898 Elizabeth Cady Stanton published her autobiography, entitled Eighty Years and More. *She predicted in the book that one day the subjugation of women would be abolished, and she noted the progress that had been achieved since the Seneca Falls Women's Rights Convention, held 50 years earlier.*

lost her sight completely. There is some belief that she was frustrated by no longer being able to work and may have killed herself with drugs obtained from her doctor. But whether or not this account is true, what is known is that on October 26, 1902, at the age of 87, she asked her daughters to dress her and fix her thick hair that many had admired throughout her life. Now very overweight, she stood and leaned against a table for a little less than 10 minutes, seemingly imagining herself giving one last speech. Then she sat down, fell asleep with her head on the table, and died two hours later.

A 1901 photograph of Stanton's granddaughter, Nora Stanton Blatch, illustrates the advancements made in opportunities for women. At Horace Mann High School in New York City, Nora participates in an ironworking class—a course of study that would have been unheard of for women in the time of her grandmother.

The radical feminist died peacefully, although she had seen only some of her life's work reach fruition. Her autobiography, finished approximately seven years before her death, ends with hopeful words. She predicts that in time her work to expose the extent of religious institutions' degradation of women would be recognized and that the subjugation of women would be abolished. Looking back on the 1848 Seneca Falls convention, she focuses on the progress that has been made:

> [W]e were unsparingly ridiculed by the press and pulpit both in England and America. But now many conventions are held each year in both countries to discuss the same

ideas; social customs have changed; laws have been modified; municipal suffrage has been granted to women in England and some of her colonies; school suffrage has been granted to women in half of our States, municipal suffrage in Kansas, and full suffrage in four States of the Union. . . . That first convention, considered a 'grave mistake' in 1848, is now referred to as 'a grand step in progress.'

It would not be until 1920 that a Constitutional amendment granting women the right to vote would be passed and ratified by the states—18 years after Elizabeth's death and a formidable 72 years after the plea was first made at the 1848 Seneca Falls convention she had spearheaded.

Additionally, it would not be until the 1960s that the women's movement would significantly reorganize to renew the fight for social change and equality—the very issues that Elizabeth had espoused throughout her life. By then more than 58 years had passed since her death and more than 112 years since the Seneca Falls convention.

"It is impossible for any one to tell what people are ready to hear," Elizabeth had said in her speech at the convention in which the NWSA and AWSA merged. Years before she had given up on waiting for the public to be ready for new ideas. Instead, she had decided to always speak up for what she thought was right and then manage the consequences. "[P]erhaps the very thing you fear," she had said, "is exactly what should be done."

CHRONOLOGY

1815	Elizabeth Cady born on November 12 in Johnstown, New York, to Daniel and Margaret Cady
1830	Graduates from Johnstown Academy
1833	Graduates from Troy Female Seminary in Troy, New York
1840	Marries Henry Stanton, an executive of the American Anti-Slavery Society, on May 11; with Henry attends World Anti-Slavery Convention
1841	Returns to Johnstown, where Henry studies law with Elizabeth's father
1842	Gives birth to first son, Daniel Cady
1843	Moves to Boston, Massachusetts, where Henry Stanton starts to practice law
1844	Gives birth to Henry
1845	Gives birth to Gerrit Smith
1847	Moves to Seneca Falls, New York
1848	Spearheads first woman's suffrage convention in Seneca Falls on July 19 and 20; begins to write and speak on the issue of women's rights
1851	Gives birth to Theodore; meets Susan B. Anthony, who becomes a lifelong friend and collaborator
1852	Becomes president of newly formed New York Woman's Temperance Society; gives birth to first daughter, Margaret
1856	Gives birth to Harriot
1859	Gives birth to last child, Robert; Elizabeth's father dies
1862	Moves to New York City when husband gets political appointment as deputy collector of the New York Customs House
1863	Cofounds the National Women's Loyal League
1866	Forms American Equal Rights Association with Anthony; becomes first woman to run for U.S. Congress

1868	Launches the *Revolution*, a women's rights newspaper, with Anthony; family moves to Tenafly, New Jersey
1869	Forms National Woman Suffrage Association with Anthony; becomes traveling speaker for New York Bureau, a position that will continue each year (from October until June) for 12 years
1872	Under duress because of controversial association with Victoria Woodhull, resigns as NWSA president
1876	Writes new declaration of women's rights for centennial celebration of America's independence; once again becomes president of NWSA and holds that position until 1890
1880–86	Coedits the first three volumes of the *History of Woman Suffrage*
1887	Husband Henry Stanton dies
1890	NWSA and AWSA merge and become the National American Woman Suffrage Association (NAWSA); becomes president and remains so for two years
1891	Moves into New York City apartment with two of her children
1895	Organizes and coedits *The Woman's Bible*, part 1
1898	Publishes her autobiography, *Eighty Years and More;* completes part 2 of *The Woman's Bible*
1902	Dies on October 26
1920	Constitutional amendment granting women the right to vote is ratified
1980	Congress designates various sites in Seneca Falls, New York, as a national historical park for women's rights

THE ROAD TO WOMEN'S RIGHTS IN THE UNITED STATES

1776   Abigail Adams asks husband John to "remember the Ladies" when formulating the new nation's government; the U.S. Declaration of Independence states that "all men are created equal"

1821   Emma Hart Willard founds the Troy Female Seminary in New York, which is the first school of higher education for women

1833   Oberlin College, Ohio, is the first college to open its doors to men and women, black and white

1836   Angelina and Sarah Grimké begin speaking publicly against slavery

1837   First Anti-Slavery Convention of American Women held in New York City; Mary Lyon founds Mount Holyoke College, first four-year college for women only

1839   American Anti-Slavery Society votes to allow women within its organization; Mississippi passes the first Married Woman's Property Act

1840   World Anti-Slavery Convention held in London; women delegates are not allowed to participate

1844   First labor association for women—Lowell Female Labor Reform Association—established in Massachusetts

1848   At first public convention on women's rights, in Seneca Falls, New York, participants sign a Declaration of Sentiments and Resolutions that lists women's grievances

1849   Escaped slave Harriet Tubman leads first of many groups of slaves to freedom via the Underground Railroad

1850   Female Medical College of Pennsylvania opens its doors

1851   At women's rights convention in Ohio, Sojourner Truth delivers "Ain't I a Woman?" speech

1852   Harriet Beecher Stowe publishes *Uncle Tom's Cabin*, an immediate best-seller that shapes the nation's attitude toward slavery

1861–65 American Civil War effectively halts suffrage activity for women

1866   Elizabeth Cady Stanton, Susan B. Anthony, and Lucy Stone found the American Equal Rights Association

1869   The women's rights movement splits; Susan B. Anthony and Elizabeth Cady Stanton form the National Woman Suffrage Association (NWSA); Lucy Stone, Henry Blackwell, and Julia Ward Howe organize the American Woman Suffrage Association (AWSA)

THE ROAD TO WOMEN'S RIGHTS IN THE UNITED STATES

1870   Fifteenth Amendment is ratified, giving vote to black men but not
        women

1872   Susan B. Anthony is arrested for voting; she hopes the arrest will
        lead to a trial in which the wording of the Fourteenth Amend-
        ment will be interpreted as guaranteeing women the right to vote

1875   The U.S. Supreme Court rules the Fourteenth Amendment does
        not apply to women

1878   A woman suffrage amendment is introduced in the U.S. Congress
        but does not pass

1884   Belva Lockwood, the first female lawyer to practice before the U.S.
        Supreme Court, runs for president on National Equal Rights
        Party ticket

1890   The NWSA and AWSA unite as the National American Woman
        Suffrage Association (NAWSA)

1891   Ida B. Wells initiates nationwide antilynching campaign after three
        black businessmen are murdered in Memphis, Tennessee

1893   Colorado becomes the first state to adopt a state amendment giving
        women the right to vote

1896   National Association of Colored Women (NACW) is formed in
        Washington, D.C.; first large woman suffrage march is held in
        New York City

1903   Women's Trade Union League of New York established; group works
        for unionization of working women and for suffrage

1909–10 The largest strike of women workers is held, predominantly in New
        York among shirtwaist makers

1915   Suffragists gather more than half a million signatures on petitions to
        present to Congress; 40 thousand march in New York City

1916   Jeanette Rankin of Montana becomes first woman elected to U.S.
        House of Representatives

1919   Nineteenth Amendment, guaranteeing women's right to vote in
        every state and federal election, passes House and Senate and
        goes to states for ratification

1920   The Nineteenth Amendment is ratified; NAWSA organization now
        becomes League of Women Voters

THE ROAD TO WOMEN'S RIGHTS IN THE UNITED STATES

1933   Frances Perkins appointed secretary of labor by President Franklin D. Roosevelt, becoming the first woman to hold a cabinet position

1941–45 Women begin performing "men's" jobs in factories when United States enters World War II

1953   Oveta Culp Hobby becomes first woman secretary of health, education, and welfare

1964   Civil Rights Act of 1964 passes, prohibiting discrimination by gender in employment

1968   Shirley Chisholm is first black woman elected to U.S. House of Representatives

1972   Civil Rights Act passes, prohibiting discrimination by sex in education; Equal Rights Amendment (ERA) is passed and sent to states for ratification

1977   First National Women's Conference, organized in part by Bella Abzug, is held in Houston, Texas

1980   Census Bureau allows for first time that women can be "heads of household"

1981   Sandra Day O'Connor is first woman appointed to U.S. Supreme Court

1982   The ERA falls three states short of ratification

1984   Geraldine Ferraro becomes first female vice presidential candidate nominated by a major political party; runs on Democratic ticket with Walter Mondale

1986   U.S. Supreme Court rules that sexual harassment constitutes sex discrimination and is therefore illegal

1993   Janet Reno becomes first female U.S. attorney general; Carol Mosley-Braun is first black woman to serve in U.S. Senate

1996   Madeleine Albright becomes first female U.S. secretary of state

FURTHER READING

Banner, Lois W. *Elizabeth Cady Stanton: A Radical for Woman's Rights.* New York: Addison-Wesley Publishing, 1998.

Cullen-DuPont, Kathryn. *Elizabeth Cady Stanton and Women's Liberty.* New York: Facts on File, 1992.

Dubois, Ellen Carol, ed. *The Elizabeth Cady Stanton–Susan B. Anthony Reader: Correspondence, Writings, Speeches.* Northeastern University Press: Boston, 1992.

Great American Women's Speeches: Lucretia Mott/Sojourner Truth/Ernestine Rose/Lucy Stone/Susan B. Anthony/ Elizabeth Cady Stanton/Carrie Chapman Catt. Performed by Eileen Heckart. Scranton, Penn.: Harper Audio, 1995. Audiotape.

Hakim, Joy. *Liberty for All?* New York: Oxford University Press, 1994.

Henry, Christopher E. *Forever Free: From the Emancipation Proclamation to the Civil Rights Bill of 1875 (1863–1875).* Philadelphia: Chelsea House, 1995.

Matthews, Jan V. *Women's Struggle for Equality: The First Phase, 1828–1876.* Chicago: Ivan R. Dee, 1997.

Stanton, Elizabeth Cady. *Eighty Years and More: Reminiscences, 1815–1897.* New York: T. Fisher Urwin, 1898.

Stanton, Theodore, and Stanton, Harriot Blatch. *Elizabeth Cady Stanton as Revealed in Her Letters, Diary, and Reminiscences.* New York: Harper and Brothers, 1922.

Ward, Geoffrey C. *Not for Ourselves Alone: The Story of Elizabeth Cady Stanton and Susan B. Anthony: An Illustrated History.* New York: A. A. Knopf, 1999.

Websites

National American Woman Suffrage Association
http://lcweb2.loc.gov/ammem/rbnawsahtml/nawshome.html

National Women's History Museum
http://www.nwhm.org

National Women's History Project
http://www.feminist.com/suffrage.htm

Woman Suffrage and the 19th Amendment
http://www.nara.gov/education/teaching/woman/home.html

Women's Rights National Historical Park
http://www.nps.gov/wori

INDEX

PICTURE CREDITS

Pamela Loos has written numerous magazine articles. After graduating from Rutgers University she taught high school, and ever since has pursued a career in publishing.

Matina S. Horner was president of Radcliffe College and associate professor of psychology and social relations at Harvard University. She is best known for her studies of women's motivation, achievement, and personality development. Dr. Horner has served on several national boards and advisory councils, including those of the National Science Foundation, Time Inc., and the Women's Research and Education Institute. She earned her B.A. from Bryn Mawr College and her Ph.D. from the University of Michigan, and holds honorary degrees from many colleges and universities, including Mount Holyoke, Smith, Tufts, and the University of Pennsylvania.

The Sacred Place

The
Sacred Place

The Ancient Origins of Holy
and Mystical Sites

Paul Devereux

CASSELL&CO

For Mike, Jean, Karen, Andrea
and Patrick Horsbrough

First published in the United Kingdom in 2000 by Cassell & Co.
A Member of the Orion Publishing Group

Distributed in the United States of America by Sterling Publishing Co., Inc.
387 Park Avenue South, New York, NY 10016–8810

A CIP catalogue record for this book is available from the British Library

ISBN 0 304 35591 7

Designed by Richard Carr
Printed and bound in China through Colorcraft Ltd.

Cassell & Co.
Wellington House
125 Strand
London WC2R 0BB

Frontispiece: *The Pyramid of the Sun, Teotihucan, Mexico, viewed from the Pyramid of the Moon.*

contents

ACKNOWLEDGEMENTS

I want to especially thank: Damian Walter for being a perfect library angel; the Lifebridge Foundation of New York for enabling me to travel to various sacred places for study and photography in support of an ongoing project, some pictures from which are used here; Peter Walker for his wonderful help in Manitoba; my son Solomon for his assistance in Mexico; my wife Charla for sharing some scary fieldwork in Crete, and Richard Bradley for being one of the most clear-sighted and inspiring archaeologists of his generation.

Most of the photographs in this book are my own; those from other sources are credited in the captions. I thank all these individuals and institutions, but I must single out the following who have been particularly helpful and generous: Stuart Abraham; Chris Ashton; Richard Bradley; Thomas Dowson; John Glover; Brian Larkman; Robert Wallis, and David Whitley.

Richard Bradley

preface

This book charts the broad, generalized change of the sacred place from natural to artificial, from its ancient, primary form as a natural feature of the unaltered landscape, through the first embellishments of such locations by human beings, to full monumentalization and the building of temples.

If it can be so put, this work attempts a 'natural history' of the sacred place – but only up to a point. There is no intention of following the entire shift of sacred place from natural origins to modern places of worship. Quite the contrary, in fact: this book focuses on sacred place when sanctity was still earthbound, still localized; when the balance between physical location and the workings of the human mind were still in some kind of equilibrium. Over recent millennia that equilibrium has become increasingly distorted. As ideas of sacredness have become more complex, more mentally constructed and more dogma bound, so religion has become increasingly abstracted from place. The global religions in their modern manifestations may have things to say about spirituality as they see it, but they have increasingly less to say about the inherent sanctity of place. Their gods are largely 'off Earth' altogether, and today most of us inhabit what the ancient mind would have considered to be a soulless geography. *The Sacred Place* focuses on smaller, localized spirituality – the ancient sense of sacred place. As a consequence, the story it tells comes to an end while monuments and temples still made reference to their natural surroundings, when they still acknowledged the old, natural sacred places.

This story does not follow a single, simple timeline because the change from venerated natural place to artificial sacred monument has been something of an untidy affair. It has happened in varying ways at different times around the world, and in some cultures it never happened at all. In most instances natural places were still being resorted to even when constructed monuments and architectural temples were in use. For this reason, therefore, any attempt to organize a look at sacred place with a degree of coherence, as this book aims to do, has, to some extent, to be an artificial exercise. Given that qualification, however, we have attempted to minimize such problems by opting for a looser, four-part approach. The first, introductory section takes a comprehensive look at the nature of sacred place, including psychological, perceptual, cultural, archaeological and anthropological aspects: the 'theory' of the matter, if you will. Working from that base, the next three parts of the book provide a 'hands-on' look at three selected, broad areas that will effectively tell the story of the sacred place: first, the use of natural places for sacred purposes and the early signs of human alteration or embellishment of such locations; next, the wide use of stones – megaliths – in the monumentalization of sacred place; and finally, the marrying of artificial and natural features in the creation of ancient sacred geographies.

Let us then take time out from our hurried, modern world and return to the old places for a while. Let us re-collect ourselves.

ancient mind, holy land

Brain, mind and place – Perception of place: ancient, modern and perennial – *Genius loci* – Sensing the sacred – A world of venerated places – Dreaming the land – The meeting point – Being here

'A megalith in a rural setting, in fields or woods, always has a distinctive atmosphere and character about it. The same tomb changes and alters its character according to the weather conditions, the qualities of light, the seasons of the year. It is never the same place twice.'

CHRISTOPHER TILLEY

Lanyon Quoit dolmen, Cornwall, England.

It is all too easy to think of sacred place almost as if it were a commodity on a supermarket shelf – 'Over in that aisle are sacred places; over here in this aisle you'll find a good selection of non-sacred places' – but sacred places are not cans of beans that can be labelled so simply. They result from a complex interaction between physical location and human mental processes, which are framed by cultural beliefs and perceptions. The concept of the sacred place – especially ancient sacred place, which is the subject of this book – requires the consideration of the sense of sanctity held by the human mind and how that has been applied to physical geography. Exploring this curious ancient human trait leads to matters about which we rarely think today, living as we do in a world where place is merely a location, relegated to a passive role of being simply where something is situated or where an action 'takes place' (as we say). The significance of place is today reduced to economics, ownership or mere mundane utility. At the cultural level we no longer have places that we view as intrinsically sacred in their own right. We may erect

An aura of sanctity. The strange, visually arresting conical hill of Glastonbury Tor rising out of the moody Somerset Levels must always have inspired a sense of the sacred – not for nothing has Glastonbury been called the 'Holyest Earthe'. It was frequented by prehistoric peoples, became associated with the fairy king and the Celtic underworld, Annwn, was implicated in the Arthurian mythos and, as can be seen by the ruined church on the summit of the mystical Tor, became an important Christian shrine site. It remains a major pilgrimage centre for Christians and New Age people alike.

a church, mosque, temple or other 'place' of worship and consider that to be holy, but nowadays such buildings are rarely placed according to any spiritual imperative – they just happen to be where they are, and we think no more about it.

A further complexity when sacred places of antiquity are considered is that they derived from the perceptions and sensibilities of the ancient mind, a mind that apprehended the world in ways sometimes quite different from those of the modern mind. Ancient sacred places often belong to peoples, beliefs, traditions, religions and rituals that no longer exist. Nevertheless, as this introductory section will try to show, we can to some extent learn to recognize the old ways of thought.

There are, then, two basic factors involved in an understanding of sacred place: first, the physical nature and characteristics of such locations; second, the mentality that perceives them as sacred. The sacred place is neither mind nor locality, but the sum of both.

Certain sacred places can retain their aura of sanctity simply because our senses can react in the same ways as they did in our ancient forebears. They provoke a sense of the spiritual within us now as then, because even though the way our minds work may differ from those of our ancestors, to a large extent the functions of our brains and psychological impressions span the ages. It could perhaps be an inborn need to experience place in such meaningful ways that explains why so many of us are attracted to powerful sacred places of antiquity. Such moments of contact afford us brief respite from the remorselessly secularized geography of the modern world. Sometimes we need holidays for our souls, not just for our bodies and minds.

This part of the book will follow up these matters in a little more depth to prepare us for the wide-ranging exploration we will be making of the many ways

in which the sacred place manifested itself in antiquity, how it originated in the natural world and how it emerged into human culture.

A Place in Mind

A place can have a sacred dimension, then, only by interaction with the human brain, mind and senses, but we usually forget that our experience of all places involves such interaction – a process we experience rather than think about. As Stephen Feld and Keith Basso (1996) have observed, the phenomenon of place is 'a powerful fusion of self, space and time'.

MIND MAPPING

Why does a familiar room seem familiar to us? To put that another way, why do we notice a difference if someone has moved the furniture around in our absence? We would say because we 'remember' what the room was like when we were last in it. But this glosses over a complex process. Every time we enter a place, indoors or out, our brain maps it – quite literally. Brain scientists John O'Keefe and Lynn Nadel (1978) identified a brain structure called the hippocampus as one of the main areas where such 'cognitive mapping' takes place. This process constantly updates our mental charts of the places in which we find ourselves so that we can become aware of changes in our environment. To this fundamental processing, other perceptions have to be added to our sense of place. Our mental archivist has to drag out what we know about a place we are experiencing – memorial information. If it is a tree, do we know its name? If it is a building, what do we know about the style of its architecture, the architect, the function of such buildings? Can we identify that range of distant mountains? What is its name? Our onboard archivist has to shuffle through the memories we may have of the maps and photographs we have seen of the region and everything we might have read about it. Then there is personal memory. Does that room, building, tree, mountain range or whatever hold specific memories for us. ('This is the room in which I last saw my mother alive.' 'That is the tree in whose shade I sat with my grandfather on happy summer days in childhood.' 'That is the building in which I got married.') Then there is the information pouring in from the senses: the nature of the light, the smell of the place, the sounds associated with it. Yet a further layer in the sensing of a place involves emotional responses: does it depress, inspire, disappoint, frighten, reassure,

Many first-time visitors to Stonehenge complain that the monument seems much smaller than they had expected from seeing photographs.

calm? Then there are psychological filters that colour our sense of a place: what are the aesthetics of the place – is it light-filled, soaring, beautiful and exquisite, or is it confusing, ugly, gloomy, eerie or boring?

All the above and thousands of other factors pump up our perceptions when we encounter a place – and all in the twinkling of an eye, so that we are barely aware of the process. We move from place to place (all our lives, for we are never out of place) and 'never give it another thought'. But we do 'give it another thought', subliminally and all the time. Occasionally we become more aware of this processing, such as when we are somewhere we have never been and our internal archivist cannot find any memorial files. Then we create 'first impressions' – that is, our brains start mapping the new environment for our minds to draw on later if necessary. Again, we can occasionally

glimpse the behind-the-scenes processing of place – like that fleeting sensation when returning home from a fairly long trip and the old place seems just slightly unfamiliar. For a few moments the mental map-maker has to re-adjust co-ordinates. A similar kind of dissonance can occur when we physically visit a place for the first time after having been familiar with photographs of it. Stonehenge, the Eiffel Tower, the pyramids at Giza, the White House and other such locations can seem somehow 'different' when we actually experience them from how we had 'pictured' them in our mind. This is because our brains have conducted some preliminary 'mapping' from the minimal data in the photographs. When we are physically on site a welter of fresh information causes the earlier cognitive map

When Sigmund Freud stood for the first time before the Parthenon on the Acropolis at Athens he had a strong sensation of unreality. 'So all this really does exist, just as we learned at school,' he thought to himself. Freud found the source of his odd feeling of alienation to be his schoolboy doubts that he would ever see the Acropolis. His mental image was different from the actual physical experience of being there. 'The situation included myself, the Acropolis and my perception of it,' he wrote many years later.

of the place to be modified. The great psychologist Sigmund Freud actually commented on such a feeling – a curious sense of alienation – when he first visited the Acropolis in Athens. Another well-known occurrence is to revisit a place known in childhood. Geographer Yi-Fu Tuan has described what happened when he returned to Sydney, Australia, and wandered around a childhood haunt there:

The beach, the promenade and a little playground with its row of swings remained much the same ... Although the physical place had not altered, my perception of it had. I saw the beach one way as a child; as an adult, I saw it in quite another way, with different focuses and values.

(Tuan 1995)

The body, the place that carries our mind around, is also mapped in the brain, although it is an elusive map, as neuroscientists have found that given parts of the body are mapped by certain brain cells one week, then by others another! So as well as mapping the place one's body is in, the brain also maps the body in relation to the place. We sense and 'measure' the space we inhabit in relation to our body – another level of cognitive mapping that has had profound implications for sacred places, as we shall note later. We are so unfamiliar with this form of 'body sensing' in our modern culture that environmental psychologist James Gibson had to invent a term, 'haptic perception', to describe how the body senses the space around it, using the joints in its limbs as additional 'sense receptors' and its tendency literally to get in touch with the environment.

PLACE AND MEMORY

It has long been known that place shares a special relationship with memory. As far back as classical times there was a celebrated memorizing technique known as 'the method of *loci* (places)'. In this, a person commits to memory the layout of a familiar building, the arrangement of islands in an often visited bay, a row of houses and shops in a well-walked street or some other locale known to them, with numerous smaller places (rooms, islands, doorways or whatever) nested within it. Then, in order to remember a list, a set of topics, a range of themes for a lecture or what-

ever needs to be recalled in an orderly way, the person mentally 'walks through' the memorised locale, 'placing' each item to be remembered in separate spots within the mental scene. To retrieve the items, the person has simply to walk back in the same fashion through the mental scene. In actuality, the method involves the placing of transient items of memory in the more secure memorial context of a real place.

This process was literalized in the Renaissance era, when Neoplatonic mystics and magicians followed and adapted ideas put forward in the first century BC by the Roman architect Vitruvius. Using astrological schemes and magical principles involving proportion and shape, parts of houses were designed and embellished even by such as Francis Bacon to facilitate memory (Sack 1976). Not only 'memory rooms' but 'memory theatres' were built to complex schemes, using separate areas or cells emblazoned with mystic glyphs and symbols. It has even been suggested that Shakespeare's Globe Theatre in London was constructed on such magical principles in order to aid and focus memory.

Even if one cannot nowadays accept Neoplatonic principles of magic, it remains the case that places can, in effect, 'store' memories. It is one of the most vital powers of place. Scholar Edward Casey talks of places having a 'gathering action', filling themselves with memories 'that belong as much to the place as to my brain or body' (Casey 1996). He visualizes a place as 'securely holding memories' for a person and then releasing them when the person is present.

Ancient and traditional people used the whole landscape as a mnemonic, an aid to memory, a place where they could lodge their myths and their religious, social and moral concepts. Casey refers to these as 'intensely gathered landscapes'. This is famously the case with Australian Aborigines, but it applied to many other ancient cultures as well. Anthropologist

Miriam Kahn has noted that for the Wamira of southeast Papua New Guinea:

> The landscape resounds ... with narratives of collective history and personal experiences. It provides tangible forms for the mooring of memory ... Meaning attached to landscape unfolds in language, names, stories, myths and rituals. (Kahn 1996)

The ancient Celts similarly had stories or myths associated with just about every hill, spring, copse, rock outcrop, river bend, lake, pool and aged tree in their country. A Celtic tradition called *dindsenchas* chronicled the legends and lore associated with a wide variety of places. Such 'territories of the voice', as they have been called, can reach great sophistication. Keith Basso spent many years studying the role of place-names in western Apache territory near Cibecue, Arizona, where stories attached to places were used as forms of cautionary narratives for social situations. Place stories or histories 'shot' a miscreant as if with an arrow, giving a moral tale or example from past time associated with a location to admonish and guide the wrongdoer. 'Surrounded by places ... men and women talk about them constantly, and it is from listening in on such exchanges and then trying to ascertain what has been said that interested outsiders can begin to appreciate what the encompassing landscape is really all about,' Basso notes (1996a). He recalls an incident in which a young fellow, who had been behaving foolishly for some time after being dumped by his girlfriend, asked if he could rejoin a couple of horsemen colleagues to work with them again in sorting steers and branding calves. He assured them that he had now seen the error of his ways and was ready to work once more. Basso noted that, in responding to him, the two older horsemen casually introduced references to

Many traditional peoples, such as the Australian Aborigines store their tribal memories in the landscape. If they are removed from their native territory, they suffer cultural amnesia and thus fragmentation. One place is not just like another to them. This is Blui Jabarula, last fully initiated elder of the Walbiri tribe. (John Miles)

(actual) places into their conversation, including such comments as 'So! You've returned from Trail Goes Down Between Two Hills!' or 'It's true. Trail Goes Down Between Two Hills will make you wise.' Basso realized that such references were adding rich layers of meaning to the two men's exchanges with the young man, because all three of them knew the stories associated with the places they were mentioning, and these had a relevance to the current situation. It was a conversation that was surreal only to outsiders who did not know that the landscape was also taking part in the discussion.

The cultural integrity of peoples who exteriorize their tribal memory by locating it in the landscape, in places, is particularly at risk when they are removed from their native lands.

DIFFERENT SPACE

It is perhaps becoming clear that the notion of there being an objective, external, fixed entity called 'a place', in which we simply exist, is a simplistic fiction. Our perceptions and experiences of a location are conducted *inside our heads*. (Indeed, we only ever experience a mental reconstruction of the world, concocted in the darkness of our skulls from electro-chemical signals initiated by raw data supplied by our bodily senses. We never apprehend the world 'out there' as it actually is.) The true situation is *that a place we are in actually exists in us*. The homes in which we have lived, the glades through which we have ambled, the rivers down which we have rowed, the mountains we have climbed, the ancient temples we have explored, the streets we have walked – all these exist within us. American scholar Eugene Walter has observed that while human experience makes a place, 'place locates experience in people' (Walter 1988).

It is crucial to have an understanding of the mental nature of a sense of place when we encounter ancient places and, especially, ancient sacred places. Because our perception of place is like a mirage, it is subject to cultural filtering. This means that we share the mirage of a place – or even physical reality as a whole – with our peers, the other members of our culture, because we are brought up to accept common cultural beliefs and world-views. Our perceptions, being psychologically constructed, are subject to the massaging of the signals we receive from the society in which we have grown up and the beliefs, ideas and assumptions with which they are freighted. As Yi-Fu Tuan has succinctly stated: 'Deeply held beliefs affect how one sees.' So when we encounter the perceptions of traditional and ancient people, societies still outside the ever-expanding modern mindset, we experience dissonance. We all too readily find ideas about spirits haunting the land or mythic beings appearing in certain places to be

Locals say that this waterfall in Brunei, northwestern Borneo, was inhabited by several spirits, but when the modern world got too close and installed water-control schemes nearby, they decided to leave.

purely superstition. But what this really amounts to is that these alien views do not fit into the mental constructs of reality that rule our perceptions. As far as we are concerned, we inhabit space that contains objects and places and is not filled with spirits flitting hither and thither nor haunted by the ghosts of the ancestors. If trees or rocks or waterfalls speak to us or if we encounter non-material beings at them, we are ill, we are having hallucinations, and we have to seek treatment by the 'doctors' who police our present, culturally condoned mirage of the world. This is in contrast to cultures that did (and to some extent still do) populate their world with spiritual presences of one kind or another, where a belief in an environment empty of them is considered a sickness.

The deep problems of how we understand space and place have long exercised philosophers, but because of the dissonance between ancient or traditional world-views and our own modern one, archaeologists, anthropologists and others who explore other worlds of the human mind – either in the form of surviving tribal lifeways or in the structures and artefacts earlier peoples have left behind – are finding it necessary also to ponder such matters. Edward Casey claims that while space comes first for the anthropologist, it is place that is primary for the native – and that 'the difference is by no means trivial' (Casey 1996). Modern people tend to live with an abstract, conceptual view of the world, while ancient and traditional peoples were much more closely tied to their land, to their real, intimate native places. A further crucial difference between ancient and modern is that in our culture, time is of the essence, while place was paramount for earlier peoples.

USING THE PAST SENSE

Archaeologists and anthropologists are becoming increasingly aware, then, that we have to be able temporarily to escape from our modern ways of seeing if we are to understand, interpret and experience ancient places, especially ancient sacred and monumental sites. We have to try to enter into the working of the ancient mind as best we can. As archaeologist Christopher Tilley has written, 'Archaeology is the dreamwork of the past' (Tilley 1993a). Elsewhere he observes that 'a megalith in an urban environment does not work, it has no aura ... the modern buildings surrounding the tombs detract from them as signifiers of the past, deconsecrate their space'. He continues:

> By contrast, a megalith in a rural setting, in fields or woods, always has a distinctive atmosphere and character about it. The same tomb changes and alters its character according to the weather conditions, the qualities of light, the seasons of the year. It is never the same place twice. Such tombs are nowadays best seen alone: a crowd destroys the sense of place, the relationship between the tomb and its setting in the landscape.
>
> (Tilley 1993b)

Not so very long ago it would have been virtually unheard of for archaeologists to consider such topics as 'sense of place' or to comment on the 'distinctive atmosphere' of a site, but Tilley is one of the relatively new breed of 'cognitive archaeologists' who are concerned with recovering some insight into ancient sensibility. In this way, they feel that more information can be gleaned from a prehistoric site, enabling them to get closer to understanding what it meant to the long-lost people who built and used it and so arrive at a more complete interpretation of such monuments. This process is analogous to the way that botanical and biological experts are struggling to preserve a living legacy of the biodiversity of the planet: so, too, cognitive archaeologists and

anthropologists are attempting to preserve something of the diversity of world-views that is fast being eroded as modern Western consciousness becomes increasingly global.

Prehistoric tombs are no longer to be seen as burial sites pure and simple but as monuments that 'presenced the ancestors in the landscape', Tilley argues. The ancient builders were creating 'dominant locales' and 'significant places'. Keith Basso considers that sense of place in some cultures can 'reach sacramental proportions' and, with sufficient research, 'may be found to exhibit transcultural qualities' (Basso 1996b). If this is true, it should be possible to recover it from at least some of the archaeological remains of sacred sites. One deceptively simple way that archaeologists are beginning to attempt this is to consider the view from certain types of monument. In the British Isles, for instance, some monuments, such as natural boulders with rock art engraved on them, tend to be in

locations offering wide views, and, as we shall find out later in this book, an observation as simple as this can impart information about ancient places. Other monuments seem to be related to specific landscape features, a matter we will pick up on again in Part Four. Other sites, such as standing stones, were seemingly meant to be intervisible, as were some burial mounds, while others seem to have been deliberately planned not to be seen from one another. Archaeologists are also learning the importance of physically approaching certain ancient monuments from specific directions. Tilley further notes that when a site that has a specific entrance–exit is left, the view of the surrounding landscape has inevitably been directed or controlled by the monument's builders. What is it they wanted us to see? It indicates ritualized movement through landscapes that were seen to be sacred or symbolic in some way. So what one sees, the sequence in which it is viewed, and how one was

meant first to confront a monument were all thought out by the builders of those places. If we pay careful attention, these aspects can be reconstructed by us today, and this opens up excitingly new and rewarding ways to visit ancient sacred places.

In a curiously valid sense, ancient sacred places continue to be inhabited by the spirits of our remote ancestors. They can still be contacted because the land never forgot.

Sacred Place

If 'place' is an elusive concept, 'sacred' is no better. No wonder, then, that 'sacred place' dances like a mirage before us when we try to pin it down. As we have noted, sense of place (indeed the very concept of 'a place') is a mental phenomenon, partly generated within the human mind and sometimes partly

A hunter's view. Rock art, like this on a natural boulder on Rombalds Moor, England, was placed and displayed for people on the move through the landscape, like hunter-gatherers, whose vision would scan the terrain in a way that of settled people did not. (Brian Larkman)

provoked by a place itself. Place felt or designated as being sacred is yet a deeper dimension of that complex phenomenon. The ancient Greeks were fully aware of this. They had two words for space: topos meaning the physical aspects of a place, much as we are conscious of today; and chora, a mysterious, less passive property of space, a more subtle and poetic quality. When we consider chora, place becomes an agent that provokes our sensibilities, that can stir the seeds of spirituality within us. Most of us have experienced this somewhere, sometime – in a great Gothic cathedral, perhaps, or in some sun-drenched Egyptian, Greek or other temple, at some moody, atmospheric megalithic site, on a hill or mountain, while walking along a woodland path or beside some delightful stretch of river – even in a garden, where, as the old adage has it, we are closest to God. Despite its widespread occurrence, it is a sense for which there is little cultural currency in our modern world – in fact, it is resisted – and such experiences tend to remain private or, if mentioned, are categorized as some kind of more-or-less embarrassing cliché. Plato said such an aspect of place could be grasped only by 'dreaming with our eyes open' (Walter 1988). Eugene Walter points out a number of examples in classical Greek literature where mention of *chora* is made. He cites, for instance, Sophocles' Oedipus at Colonus, when Antigone stops at a resting place with her father, Oedipus, and says: 'As for this *choros*, it is clearly a holy one.'

SPIRIT OF PLACE

Chora was merely the ancient Greek articulation of what may be a universal sense of the sacred in localized form. The Romans called it *genius loci*, spirit of place.

> The genius loci, which first appeared in Italy as a snake and later in human form, stood for the independent reality of a 'place. Above all, it symbolized the place's generative energy, and it pictured a specific, personal, spiritual presence who animated and protected a place. On the deepest level, the image of a guardian spirit provided a way of representing the energy, definition, unifying principle and continuity of place. The Roman conquerors dominated people and seized property, but in religious principle they respected the independent spiritual sovereignty of the places they occupied. Where they camped they often erected a votive tablet to the spirit of the place. (Walter 1988)

Before the Romans, the Celts similarly pictured gods, goddesses and local spirits as abiding at their shrine sites, especially in groves and at springs or wells. The Celts left little in the way of monumental architecture at such shrines, and we know about them mainly because of place-name evidence, artefacts found by archaeologists at such places and the references and artefacts relating to them produced in Romano-Celtic times (see Part Two). For instance, the healing springs of Bath, Somerset, England, were presided over by the Celtic spirit or deity Sulis, whom the Romans associated with their Minerva. They built a great spa and religious complex there, appropriating a place that was sacred long before the Roman occupation of Britain. In some of the Celtic fringe areas of Europe, such as Ireland, Brittany and the western British Isles, pagan Celtic spirits of place were transformed into local saints by Celtic Christianity.

The most ancient of religious impulses was that of animism, in which natural phenomena and the land and all within it, animate or inanimate, were seen as being suffused with spiritual qualities, as being ensouled. The classical philosophers conceived of a world soul, *anima mundi*, and spirit of place can be seen as a microcosmic version of this.

> The animus of a place does not have to be taken in any spiritualistic sense, but as the geography, the climate, the history and the character of the place, informing all who come in contact with it...... A place emanates logos, so that its specific animus is heard and perceived; animus is not merely an organ of human intelligence.
> (Moore 1987)

The Roman Great Bath, at Bath, Somerset, England.

The Tibetans use the term *gnas* to denote what is often translated as 'holy place', but Toni Huber has pointed out that the matter is a little more complex than this. It can be used to denote a more active sense, such as to exist, reside, abide or remain. The whole of the physical environment is considered by religious Tibetans to teem with a host of deities and spirit forces; these non-material entities can be mobile or fixed at specific locations. 'The term *gnas* and its compounds most often designate the abodes of all these deities and spirits and their associated states of being, variously conceived,' Huber writes (1994). *Gnas* allows Tibetans automatically to incorporate the sense of *genius loci* when they refer to sacred place. The concept is built into the terminology they use.

In Siberia spirit of place is encapsulated in the concept of the supernatural 'land master', *gazarin ezen* (Humphrey 1995). The 'master' of an area provides it with beneficent properties, unless angered, in which case the land becomes stricken with drought or pestilence. The major land masters are associated with mountains (see Part Four).

Although spirit of place can, of course, be interpreted by us today without recourse to a literal belief in a spirit or deity haunting a locality, often the most effective way to sense the qualities of an ancient holy site is to try to suspend one's modern worldview for a while when present at it. To enter an ancient mindset, no matter how briefly and imperfectly, enhances a visit to a sacred place. But we do not find this easy: a direct and literal belief in spiritual entities doubtless made the idea of sacred place fairly straightforward for ancient people, but trying to grasp its essence today is a more complex and fraught matter, although this has not stopped modern thinkers from wondering, questioning and theorizing.

ON THE NATURE OF SACRED PLACE

The German theologian Rudolf Otto tried to unpack the concept of spirit of place. He considered that the earliest association of sacredness with place would have been the occurrence of eerie feelings at specific locations, eventually leading to the belief that a 'sacred place' was characterized by its being inhabited by a non-material presence, what Otto called a *numen loci*. Otto cited Jacob's words in Genesis, 'How dreadful is this place! This is none other than the house of Elohim ...', as being instructive for the psychology of religion. He observed:

> The first sentence gives plainly the mental impression itself in all its immediacy, before reflection has permeated it ... It connotes solely the primal numinous awe, which has been undoubtedly sufficient in itself in many cases to mark out 'holy' or 'sacred' places ... There is no need ... for the experient to pass on to resolve his mere impression of the eerie and aweful into the idea of a 'numen', a divine power, dwelling in the 'aweful' place ... Worship is possible without this farther explicative process. But Jacob's second statement gives this process of explication and interpretation. (Otto 1924)

Otto also noted that the German expression *Es spukt hier* (literally, 'It haunts here') has no true subject; it is not referring to a discrete entity, such as a spirit or ghost, but is more an expression of the sense of a place as a whole, although perhaps 'just on the point of detaching and disengaging from itself a first vaguely intimated idea of a numinous something, an entity from beyond the border of "natural" experience'.

Otto's observations were widely noted, and the great psychologist Carl Jung coined the noun 'numinosity' from Otto's 'numinous'. Jung's term is probably the one we feel most comfortable using nowadays when we are trying to express that indefinable quality that is the mysterious essence of many ancient sacred places.

Another famous thought on the subject of sacred place was proffered by the religious historian Mircea Eliade when he suggested that a place was considered sacred because people saw it as embodying a 'hierophany', as was distinctly not the case with a secular spot. Eliade used the term to mean 'manifestation of the holy' (Eliade 1964). Elsewhere he elaborated:

The numinosity of a sacred place can be felt by anyone, it occurs for visitors to this natural grotto in Kimberley, Northern Territory Australia.

Among countless stones, one stone becomes sacred ... because it constitutes a hierophany or possesses mana or again because it commemorates a mythical act and so on. The object appears as a receptacle of an exterior force that differentiates it ... This force may reside in the substance of the object or in its form; a rock reveals itself to be sacred because its very existence is a hierophany ... It resists time; its reality is coupled with perenniality. (Eliade 1989)

This approach is well expressed in Mescalero Apache ideas about some of the sacred places that they consider to possess or contain a supernatural power, *diyi*. Such power places 'occur at points of intersection

between the physical and spiritual worlds' (Carmichael 1994). The sacred site is conceived of as a kind of mirror, the physical world being merely a reflection of the deeper and more real spiritual world. Transformations occur when people make spiritual journeys from one side of the mirror to the other. Carole Crumley concurs with this view concerning traditional attitudes to sacred places as being agents enabling or provoking access to spirit realms:

> Sacred places everywhere are modeled on a core set of natural places (mountains, caves, rock outcrops, springs, etc.) and embellished with culturally distinct symbols. These places are considered liminal, tucked between the mundane and spirit world; they are entry points into another consciousness. (Crumley 1999)

This view of sacred place is particularly well exemplified in the Hindu concept of the *tirtha*. This word, applied to a whole category of holy, pilgrimage places typically situated on rivers, means 'a crossing place', a 'ford'. This is not only physically descriptive of many of these places but is also deeply metaphorical. *Samsara*, the ceaseless flow of birth and death and birth again, was likened to a river and 'the far shore became an apt and powerful symbol of the goal of the spiritual traveler as well,' explains Diana Eck (1981). She points out that the term *tirtha*, coming from a Sanskrit verb meaning 'to cross over', can also signify a path or a passage in a more general sense. 'The word ... belongs to a whole family of Indo-European cognates which are the great words of passage and pilgrimage in the West: through, durch and trans, as prepositions, and all of the many passage words related to them, which in English alone include thoroughfare, transition, transform, transport and

transcend.' An ancient concept of the nature of sacred place is therefore deeply embedded in Western languages.

Scholar John E. Smith has noted that while the experience of the holy can intrude upon us in terms of time 'whether we will or not', we must go to a special place in order to realize its holiness (Smith 1992). In other words, we have to seek out sacred places, while numinous events can sometimes seemingly choose us or are, at least, random events. He feels that sacred places have an arresting function in that they 'lead us to respond in awe to the Holy'. He identifies three basic characteristics of any sacred place: it must be set apart from routine experience; it must have historic associations that remind us of the experiences of the holy had by others in the past; and it must be so structured as to direct our minds towards non-ordinary states.

Other scholars have questioned what different cultures mean by 'sacred'. Jane Hubert notes (1994) that the Maori people of New Zealand have their *waahi tapu*, sacred places, but even within their own culture groups they have different definitions and classifications of what constitutes a sacred site, and no tribe or group would be so presumptuous as to define *waahi tapu* for others. Hubert further observes that to many cultures sacred sites are seen to have a differential sanctity – greater, lesser or different. 'Although the whole landscape may be considered sacred, there are differences between this and the sacredness of sites that have particular significance. Not every stone or plot of earth can be treated with the same degree of respect. Does this mean that there are degrees of sacredness?' she asks.

A sacred place can be as small as a tiny mound of stones or a single standing stone or as broad as the eye can see – a whole mountain range, perhaps. 'Sacred place' could be said to operate at any scale, from a specific site, to a localized place, a scene or a whole landscape. Quite often one scale of sacred place is 'nested' inside the other. Nicholas Saunders reminds us that attitudes towards landscape and place 'depend, in part, on culture-specific perceptions' (Saunders 1994). That is as true for us today as for any ancient society, and that is why we cannot unload our whole modern world-view on to ancient landscapes and sites and expect to understand them. We have to try to hold our automatic, contemporary concepts in abeyance. Hubert also asks if a sacred place can lose its sanctity. As an example, she cites the deconsecration of churches in the Christian tradition. This might be due to the fact that sanctity is more of an abstract property in Christian thought and less attached to specific places. The Christian god is cosmic and all-encompassing and so theoretically cannot be tied to a specific location like a spirit of place – it is more a matter of the Church than a church on a particular site. Place did become important for the Church in a political sense, however, in that it sometimes deliberately erected churches on places of pagan worship in order to signal to a peasant or indigenous population that the Christian god was more powerful than the earlier pantheon and had 'taken over' the site of the pagan deity or spirit. Even the Vatican stands on a pagan site. (The way some Christians actually behave in church, before statues of Christ or the Virgin, for example, nevertheless suggests that for many of them the object of their worship can indeed be located.) Unlike the Church, however, sacred places are viewed by most traditional cultures as being permanent – perennial, as Eliade averred – but even some of their sites can occasionally lose their holiness. This is typically the case if a taboo is broken or if a sacred place is defiled in some way in the eyes of the local culture. The maintenance of sacred sites is also important. Australian Aboriginal places of sanctity, for instance, require the

Like other branches of Christianity, the Greek Orthodox Church often sought to place its churches on prominent, 'pagan' hilltops to display its ascendancy over the older faith. The visitor to Crete soon gets used to seeing tiny white chapels and monasteries perching on the summits of some unlikely peaks.

songs and dances belonging to them to be performed, debris to be cleared away, rocks rubbed, rock art renewed and so forth. If a place is neglected, it is said that eventually the site loses its spirit and dies, leaving the place as a mere physical feature rather than as a living spiritual node in the landscape. This is considered to have serious, negative implications for those people who have connections with the site.

In some cases the perceived holiness of a place can 'migrate' with a change of culture and religion. A place still remains and continues to be venerated, but the deities or spirits associated with it change places, so to speak, without changing place. This process is well exemplified by the continued ritual use of caves in Maya country, where Christian imagery is flimsily pasted on to the old Mayan gods.

Sometimes we can reconstruct the significance that an ancient sacred site had for the people who used it by means of ethnographical and place-name evidence or through meticulous and skilful interpretation, but some sacred places can affect us still in a direct, psychologically meaningful or spiritual way. The sanctity of various other kinds of sacred site has been lost to us, for it was bound up with cultural perceptions now inaccessible to us. In such cases it can be reasonably said that their 'sacredness' died with the people who resorted to them. It is too simplistic to think in a reductionist way about a sacred place as being merely a kind of topographical screen on to which humans project significance, and it is equally inappropriate to assume that holy sites somehow have sacredness as a more or less objective factor integral to their make-up that is missing from secular places. In actuality, sanctity of place, a specialized form of sense of place, exists in the exchange between physical place, and the human mind and body, and is modelled by the cultural context in which it occurs. All four elements contribute to the condition that we refer to as sacred place.

THE VARIETIES OF SACRED PLACE

The forms and purposes associated with ancient sacred places were many and varied. Although they warn that there were (and are) cross-cultural differences, anthropologist David Carmichael and his colleagues note that there are, nevertheless, 'broad similarities' in the nature of traditional sacred sites around the world:

> Over and over again these sacred places are connected with or are, what the Western world classes as 'natural' features of the 'landscape', such as mountain peaks, springs, rivers, woods and caves. (Carmichael et al. 1994)

Unaltered natural sites of sanctity are the most difficult for outsiders and modern researchers to identify. Unless a snippet of ethnography or a place-name alerts us, there is little to mark such places as having been considered as special. The UN's World Heritage Committee has found this matter to be problematic and has started to recognize what it calls 'Associative Landscapes', which are those with strong religious, artistic or cultural associations, with or without any material cultural evidence. The Committee had problems, for example, in evaluating the sacred status of the Tongariro National Park in New Zealand. It had considered this to be simply a natural feature, but it was a natural landscape of deep religious significance to the native Maori.

When subtle additions start to be made to natural sacred locations – be they small walls or enclosures, rock art or other embellishment – or when archaeologically tangible items – such as offerings – are found at them, they obviously become easier to recognize. A further way of identifying otherwise unmarked natural places is when they show evidence of having been used as resource areas for ritual materials: rock for ceremonial axes; pigments for body paints or rock art; metals for votive offerings; or plants for offerings or causing visionary experiences. While we would view such locations as being simply utilitarian sources, in the ancient mind the ritual material may have had special properties because the locations were themselves considered holy, having mythical or mystical significance going back to the dawn of tribal time. Again, however, without ethnographical, place-name or archaeological clues, such places and areas can be difficult to discern. In Mexico, for instance, the Wirikuta plateau is considered sacred to the Huichol Indians. For them, it is ancestral land to which they make a long, annual pilgrimage in order to collect the hallucinogenic peyote cactus that grows there, which they use for their religious rites. Without the existence of that pilgrimage and the ethnographical literature that has grown up around it, the significance of the plateau would be lost to outsiders. This is equally the case with the totemic places of the Australian Aborigines.

Various types of sacred place, both natural and monumentalized, have been noted by scholars or by indigenous peoples as having different qualities or functions. Although we will encounter numerous examples in the course of this book, we can take a quick, initial overview of some examples to obtain a working idea of the range of places that were considered holy in non-Western cultures. To begin with, the Sto:lo Indians of British Columbia, who do not have an overall term for sacred places, designate selected locations as spiritually significant, using the term *stl'itl'aqem*, meaning 'spirited spot' or 'spirited place' (Mohs 1994). These are seen, variously, as 'transformer' sites (places where a person can gain supernatural power or enter the spirit world); spirit residences; ceremonial areas; traditional landmarks (notable physical features that have been associated with events important to Sto:lo cultural history);

vision-questing places (suitable locations for the personal rite of passage of the vision-quest common to many Native American peoples and also where ceremonial regalia are lodged); places where mythical events supposedly took place; and burial sites. Much further south, in New Mexico and western Texas, the Mescalero Apaches have a similar range of sacred places. David Carmichael (1994) observes that these sites have 'very low archaeological visibility' and that Apache holy places are, as a group, among the least visible site types. 'Although the topographic setting of such sites can be distinctive, the associated spiritual events or activities often leave few or no physical remains,' Carmichael notes. This is, of course, the perennial problem with natural sacred places from the point of view of today's scholars. There are transformer sites, which in Mescalero tradition include burial places and are considered rather dangerous; places of 'intersection' (see above); and resource areas.

The ancient and recent dead … More than 1500 years ago the Hopewell people of what is now Ohio built this huge mound, one of their many great earthworks. Then people from far across the ocean came and settled, founded a town called Marietta, and interred their dead around the ancient Indian mound.

A great variety of natural features, such as peaks, caves and springs, is identified with such locations, and all are considered places of power. Throughout the Americas, indeed, prehistoric peoples venerated caves, rock outcrops, boulders, mountains, trees and water sites as sacred places, carved and painted symbols on rocks, built earthen mounds, constructed stone pyramids mimicking holy mountains and created remarkable spiritual geographies by emblazoning whole landscapes with markings ranging from mysterious straight lines to effigies and seemingly crazy patterns (see Part Four).

In Madagascar a site is considered sacred (*masina* or *manan-kasina*) when it is inhabited by qualities referred to as 'things' (*zavatra*), spirits or ancestral spirits. These sites take numerous forms, the best known and most important of which are the tombs and palaces of ancient chiefs or kings, who were deified. Natural places – caves, lakes, trees, springs – also figure, as do upright stones and sacred areas encircled by wooden fences or marked by memorial poles. A common writer's error is to mistype 'scared' for 'sacred': this is not without some irony, for sacred sites are often regarded as places of fear, and in the case of Madagascan sites Chantal Radimilahy (1994) specially notes that 'some places are more feared than venerated'. On the African mainland the Nso' of Cameroon have a variety of sites where prayers can be offered. Several decades of Christianization have modified traditional beliefs and churches, and the places of worship of other religions are treated with respect and reverence, but in Cameroon's western grassfields other places or spots are still considered to be powerful, inhabited by God or the ancestors. These places can range from areas without any buildings on them to specific structures in or around a chief's palace or state house; sites belonging to healers; graveyards; special assembly halls and cult houses;

and certain waterfalls, pools in rivers marked by raffia ropes tied across them, and by special trees.

The Bantu-speaking Busuku of Kenya, to take another African example, traditionally have a belief in a supernatural power and ancestral spirits. They have three main types of sacred site: a small – even tiny – hut-like sacrificial shrine dedicated to the ancestors and made from twigs placed in front of a dwelling or nearby ant-hill; another, vault-like, shrine would be built behind a house, underneath its eaves; and the third kind of holy place was the grave, which for the Busuku takes the form of an oblong earthen mound. The most sacred of this latter type of site are the grave mounds of elderly people, especially men. The central post from the dead person's house and a white stone were traditionally placed as markers on these graves, and ceremonies involved splitting the post and taking the stone to the house of the eldest surviving son of the deceased. Elsewhere in Africa there were, of course, many other holy places, such as in Botswana and Zimbabwe, where there are networks of 'land shrines' (Werbner 1989), used for offerings, trance possession and oracular functions related to the Mwali cult. These shrines, depending on their regional status, take the form of a circular clearing around selected trees or clearings with huts. Nigerian sites include stepped pyramids built out of clay in honour of the Earth mother, Ala. In Africa, from the Sahara to the Cape, caves and rock shelters were painted or engraved with images from the remotest times, marking them out as ritual or sacred places for many different peoples. In Egypt, in addition to the well-known pyramids and temple structures, there were also pre-dynastic rock-hewn temples and, as we shall note below, a veneration of natural forms.

The ancient reindeer-herding peoples far away to the north, in arctic Russia near the Barents Sea, also had their shrine sites. Russian archaeologists have

Old drawing of part of the megalithic temple of Mnajdra, Malta.
(James Fergusson 1901)

found sanctuaries and sacrificial places with a wide variety of votive offerings, as we shall describe later on in the book, and, as we shall also see, in Ireland, the British Isles and western mainland Europe there remains a rich variety of ancient sacred places from many periods of history and prehistory. In Mediterranean Europe there are megalithic temples, such as those on Malta, sacred mountains and peak sanctuaries in Greece and Crete, ritual caves, holy wells, springs and all the usual sanctified natural places. In the Middle East there are again standing stones and great ancient temples and holy cities, such as Baalbek in Lebanon or the rock-hewn Petra, 'half as old as time', in Jordan, and rock-cut shrines like that of Yazilikaya ('written or carved rock'), in Turkey. In Iraq and Iran – ancient Persia – there are the remains of temples, stepped pyramids or ziggurats, and ceremonial shrines like Persepolis, emerging out of a most rich and ancient cultural setting.

In Tibet and Himalayan regions caves and holy mountains again figure prominently, as do carved boulders, sacred rock outcrops, stone mounds or cairns, holy pools and temple sites. China and southeast Asia also have sacred caves, trees and groves, holy mountains, great necropolises, like the Ming tombs complex near Beijing, and impressive temple complexes like those at Angkor, Cambodia, and Borobudur, Java. Sometimes the sacred places were more subtle, however: in Japan, some locations were considered to be hallowed simply because they had been visited by certain powerful, charismatic holy men.

The South Sea islanders of the Pacific generally recognize natural sacred places and have what we might call minimalist shrines and holy sites, but there are some instances of rock art, as well as megalithic features on some islands, such as the famous statues on Easter Island and, less well known, a Stonehenge-like trilithon on Tongatabu Island, Tonga; extraordinary 'islands' created by tall-walled enclosures constructed of columns of basalt off Ponape in the Caroline Islands; and a range of lesser stone features, such as monoliths, platforms and dolmen-like structures, on other islands. Australia has a rich legacy of ancient Aboriginal rock art located in various places on the continent, and there is a profound indigenous use of natural features – rock outcrops, water soaks, trees, quartz pavements, caves, crevices, hills – as mythic and totemic places in a conceptualized sacred topography, criss-crossed by invisible 'dreaming' tracks or routes popularized in Western literature as 'songlines'. This legacy is fairly well known to Western scholars because contact between Europeans and Aborigines occurred relatively recently, and Aboriginal tribal cosmology, knowledge and related concepts were recorded. Parts of Aboriginal sacred geography – what some anthropologists would technically refer to as a 'cognized landscape' – still survive, although in a patchy fashion. In New Zealand the indigenous Maori people count among their sacred places burial grounds, altars, mauri stones and trees,

Aboriginal cave painting site in Arnhem Land, Australia. It is obvious why this place caught the ancient eye. (John Miles)

carved poles representing the ancestors, rock art sites and a range of natural places, including certain caves, mudflats, sacred mountains, water sources and places where significant events took place.

WHAT YOU SEE AND WHAT YOU GET

An especially important type of early sacred place are natural landscape features that offer the visual resemblance of a face, figure, animal or other likeness. Such natural images allowed an ancient society to see its mythology emblazoned on its territorial topography. This prompted a deep interaction between mind and land, for the very landscape became mythically alive, turning it into a kind of holy script. The forms of the gods and creation heroes were seen in the landscape – 'the lineaments of legend in the topography,' as anthropologist Lucien Levy-Bruhl described it (1983). The scale of features recognized by this 'Dreamtime' mode of perception could be quite variable, ranging from a small rock, single boulder or modest outcrop looking like a human profile or animal form, to a whole hillside looking like the head of a mythical being or a mountain range suggesting the breasts or reclining body of an Earth Mother goddess. The forms of mythic personages in landscapes features were the simulacra of culture heroes, deities or totemic beings.

Throughout the Americas people venerated simulacra, be it the Apaches seeing the profiles of mythic heroes in the Chisos Mountains, Texas; the Ute (and probably the ancient Anasazi before them) seeing the form of a sleeping chieftain in Ute Mountain, Colorado; the Ashinanabe making offerings at anthropomorphic and zoomorphic rocks in the sacred boulder mosaic landscapes of Manitoba and countless other examples.

In Asia, Buddhist sacred places similarly included the recognition of simulacra. For example, in the Himalayan sacred landscape of Karzha, in Lahul, Himachal Pradesh, India, anthropologist Elisabeth Stutchbury noted the deep religious significance of mountain simulacra. An eighteenth-century poem about the peak of Drilburi by a yogin-saint lauds the mountain as a manifestation of the Buddhist Pure Lands and contains the lines:

> The mountain to the right is like a pile of jewels
> The mountain to the left like the fierce deity King of Wrath
> The mountain in front like the triangle of origin piled up
> The mountain behind like a crouching lion.

SIMULACRA

A simulacrum is the illusory image of a face, castle, animal, human figure or other shape or form seen in the chance configurations of clouds, the coals of a fire, the bark of a tree, reflections in water, the cracks, crevices and projections of a rock face or other surface. Strindberg saw heads as if sculpted out of marble by a spectral Michelangelo in the folds and creases of a rumpled pillow; Leonardo da Vinci advised his students to study the 'exquisite landscapes' formed by the mouldy damp stains on his studio walls; the French poet Antonin Artaud, on the verge of madness, repeatedly saw 'signs, forms and natural effigies' in the plays of light and shadow on crags and rock faces in Mexico. It is in the nature of human beings to seek patterns in randomness, and the images that result can sometimes tell us more than any picture we

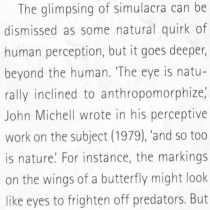

might artfully create. A face that is a simulacrum, for instance, can possess profound and even disturbing depths, as if regarding us from out of the well of the unconscious mind.

The glimpsing of simulacra can be dismissed as some natural quirk of human perception, but it goes deeper, beyond the human. 'The eye is naturally inclined to anthropomorphize,' John Michell wrote in his perceptive work on the subject (1979), 'and so too is nature.' For instance, the markings on the wings of a butterfly might look like eyes to frighten off predators. But where is the mind in nature to create such simulacra? Simulacra are a by-product of a deep reflex in nature, and many ancient peoples used it to see their gods. And we can still see those gods today if we look quietly, carefully, as if through ancient eyes.

The arrangement and suggested imagery of the mountain peaks were turned into a mandala of meaning. In the same landscape a double-peaked mountain and a glacier combine to form the image of a Buddhist deity, and pilgrims come to meditate on the vast, natural image. Another mountain configuration in the region looks like a woman reclining on her back, her hair flowing out beside her. 'It seems that few peaks are not imbued with meaning through the perceived presence of a deity or some other being which not only gives form and shape to the geographical feature, but is seen to emanate the energy of that form,' Stutchbury observes (1994). In

Karzha this mode of geographical perception is linked with observations in which the annual progression of the sun is associated with particular skyline features and is extended into a tradition called *satalegpa*, a form of landscape divination that is slightly akin to the Chinese *feng shui* and that, among other things, places attention on the specific geographical location of buildings. So the temple of Dodrup Chen, for instance, is situated within topography said to look like a specific Dzogchen master sitting in a meditation posture.

Fairly recent work by Egyptologist V.A. Donohue has revealed the existence along the Nile of natural

BUFFALO ROCK

This natural boulder (above) is surrounded by an ancient 'petroform' sacred landscape in Manitoba, Canada (see Part Four). It is called Buffalo Rock by the Indians, and offerings are still made at it. Its shape certainly echoes the characteristic form of the buffalo (below).

A 'proto-sphinx' seen in the modified profile of this natural outcrop containing a rock-hewn temple. Egypt. (Anthony Donohue)

configurations in cliff-faces, some of them probably slightly modified, resembling images in Egyptian mythology and kingly iconography (Donohue 1992). It could even be that these natural simulacra actually promoted visual ideas that were incorporated into dynastic symbolism, thus helping to shape Egypt's myths and religion and giving the lie to the popular misconception that the high civilization of ancient Egypt arrived suddenly and 'ready made' in the Nile valley. Rock face imagery has been identified by Donohue at several locations along the Nile in association with temples. Among the simulacra that have been noted are resemblances of cobras, pharaohs and the profiles of gods and proto-sphinxes. For instance, a cobra (associated with pharaonic iconography) rears above the image of a pharaoh in the cliff-face behind the temple of Hatshepsut, at Deir el-Bahri, in the Valley of the Kings. These images were seemingly not noticed for thousands of years because they are heavily eroded and, probably in no small measure, because no one was looking for them until Donohue made a fortuitous observation.

Prehistoric European 'Dreamtime' landscapes also include such natural mythic imagery, like twin-peaked mountains known as 'paps' or breasts in Scotland and Ireland. We will see later (Part Four) how at least one of these topographical features was the focus of Stone Age religious attention.

The Paps of Anu, Killarney, Ireland.

CENTRES OF THE WORLD

All the types of sacred place summarized in the preceding pages and more besides, relate or related to a range of purposes. These include, variously: worship and the expression of devotion; spiritual cleansing and purification; the offering of sacrifices and prayers to deities and otherwise petitioning or placating the gods, spirits of the ancestors or other forms of spiritual entity; seeking oracular wisdom or other divinatory information; entering trance and dream states so as to 'cross over' into the spirit realm or receive visions; receiving healing; obtaining ritual materials; conducting initiatory rituals or other rites of passage; entreating animal master spirits or totemic entities; ceremonially remembering and re-enacting the tribal myths; performing funerary rituals and, generally, burying the dead. There are probably even more purposes associated with places designated as being holy, but these are the prime ones. There is, however, another, specific and important class of sacred site: cosmological places. These symbolize an *axis mundi*

or world axis – they were the centre of the world. This was a crucial concept for the ancient mind; indeed, it is archetypal. Projected outwards into the world it provided a point of reference in time and space as well as helping to augment tribal identity; projected inwards it provided an image that structured the cosmology of a people.

In the outer world the *axis mundi* was a ceremonial and conceptual centre, a 'world navel', the point of intersection of the cardinal directions. Classically, it was symbolized in ancient Greece by a domed stone known as an *omphalos*, and such *omphaloi* were to be found at numerous Greek temples, such as Delphi and Delos (Devereux 2000a). The somewhat mysterious Etruscans represented the world navel as a pit or circular trench dug into the ground from which they would lay out the street grid of their towns, a practice adopted by their more powerful neighbours, the Romans. In Roman towns and camps this centre point, or *mundus*, was where the primary roads from the four cardinal directions crossed – the central squares

QUARTERING THE WORLD

The quartered circle, which appeared in various forms, was the symbol for the Four Directions for American Indians throughout much of the Americas. The Lakotas referred to the sign as 'the sacred hoop' and as the 'wind centre'. The outer circle was the encompassing horizon, the crossing lines represented the winds from the Four Directions and the small central circle was 'here'. During ceremonies the Osage painted their version on their faces so that the nose formed the centre point, while the Pawnee made the top of the head the centre point.

and 'high crosses' of medieval and later European towns are vestiges of this. Jerusalem has been considered a world navel for centuries by Judaism, Christianity and Islam. Medieval Christian maps placed Jerusalem at their centres, and some literally showed it as Christ's navel. Being archetypal, the concept of an *axis mundi* is, naturally, cross-cultural, occurring with traditional peoples around the world and from many eras. So, for instance, it is widespread in the Americas, where virtually all the native peoples possessed a powerful image of directionality, often expressed in symbols and cosmologies based on the idea of the Four Directions or, in some cases, the Six

Directions: up and down, as well as north, south, east and west, although these did not always concur with our modern compass directions. The Pueblo sunwatcher priest would use gestures to express the Six Directions by pointing to the place of sunset on the summer solstice, the place of sunset on the winter solstice, then the sunrises at those times, finishing by gesturing overhead and at the ground.

The Pueblo Indians of the American southwest talk of *itiwanna* ('centre place'), the midmost place of the Earth Mother, and they have myths that explain how the First People emerged from the ground and were led to Centre Place. The Tewa Indians of New Mexico, who view their pueblo or village centres as 'Earth mother, Earth navel, middle place', a spot marked by a ring of stones, also consider that there is a *nan sipu* ('Earth navel') on the peak of each of their sacred mountains. Far to the south the minds of the ancient Maya were equally drenched in the imagery of directionality. They, too, had a concept of the world navel – *mixik' balamil* – which they identified with specific hills and mountains, among other things, and which governed the central surveying point in Mayan ceremonial cities (Freidel *et al.* 1993). The Mayan world was created by the Vaxak-Men, the gods who support it at its corners and who designated its centre. This cosmological concept even influenced how fields were laid out, as was the case with other Native American Indian peoples.

The image of the tree was also a key symbol of the *axis mundi* in numerous other ancient cultures, its most famous manifestation probably being Yggdrasil, the World Ash of Norse tradition, with its roots in the underworld and its branches in the upper world of the gods. In actual ceremonial manifestation the great cosmic axis was typically represented by a pole. The merry maypole of Europe carries ancient echoes of the World Tree, and the 'cosmic axis' is present even in some Australian Aboriginal traditions. The

Achilpas, one of the Aranda tribes, used to carry a ritual pole said to have been fashioned by a creator being, Numbakula. The land around where it was erected became habitable and was transformed into a 'world'. The Achilpas used to erect it and determine the direction of their next wanderings from the direction in which it leaned. In this way, they were always 'in the world' – they carried their centre with them. Any damage to the pole was considered to be a catastrophe, and its loss would mean the emergence of

This now-leaning column in the ancient Mayan city of Uxmal represents the Ya' axche Cab, *the Central Tree or* axis mundi *of Mayan mythology. It was originally stuccoed and painted with hieroglyphs and symbols.*

chaos. An Achilpan myth records a once-upon-a-time when the pole was broken, causing the tribe to wander aimlessly, until eventually all its members sat down and allowed themselves to die.

The world axis was represented by numerous other physical features in the ancient world. Mountains were commonly so designated. The classic example is the Hindus' mythical Mount Meru, the Buddhists' Sumeru, physically symbolized by Mount Kailas in the Himalayas. But any hill or mountain served the purpose for different cultures – Harney Peak in South Dakota, as a case in point, was famously where the Sioux holy man, Black Elk, was transported during his Great Vision and became for him the mystical centre of the world during his experience, which was replete with references to the Directions (Neihardt 1972). The Aztecs in the Valley of Mexico selected Mount Tlaloc as their axial mountain. They approached a platform area on its 4000-metre (13,100-foot) high summit by a monumental processional way. Although no buildings that may have been erected on the summit have survived, it has been noted that outcrops of basalt rocks project out of the platform at the inter-cardinal (northeast–southwest, southeast–northwest) points. Another boulder stands in the centre of the platform area. (The Tlaloc rainmaking ritual took place at this site, in which, according to Aztec documentation, four Tlaloc figures were placed at each corner, with a fifth in the centre.) A deep shaft was cut into the bedrock on the eastern side of the platform, forming an Earth navel.

The Pole Star, Polaris, was also an often-used physical symbol for the world axis, in northern Eurasia, North America and even as far south as central India, where the ceremonial city of Vijayanagara had its main axis aligned to it. To the Siberians it was the Nail Star, the fixed point around which the heavens

Modern maypoles, like this Maibaum *in Speyer, Germany, carry echoes of the World Tree,* axis mundi, *symbolism.*

rotated. The Saami of Lapland also saw the Milky Way as an axis that connected the worlds and was sometimes represented in the imagery decorating the skins of shamans' drums as a pillar. Inwardly – that is, mythically, as a cosmological metaphor – the world axis was similarly envisaged in various guises by

different societies: trees, ladders, spindles, ropes, arrow shafts, celestial mountains and more besides. The essential pattern was of some kind of vertical axis that linked the three worlds – the underworld of the dead and chthonic forces; the middle, human, plane; and the heavens. This 'three-world' image belonged to shamanism and could be greatly embellished depending on the tribal society, perhaps involving seven or nine 'worlds' or planes. When the shaman went into a trance, it was thought that he or she went on a spirit journey, climbing or descending the tree – or whatever the axis was visualized as being – allowing passage to the otherworlds.

At heart, then, the world axis archetype related in a psychological sense to a mapping of the altered states of consciousness encountered in shamanic trance. The image is archetypal because it has a physiological basis and, for that matter, a neurophysiological basis as well: we recall that the brain maps the body and situates it in space. In discussing 'the importance of bodily structure for emplacement', Edward Casey (1996) cites the philosopher Immanuel Kant, who stated that 'our geographical knowledge and even our commonest knowledge of the position of places' would be of no use to us if we could not make 'reference to the sides of our bodies'. What Casey refers to as the 'fleshly monolith' of our bodies is the world axis in a psychological and perceptual sense. To this bilaterality of the body and brain (right- and left-handedness) must be added the first sense of our perception – that it is egocentric, a factor that the experimental psychologist Jean Piaget found ruled the perception of infants. Although we abstractly 'know' that any one of us is just an individual locus of consciousness wandering around in unstructured, unbounded space, the actual, embodied experience we have is that we are at the centre, with the world arranged in diminishing distances from us in all direc-

SHAMANISM

Shamanism is associated with tribal societies, and it was one of the first expressions of human spirituality, emerging from, or merging with, animism and totemism. A shaman could be a man or woman, depending on the culture. He or she was the healer, seer, mystic, priest, conjuror and entertainer of the tribe. By means of ecstatic trance, the shaman could make contact with the spirits and the gods and could travel in the underworld and the heaven world. This was done for various purposes, such as seeking the lost or trapped souls of sick tribal members, escorting the newly dead to the otherworld and gaining supernatural powers to aid in healing, divination and the protection of the tribe from inimical outer forces. The shaman was an expert in the technology of consciousness and could use many methods for entering trance, typically drumming, chanting, dancing, shaking and the taking of mind-altering drugs. The crux of shamanism was

ecstasy – that is, the flight of the shaman's spirit from the body, what we would today call an out-of-body experience. The shaman would go on an aerial journey, a soul flight, to the otherworlds.

In some societies, the shaman was a solitary figure, feared as much as respected, yet in others he might be a central figure, even a chieftain or part of the ruling elite. In some tribes, like those traditional ones still surviving in the rainforests of Central and South America, numerous members could enter shamanic ecstasy, if they had been properly initiated.

Technically speaking, shamanism belongs to Siberia, which is where the term originated, but most anthropologists nowadays use it to describe any form of healing and divination using ecstatic techniques anywhere in the world. Because they did not all use the ecstatic method, some sorcerers and spirit doctors were not shamans.

tions. One has only to gaze around at the horizon when we are on the ocean or in a wide, open landscape. It feels as if it is encircling us, although we intellectually know it is not. In other words, our embodied view of space is given an automatic, centred structure. It is where the fundamental concepts of 'here' and 'there' come from. As archaeologist Julian Thomas has put it:

We can measure our physical bodies and express our proximity to other things in quantitative terms, but this is really only a secondary issue. The measurement of space in relation to the

human body relies on a much more fundamental understanding of things: the qualitative distinction between that which is 'closer' and that which is 'further away' from us. When we say that we feel emotionally distanced from something or that we have become very close to someone, we are not simply using a spatial metaphor in order to express more metaphysical relationships. On the contrary, our perception of space relies on a more fundamental human ability to experience relationality. This results in a spatial order which is centred on the human body ... This spatial order, which we might call 'experiential space',

This 15-metre (50-foot) tall stalagmite forms a natural pillar-like or phallic axis mundi *within the Muang On Cave in Chiang Mai, Thailand. (Chris Ashton)*

has a certain priority, in that geometrical space can only be discovered through first existing in experiential space ... human beings are oriented in relation to the world as it is understood rather than as it is revealed by empirical science.

(Thomas 1996)

What Thomas calls 'experiential space' geographer Yi-Fu Tuan refers to as 'symbolic space'. 'The space based on a grid of centre-periphery and the cardinal points, its scale ranging from a small object ... to a large country, seems to be deeply congenial to human practice, mind and imagination, for it occurs worldwide,' Tuan observes (1995). 'Wherever it occurs, the spatial frame of center and cardinal points is loaded with other symbols, which may include combinations of color, animal, seasonal or meteorological phenomena, and human social categories and activities ... Symbolic space is geography elevated and transfigured.'

These two facts of human structure and cognition – bilaterality and centric perception – constitute what Jung called the archetype of quaternity: 'the centering process and a radial arrangement that usually followed some quaternary system' (Jung 1954) – the Four Directions. Indeed, the Six Directions: we have 'above' and 'below', our heads in the clouds and the ground beneath our feet, as well as front, back and sides. It is this fundamental relational form of cognitive mapping that was projected on to the physical environment, became formalized in rituals and structures, and that permeates the ancient cosmological models. As Eliade has noted with regard to what he termed 'sacred space', any orientation implies acquiring a fixed point: 'It is for this reason that religious man has always sought to fix his abode at the "center of the world (1992) ... The discovery or projection of a fixed point – the center – is equivalent to the creation of the world.'

Part of Templo Mayor, excavated out of the heart of modern Mexico City. It is hard now to appreciate the grandeur of this mighty temple complex of the Aztecs.

The centre of the world can be anywhere because wherever we go we are always at the centre of our world. We are always 'here', wherever 'here' is. The directionality that became formalized in social beliefs and systems was a perceptual tool that took on astronomical (therefore temporal) and cardinal (spatial) aspects only after the fact.

The archetype of the world axis not only produced cosmological models and rituals and was projected on to natural features like trees and mountains, it also gave rise to specific monumental structures. Hindu temples in Indian cities traditionally represent Mount Meru, for example, and they are oriented to the cardinal points. Templo Mayor, the remains of the Aztec capital Tenochtitlán, now beneath modern Mexico City, was arranged as the centre of the Aztec cosmos oriented to the Four Directions, the quartering of the world. In southern Illinois the Mississippian Indians' Monks Mound, a giant earthen pyramid, has specialised small mounds laid out around it marking the Four Directions.

Summary

The form taken by places designated as sacred can be seen to break down into a number of basic types or categories:

⚸ Unaltered natural places that were prominent features of the landscape, resembled faces, human or animal forms or were otherwise distinctive, or were shadowy, liminal places such as caves and springs that connected with the underworld.

⚸ Simple areas that had no distinguishing characteristics and were regarded as sacred simply by dint of some cultural factor (such as being where a battle or famous death occurred, plant resource areas, places of divination or healing, unmarked vision-questing sites and so forth) that is not visible after the fact to archaeological or other forms of physical investigation.

⚸ Slightly modified natural places, such as rock art on boulders or cave walls, the creation of subtle walling, enclosures or platforms, the placing of offerings, the digging of pits, the re-arrangement of naturally distributed rocks, the working of resources such as flint, chalk and the like.

⚸ Basic monuments of earth, stone, timber – such as the creation of burial mounds, the digging of ditches and banks to enclose ritual or ceremonial areas, the erection of standing stones or timber posts.

⚸ Larger and more complex megalithic and earthen ceremonial and ritual structures.

⚸ Sophisticated architectural features like Egyptian, Greek or Mayan temples and ceremonial cities.

⚸ Ground markings, alignments of stones, modification or incorporation of topographical features, stones and posts and openings with astronomical orientations and so on to create sacred landscapes.

Regarding the rôles performed by sacred places, we can perhaps summarize by saying such places were locations that, variously,

⚸ represented a mythic or spiritual presence in the landscape;

⚸ marked where spirits or deities dwelled;

⚸ were where a sense of the numinous was provoked;

⚸ were for the worship of supernatural powers and other spiritual and ritual activities;

⚸ memorialized a historic, mythic or otherwise important event;

⚸ were for burial, the placing of the ancestors in the landscape;

⚸ created a funerary geography for ritual and ceremony;

⚸ mapped an otherworld geography;

⚸ were for consulting the gods;

⚸ represented a cosmological feature;

⚸ linked heaven and Earth by means of astronomical orientation, for ceremonial purposes based on astrological or cosmological principles.

UNEVEN EVOLUTION

It is clear that there has been a broad development of the sacred site from the earliest times, when natural places in the landscape were the focus of religious attention, through various kinds of monumentalization to the building of architectural structures. It would be wrong, however, to see that broad, generalized development as a neat, single thread of 'evolution'. Sacred place did not simply start out as a cave and end up as the place of worship on a city street corner today. For instance, when there was the use of sophisticated architectural temples, whether in Greece, the Yucatán or elsewhere, veneration at cave shrines and peak sanctuaries was often still taking place. In many cultures the roles and nature of certain places changed and migrated with the coming and going of cultures and gods. And, of course, different cultures have changed in different ways in different places and at differing paces, so to this day there are still some people making offerings at natural holy places, while others visit places of worship built of concrete and steel located in downtown urban areas. Ironically, the most direct and purest forms of spiritual expression are probably found with those closest to nature, who still use trees, sacred waters and holy rocks. The rest of this book follows the emergence of the sacred place from such natural locations, but only to the point where constructed monuments and temples still held a relationship with the topography, the natural features, around them. In short, it traces the story of the sacred place only while the *genius loci* could still dwell within it.

Holy hills, sacred places: Loughcrew, Ireland.

natural places, early signs

Conjuring the spirits – A place with a view – Seeing through ancient eyes – The archaeology of natural sacred places – Offerings to the gods – Making markings – Slipping through the cracks – Dead men walking – Descent to the underworld – Peak experiences – Turning over ancient leaves – The waters of life

'A giant stalagmite in the remarkable likeness of a great tree – a stone axis mundi *wrought by nature, surrounded by offerings that have lain undisturbed for a thousand years.'*

Balankanché, Yucatán, Mexico.

The first sacred places were natural places. The Earth itself provided the primary points of sanctity. No matter what form of monument or sacred site later developed in their cultures, all human groups started out by selecting certain natural places as special, and such locations were still often being revered long after constructed, more architectural holy places had been built in the same territories. The impulse that today may take us into a church, a mosque, a temple or other developed, sophisticated place of worship found its first realization in the caves, groves, mountains, gorges, rivers, springs and other natural places that spoke of spirituality to our distant forebears.

This striking natural simulacrum of a head on the top of Carn Brae in Cornwall, England, is known locally as the Giant. It looks towards another hill, St Agnes Beacon, 10 kilometres (6 miles) distant, also inhabited by a giant, according to a Cornish legend, which states that the two hilltop beings threw rocks at one another. There are the barely visible remains of a 5000-year-old settlement on the summit of Carn Brae, and it is hard to believe that the neolithic people who used it did not mythologize this natural feature.

Where they can still be identified, it is the natural ancient sacred places that most often still retain the power to affect us directly at psychological or numinous levels, even if we cannot now share the specifically cultural, religious ideas with which the ancients clothed that primal response at such locations. For instance, one may not now believe in the Greek pantheon and Zeus may be diminished to a thunderstorm, but the Dictaean Cave in Crete, identified in myth as Zeus's birthplace, will nevertheless still trigger a reaction of awe in the modern visitor. Even the places of worship belonging to the relatively newfangled world religions work best for us at the psycho-spiritual level – the gut level, even – when they emulate natural places. So Gothic cathedrals, for example, were designed to reproduce the sensation of being in a forest of tall trees, with soaring space defined by trunk-like columns reaching to the roof, arching over like a forest canopy; a cool, dim place, with occasional gleams of light. A mosque glitters and shines with the intricacy of natural forms and otherworld glamour – the garden of paradise. In other ancient religions, as we shall see in due course, pyramids were metaphorical mountains.

In the absence of ethnological or archaeological clues, how do we recognize an unaltered natural place today that was considered holy in times past? To a large extent, it has to be by means of our inbuilt abilities of recognition – recognition of what have been called *loci consecrati*. Such a sensibility is in our cells; it is in our psychology. It is an essentially universal sense, responding to the basic properties underlying whatever cultural religious veneers were invested in such places. Obvious qualities that could denote a natural place as formerly being considered holy include its prominence in the landscape, making it a focus, a centre of perception – a simple landmark, in fact. Another, sometimes related, characteristic was mentioned in Part One: the unusual shape of a hill, mountain or rock outcrop, perhaps resembling a human or animal form or some symbolically significant icon. Levy-Bruhl noted that for New Guinea natives and Australian Aborigines remarkable features of the landscape were 'indications ... of the presence and the activity (in the past and now) of the mythic ancestors'. This was equally true of many other ancient cultures around the world. Archaeologist Richard Bradley has observed that in Lapland, Saami sacred places – sacrificial sites or *siejddes* – 'are often characterized by rock formations that bear a certain resemblance to humans, animals or birds' (Bradley 2000). Similarly, the Wintu Indians of California consider that 'rock features of unusual configuration' harbour indwelling spirits (Theodoratus and Lapena 1994). The Inca of the Andes sometimes selected (or recognized) a sacred place or huaca because of:

> ....its state of difference, an arresting visual characteristic or peculiar feature ... A stone is marked for its resemblance to a human being and another for a shape in the manner of a falcon.
>
> (Guchte 1999)

Other clues to the possible former sanctity of a natural feature or area include aesthetic characteristics that give rise to psychological effects, such as awesome natural sounds created by the roar of waterfalls and streams, the rush of wind through trees and rock crevices, the occurrence of strange echoes or the effect of light at a place – it might be shrouded by foliage or hemmed in by tall rocks that create an eerie gloom. Again, dramatic and dangerous locations associated with the power of the Earth were commonly equated with holiness – in antiquity, for example, offerings were made in the volcanic craters of Mount Etna. In contrast, to many early and traditional peoples waters bubbling gently from a spring indicated the presence of the ancestors beneath the ground. Another important type of spot typically selected in ancient times for its numinous potential was that which exists in a liminal position – that is, a 'betwixt and between' or marginal kind of place. Caves, facilitating the lightness/darkness and world/underworld (thus living/dead) interface, are classic sites of this sort. Cave mouths in particular offer the marginal experience; in some caves with rock art, such as in western Norway, the imagery begins precisely where the last of the daylight fades away. Woodland groves similarly offer a liminal experience expressed in terms of light, shade and soft green gloom. Shorelines are another example of liminal or marginal territory that was considered suitable for shrine sites, as was the border between cultivated land and wilderness, and this carried the deeper social significance of the boundary between settled, agricultural and nomadic, herding and hunting lifestyles. Rivers, too, were seen as liminal features by some ancient people, including the Saami and the Greeks. They were boundaries between the living and dead – the famous example in Greek mythology being the River Styx, across which the soul was ferried on its way to the underworld. We will also recall that in Part One it was noted that the Hindu idea of a sacred place as being a crossing-over point, a *tirtha*, was similarly associated with rivers, both physically in many cases and metaphorically.

While many of us today can enjoy a vista from a lookout spot – the sort of places often marked on our more scenic roads with signs and parking areas – we tend not to realize that such locations were often considered as sacred spots in their own right by ancient people – Shinto *torii* gates in Japan, for instance, can mark just such places. Shrines, sanctuaries and other sites of this kind were particularly common in societies that were 'on the move', so to speak – nomadic peoples, hunter-gatherers and herders. They would have seen the land differently from more settled and sedentary societies or a culture such as our own that has demythologized its surroundings. Above all, they would have experienced the topography at slow walking speed and therefore tended to register things – places, views, landforms, sightlines – that modern people move too fast to notice. Even when we are walking in the countryside, we can all too often become preoccupied with our thoughts, because we keep our minds locked tightly in our brains behind our eyes, affecting how they see – or don't see. The ancients more readily spread out their minds, their memories, their myths, in front of their eyes, in the land. Land was mind, was memory. Piers Vitebsky has commented that in a shamanic culture 'mapping one's mental state on to a geography of somewhere outside oneself is not just the privilege of the shaman, but is a basic way of talking about one's emotions and social relationships' (cited in Walter 1995). Some of the natural sacred places on ancient routes through the land are simple boulders or rock outcrops, and some of them became marked with rock art. As mentioned in Part One, it has been increasingly noted by archaeologists that such locations are frequently at points providing sweeping vistas. 'Hunter-gatherers recognize their territories by monitoring the paths running between specific places,' writes Richard Bradley (1993). 'Some of those places overlook the surrounding land, so that people may think of their territories in term of the views seen from them.' Sven Ouzman (1998) additionally observes that 'the actual journey between rock art locales may have been considered just as important as the locales'. Archaeologist Christopher Tilley has called walking a form of 'topographical language' and has noted that to some types of society walking 'is the medium and

outcome of a spatial practice, a mode of existence in the world ... the view from a locale makes sense of its positioning' (1994) and talks about 'where the walk meets the place' (1993a). He describes the practice of Gabbra camel-herders of the Kenya–Ethiopian borderlands who undertake periodic pilgrimages to holy mountain sites. These *jila* journeys are not the shortest routes to a mountain 'but rather a prescribed walk in which it can be approached and seen from the propitious direction' (1993a). Networks of paths and routes have special significance for people who travel through a landscape rather than settle in it. Without compromising pragmatic concerns, such as the sources of water, the locations of food plants or the movement of animals, paths were ways through the land linking landmarks invested with mythic meaning, of which water, animal migration and food resources were made part. Sacred places in such circumstances therefore tend to become 'stations' on a journey, punctuation marks in a topographical narrative. This is very much the case with Australian Aboriginal dreaming tracks or 'songlines' as they were popularized by Bruce Chatwin. Further, in addition to being a physical feature, the path or way can become a metaphor used in social and religious contexts in tribal, small-scale communities and even in larger, more complex societies. All in all, it is easy for the seeker of natural sacred places to overlook the overlook, if one can put it that way.

If there is to be an archaeology of natural places, as Richard Bradley contends there needs to be, we will have to develop the ability to enter past ways of thinking, seeing and feeling, as was discussed in Part One. Methods of training archaeologists to use their

Between light and dark: this cavern of the Lol-Tun cave system in the Yucatán, Mexico, and sacred to the Maya, dramatically displays the 'liminal' nature possessed by many ancient, holy places.

intuitive senses more effectively and temporarily to suspend their modern, culturally fashioned perceptions will have to be devised. (To a limited extent, this is already beginning to happen with 'cognitive archaeology', as was indicated in Part One.) We need to be able to put ourselves in the same mind-space as the ancient people who inhabited a given landscape in order to be able to experience it as they did – at least to some degree. If we are to train our eyes to see in such ancient ways, we have to be able to modify our whole perceptual processes and psychological sensibilities, no matter how fleetingly. In those moments we can glimpse the land as our ancestors did: as a holy land, drenched in myth and spiritual significance. Places in it that were formerly perceived as sacred will become self-evident. It would also be ideal – if unlikely in practical terms today – to experience those places in trance states in order fully to appreciate them in the ancient manner. The production of visionary states was a key aim of primary religious practices, and many sacred places, both natural and monumental, were surely used in states of ecstasy. Think about that. How does the simulacrum of a figure seen in a rock outcrop appear in an altered mind-state? Does it seem to move or gesture? Does it speak? Does the roar of a sacred waterfall become a chorus of spirits? Do the gods utter divine wisdom in the winds howling through mountaintop crannies, and do the ancestors whisper messages to their descendants in the rustling of the leaves in a sacred grove?

In short, the only approach for a person trying to identify unmarked natural sacred places is carefully to study and experience a landscape known to have been used by ancient peoples in order to locate features that still possess a haunting numinosity or that provide visual or acoustic clues and cues. The trained and disciplined use of subjectivity is needed to obtain objective information.

AGES BEFORE HISTORY

Throughout this book there are references to periods of prehistory, such as the neolithic. Here is a quick reminder of the broad, extremely generalized divisions usually given to prehistoric time when dealing in a European context.

Palaeolithic (Old Stone Age): ?600,000–18,000 BC
  Lower Palaeolithic: 600,000–90,000 BC
  Middle Palaeolithic: 90,000–40,000 BC
  Upper Palaeolithic: 40,000–8000 BC
Mesolithic (Middle Stone Age): transitional, 8000–4500 BC
Neolithic (New Stone Age): 8000–2000 BC
Bronze Age: 2000–900 BC
Iron Age: 900 BC – Historical era

The transitions from one era to another were gradual and diffuse. There were overlaps, and the actual periods vary significantly from one part of Europe to another. Moreover, these divisions of prehistoric time refer only to observable technological changes in the archaeological record and do not relate to cultural changes. It is important to remember, therefore, that these are very general divisions and are not scientifically exact dating. It is simply a working guide for non-specialists.

In landscapes that possess prehistoric or proto-historic monuments it can often be assumed that they relate in one way or another to natural locales that were seen as being sacred prior to the building of the monuments. These can sometimes be identified by tracing outwards from the monument. As Bradley observes, monuments can make 'explicit reference to features in the wider landscape'. He continues:

> They may be aligned on the heavenly bodies, but they can also be orientated towards hills or rock outcrops. Sometimes the relationship is even closer. For example, it seems as if one group of Swedish megaliths was constructed to imitate the appearance of nearby mountains – a connection that even extended to the choice of materials used to build them. (Bradley 2000)

In Parts Three and Four we will show actual examples of such reconstructions of ancient visions of the landscape, of sacred geographies.

There are some sacred sites, however, that we can never recognize, unless we are knowledgeable about the history and beliefs of an ancient society; places whose location and significance are inaccessible to us unless we know the ethnology of the tribe or society concerned. These are locales that were considered to be sacred or supernaturally powerful for specific cultural reasons, rather than ones that activate the kind of universal sensibilities we have been discussing. In Part One we noted some of the cultural reasons a site could become viewed as being hallowed, such as it being where an important historic or mythical person died or was believed to have died or where a legendary battle or struggle took place. To these we might add other culturally based reasons, such as places associated with illness caused by spirit attacks; usually dangerous or almost inaccessible spots to which a shaman is believed to travel in trance (Walter 1995); places noted for spirit appearances; or locations with cosmological associations for a society, such as places of emergence. Certain places might also have been considered sacred because they defined territorial

boundaries, invisible to the researcher who did not know the landscape had even been an ancient territory. Finally, we should not forget that 'everyday landscapes' that we would view in strictly mundane terms could also be experienced as sacred by ancient peoples.

Although most of these sites may be lost to us without the required ethnological information, our concern in this part of the book is with natural sacred places that have been identified.

First Signs

Objective ways of gaining knowledge leading to the identification of natural sacred places of antiquity can be garnered by a number of approaches. A key one is ethnology, as indicated above, when the study of a traditional society or tribe leads to the discovery of its early use of landscape features for religious purposes. But, of course, many sacred places belonged to long-lost societies for which there can be no ethnology. Sometimes, however, such people left a faint echo in the landscape in the form of place-names, the study of which is called onomastics. This is a 'softer' approach, perhaps, but can nevertheless give indications of natural places that were venerated or where rituals occurred. The Celtic scholar Anne Ross has emphasized that place-names can persist for a very long time in a landscape. Ross, a Gaelic-speaker, found that virtually every rock, peak and stream in the remote Scottish valley of Glen Lyon had a Gaelic name denoting its mythological, sacred nature. (Remarkably, an annual ritual is enacted in the glen that almost certainly dates back to the Iron Age, as we shall note in Part Three.) Another scholar, Hilda Ellis Davidson, has similarly observed that the evidence of Scandinavian place-names 'shows how many local sites were dedicated to a god or goddess, so that they must in some sense have been holy ground' (Davidson 1967). She notes, for example, that pagan deities such as Ull and Njord, which have scant literary references, have inspired many place-names that date to a period before the Viking era. In an English context Della Hooke (1998) has found that some river names are 'amazingly old' and 'seem to have been adopted from the neolithic people who occupied these islands in the prehistoric period'. (In Part Four we will discover a probable neolithic river name surviving in the sacred geography of the Avebury complex in Wiltshire.) Hooke points out that it can be a fascinating exercise to examine ancient

Sancreed well, Cornwall, has the 'atmosphere' typical of ancient Celtic holy wells.

place-names in one's own landscape for pre-indus-trial place-names commonly related to the physical appearance of a place, the topography, and to look closely at the lie of the land to divine their meaning. The place-name Weedon, for instance, which occurs in several English localities, consists of the Anglo-Saxon words *weoh* and *dun* denoting a shrine in a hilltop situation. Harrowden names, found notably in Bedfordshire and Northamptonshire, make a similar ancient reference.

Celtic sacred sites can be notoriously difficult to identify, because they were commonly natural places, such as woodland groves and wells or springs. Although the Celts also constructed shrine sites of various kinds, the natural locations may have had just minimal artefacts, like wooden effigies, associated with them. These have survived at a few sites, but most are long lost along with the sites themselves. Many holy wells and springs have survived as physical features down the ages (a good number of them becoming Christianized), but the locations of Celtic sacred clearings in woodland are especially difficult to establish. Here, place-name evidence is of particular importance. The Celtic word for sanctuary, *nemeton*, appears in Old Irish as *nemed* and *fidnemed* ('sacred grove'). Elements of this ancient word became widely appropriated in place-names – especially Romanized place-names – in the Celtic fringe of Europe. For example, Nanterre, at the foot of Mount Valèrien in France, derives its name from Nemetodorum. There was Vernemet(on), a sacred grove formerly somewhere in the vicinity of the central English city of Leicester, and at Buxton in Derbyshire there was a holy spring called Aquae Arnemetiae, a dedication to Arnemetia, the patron goddess of the spring and sacred grove. Nymet place-names in south-west England, such as Nymet Tracey and Nymet Rowland, both in Devon, also probably relate to former sacred groves.

In addition to ethnological and folkloric approaches, there can also be archaeological clues to a natural site's importance in ancient times. There are three main strands of this kind of evidence: offerings or votive deposits at venerated sites; various kinds of change to, or embellishment of, natural places, including the taking of ritual materials from them; and a 'special case' of embellishment, the engraving or painting of natural rock surfaces – rock art. Collectively, these provide the early signs of the sanctity associated with natural places; they bring them into archaeological visibility.

MAKING A DEPOSIT

The pre-Christian sacred sites of the Saami of Lapland were in the main selected natural places. These were of many kinds, including lakes (often associated with the ancestral spirits of women); rivers; mountaintops (associated with specific gods), some displaying distinctive profiles; trees, 'possessing perhaps humanoid characteristics' (Fjellström 1983); waterfalls; naturally shaped *seite* stones displaying remarkable forms; cliff-ledges; peninsulas; caves; islets; and prominent boulders and rock formations, these last also often being in unusual shapes, perhaps suggestive of human or animal forms. Many of these sites have been archaeologically recognized only because they had sacrificial deposits or votive offerings at them, and they are commonly referred to as 'sacrificial sites' in the literature, although one Swedish scholar, Rolf Kjellström, has written that he feels that there ought to be more distinction made between sacrificial sites and what he terms cult-places. To date about 500 Saami natural sacred places have been recorded, often in remote locations along the migratory routes taken by the Saami with their reindeer herds, in hunting grounds, by waters that were fished and at dwelling sites. The pagan Saami, a shamanistic and animistic

A Saami sacrificial site or siejdde at Alta, northern Norway. (Richard Bradley)

people, saw the landscape as being inhabited by spirits and deities, and their sites mark the presence of such entities at certain places. They worshipped regional deities, ancestral spirits and the deities of the sun, moon, thunder and other elements. Sacrificial deposits were made for various reasons, including gifts to the gods, in thanksgiving – perhaps for a successful hunt – or in propitiation, to placate a god for some misdeed or to gain a regional deity's favour for the fertility of the reindeer or fish or for some undertaking.

In Saami pagan tradition (Christianity did not start to make an impact in Lapland until c.1000) sacrificial offerings consisted primarily of metal or wood artefacts, bones of reindeer, bear (in 'bear graves') and other creatures to a lesser degree, and horn. Other materials, such as quartz, flint and glass, have also been found, however, as well as food items, such as fish, milk, cheese and porridge (as a cereal offering to the sun-goddess Bieve). Metal objects – buckles, rings, chains, pendants, clasps, sheet metal, iron arrow points, knives, silver coins – seem to have been deposited between AD c.950 and 1350 but frequently at sites where sacrificial rituals had probably taken place for much longer. Many of the metal items originated from trading with other countries, but others, especially pewter objects, were made by the Saami. Certain metals were believed to have had special powers. Brass, for instance, was considered very sacred, and brass rings for the sun-goddess and brass pointers as used by shamans on their drums for divination have been found as deposits. Idols were placed at some sites, and these were of stone or wood. The stone effigies were almost always unworked rocks that happened to bear anthropomorphic likenesses or were of unusual colour – so an effigy could be built from, say, a large, dark rock representing the body, surmounted by a smaller white stone as the head (Bradley 2000). Few wooden idols have survived, but from those that have it seems that they were often carved from the boles of trees; the carving was frequently quite minimal and used simply to enhance naturally occurring suggestive forms already displayed by the piece of wood. A more basic kind of wooden idol consisted simply of a tree trunk placed with its roots uppermost or a log with a cleft cut at one end. Horn deposits were typically of reindeer antlers, although some votive objects were also fashioned from horn.

To give a 'feel' for these sites *in situ* we can look briefly at a few examples of find-spots that marked Saami natural sacred places. Vidjakuoika is situated near rapids in Vuojatätno River, in Jokkmokk, Swedish Lapland. Deposited there were forty *seite* stones, a thick layer of reindeer bone and horn, iron arrowheads and bronze sheets. The marrowbones in the deposit had been split, indicating that sacrificial meals had taken place at the site. The place-name

An old depiction of a Saami worshipping at a sacrificial site
(J. Schefferus, 1673)

element *vidya* means 'holy'. The sacrificial site of Saivo, on a tiny island in Lake Gällivare, Sweden, was found to have a similar set of deposits, but with the bones of additional creatures, plus metal ornaments, chains and beads. Many sites can be barely noticeable, such as a concentration of bones and a piece of metal in a hole beneath the turf alongside a small boulder or wedged into a crevice between a couple of large rocks.

The practice of placing objects at natural places was, of course, widespread throughout the ancient world. Among many other areas we might cite as examples is prehistoric Britain. Deposits in caves often involved bones and Peterborough Ware – a style of neolithic pottery – as if there were some special association between the type of place and the type of deposit. Again, intact Peterborough Ware vessels have been found deposited in bogs and other wet places, locations that have a marked absence of Grooved Ware, another kind of neolithic pottery. Unbroken stone axes were frequently deposited in rivers and bogs, and the River Thames seems to have yielded an unusually high number of mace heads.

Different types of material used for votive deposits seem to have been carefully grouped together.

Grooved ware, for example, would typically accompany seashells, fossils and carved chalk items but tends not to appear with worked bone, stone axes or artefacts of polished flint. This extended to bone deposits in constructed monuments, too. For instance, animal remains in chambered cairns (stone mounds) on the Orkney Isles off Scotland's northern coast seem to have varied according to the locality in which the monument was built. So the bones of sea eagles were found in tombs on the coast or on cliffs, but those of domesticated animals were found on lower ground inland and of reindeer on higher ground. Sometimes these were 'foundation offerings', pre-dating the construction of the tombs, indicating that the place had been granted importance before any structure monumentalized it. Inside the tombs even the human skeletons were presented in different ways according to which area of the islands the monument in which they were interred was located.

Deposited axes tended to have been polished, bringing out the character of the stone and indicating that they were not being treated simply as tools. Some archaeologists have speculated that the depositing of stone axes may have been some kind of ritualized way of offering the material back to the Earth. Similarly, carved chalk objects are typically recovered from (often very deep) pits or shafts in the ground or from rock fissures and crevices.

Human bones were deposited at what were obviously considered to be significant places around the landscape in just the same manner as ceramics, animal bones, antlers or other deposits. For a long time there seems to have been no distinction between human remains, animal bones, antlers, ceramics and other objects insofar as use in deposits was concerned, even though the relationships between places and material might vary. This suggests that distinctions between culture and nature were not recognized or, at least,

were not considered important at the religious, ritual level. Everything was portable, and it was the place that mattered. The full complexity of beliefs associating certain kinds of objects with specific types of locale may not now be recoverable, but archaeologists continue to sift the evidence to see if explanatory patterns come to light. One pattern that is becoming clear is that over the ages the nature of deposits could change at given places. In some instances earlier

Ri Cruin Cairn, Kilmartin Glen, Scotland. The faint shapes of axeheads may be discerned on this cist end-slab, all their blade edges facing to the right. Detailed examination has revealed six of these carved motifs on the slab.

monuments were reused, and instead of funerary deposits other kinds of offering would be interred at them, as if the original meaning of a site had become confused or forgotten.

In the Bronze Age metal objects appeared in the offerings deposited at specific places. These objects were mainly weapons, especially axes and daggers. These are not found very often in Bronze Age burials but are frequently found in 'hoards', formally arranged deposits typically located on hilltops and in springs, bogs, rivers and lakes. Some were placed in the sides of existing burial mounds. There is clear evidence that many of the axes found in such deposits had never been hafted and in some cases the blades had been decorated – all signs that they were not 'real' weapons. Richard Bradley (2000) notes that the nature of the hoards themselves has tended to occupy more archaeological discussion than the places in which they are deposited. There are, in fact, patterns beginning to appear between the nature of the deposits and the places in which they are found, but these are detailed matters that are outside the brief of this book. A point of interest that must be noted, however, is

Bradley's observation that some kinds of rock art depiction of axes and weaponry in Britain, Spain, Portugal and other parts of Atlantic Europe may have served the same purpose as the votive depositing of the actual metal artefacts themselves. In Kilmartin Glen in Argyll, western Scotland, to take one set of examples, axeheads are found depicted on burial slabs inside monuments. Did these act as burial gifts, in lieu of the actual metal artefacts? The answer could be more subtle, as Bradley explains:

> The decorated slabs appear to be fragments taken from decorated surfaces in the open air. There is even some evidence of the outcrops from which they may have been removed. This apparently bizarre behaviour makes sense if we suppose that in such cases relics of particular places in the landscape were incorporated in the burials of the dead … The effect of depicting deposits of metalwork in the fabric of the tomb was to create an association between the funeral rite and other activities which had taken place at specialized locations in the landscape. (Bradley 1998)

Depictions of axes were also carved on the most famous megalithic monument of them all – Stonehenge.

CHANGING PLACES

The actual material of certain offerings or deposits could have had considerable bearing on the sanctity of natural places far from the location where the deposit was made, a factor it is all too easy for us to overlook. In other words, where metals and stone came from was seemingly viewed with significance. In Britain – as elsewhere – certain places were favoured as 'stone axe factories' (production sites) in neolithic times, and the products of these places circulated widely. We would think in terms of efficiency, cost

The carving of axes and daggers on a sarsen upright at Stonehenge, Wiltshire.

and labour productiveness, but these do not seem to be the principles that drove the neolithic quarrymen. They seem to have selected their resource sites at least partially for other reasons. For one thing, such places tended to 'stand out from the surrounding country because of their unusual characteristics' (Bradley 2000). Some were remote and difficult to get to. The distinctive Langdale Fells of northwestern England, as an example, had a few stone axe production sites. The outcrop of suitable rock extends for many miles, but the places chosen to access it were on dangerous ledges, high up mountains such as the conspicuous Pike o' Stickle. It seems perverse to us to select awkward and unsafe places when more convenient locations were to hand, but as Bradley notes with the Pike o' Stickle example, the production sites there commanded extensive views as they were on the steepest gradients, as if deliberately selected to be isolated from the lower ground and the mundane world. As in later ages monasteries and temples were positioned on rock pinnacles and mountaintops, so too these stone axe production sites seem to have been chosen to be close to heaven or, at least, to be in an otherworldly, rarefied spot. Pike o' Stickle may well have been a holy mountain to the neolithic people, who carefully and doubtless with appropriate ritual took away pieces of its sacred substance. That this is not unlikely is indicated by the fact that what may have been altars or ceremonial settings have been found at other production centres, like the Welsh Preseli Hills, source of the bluestones of Stonehenge (see Part Three) and a stone axe production centre. Again, there was once a sacred hilltop near present-day Locmariaquer, on the coast of Quiberon Bay, Brittany, but a few thousand years ago the coastline was inundated by the sea and the hilltop is now an islet. How do we know it was considered to be sacred? Because a double stone circle known as Er Lannic sits

The remnants of two settings of standing stones on the islet of Er Lannic, Brittany, with the cairn of Gavrinis on a nearby island visible in the distance at right. (Simant Bostock)

on it (and is partially drowned each high tide) and because there was a source of stone for axe manufacture close by. Two of the standing stones forming Er Lannic have representations of axes carved on them and, further, a hoard of unfinished axes was found buried within the stone circles. Production site and ceremonial monument are here demonstrably linked, but Er Lannic was probably erected long after the hilltop itself was first venerated for its own, natural sake. On a nearby former hilltop, now an island, stands the famed passage grave of Gavrinis, which has representations of axeheads carved on its interior stones, and similar depictions are found in many other early neolithic monuments in Brittany (Patton 1993).

Many places that could have served as production sites appear to have been ignored in favour of rocks that had a distinctive quality – colour, texture or suchlike – not to mention the remote and isolated characteristics of the production sites themselves. It is important to realize that the stone axes produced were by no means all tools or weapons – far from it, especially axes from the more unusual rock sources. The

Breton axes, for instance, are superb artefacts, sleek, polished and beautiful, and clearly and definitely ceremonial objects. Products from the Langdale Fells have been found as far afield as Ireland, where nearly half of those so far identified were discovered as deposits in rivers and bogs – again, obviously ceremonial or ritual items. A fair interpretation would be that the axes or other objects of stone or metal, such as copper and bronze, came from sacred sources, the votive items being in effect 'pieces of places' (Bradley 2000). We have seen the same idea in more recent ages, in the bringing back of tokens, soil or holy water from pilgrimage sites, as well as in the traffic of 'relics', the bones of the saints.

Le Pinacle (The Pinnacle) on the Channel Island of Jersey. An example of a natural site subtly modified by human hand. (Stuart Abraham)

The use of some natural sacred places as production sites for ritual and ceremonial artefacts seems to have been one of the first changes resulting from human activity to affect the unaltered status of such locations, but other, subtle modifications of natural features began to take place as well – the first hints of monumentalization. Bradley has made the important observation that the first peoples who started to modify natural features and then to build monuments were committing a major, irreversible act, one that must have required the overcoming of feelings of sacrilege: they were 'altering the Earth' for the first time (Bradley 1993). The earliest signs were minimal, such as at Le Pinacle (the Pinnacle), on the Channel Island of Jersey: a distinctive column of rock on the end of a promontory. Its first use was as a stone axe factory in the neolithic period, probably because the striking visual

nature of the place had made it important, thus making its rock special. Then, later, a platform was built against one side of the rock column, and a low wall was built, cutting off the end of the promontory. Deposits of items such as copper axes and fine pottery were made in this restricted zone, probably revealing it to have become part of an artificially denoted 'sacred space'.

Similar events occurred on the virtually treeless, granite upland of Bodmin Moor in Cornwall, southwest England, considered to be a 'fossil' prehistoric land-scape by archaeologists. A brown and bleak plateau, the moor can nevertheless provide quite dramatic panoramas, its wide spaces being punctuated by ridges and occasional hills, whose eroded summits display craggy 'tors' or rock stacks surrounded by litters of loose rocks, forming distinctive landmarks. These in turn form vantage points, providing open vistas. Archaeologists have found flint scatters indicating paths of movement across the moor by mesolithic people and suggesting that they found springs, marshes, some of the more prominent craggy tors and a curious shallow lakelet, known as Dozmary Pool, of importance. Archaeologist Christopher Tilley observes:

> In the past, as today, the Tors would be named and significant places invested with meaning, between which people moved. It is not hard to imagine that the fabulously weathered Tors would be great sources of symbolic potency and power ... The Tors were, in effect, non-domesti-cated 'megaliths' or stone monuments, sculptured by the elements and imbued with cultural signif-icance in the mesolithic imagination in the forms of stories, myths and events of cosmological import. (Tilley 1996)

Actually, Tilley expresses the chain of associations here somewhat backwards: the later megalithic monu-

Above: Showery Tor, Bodmin Moor, Cornwall. The minimalist prehistoric walling made from rock cobbles is visible in foreground. (Simant Bostock)

Below: The weirdly weathered Cheesewring, also on Bodmin Moor. Note the prehistoric walling at left.

ments were made to relate to the original, natural places, being seen as 'domesticated' tors and holy outcrops, rather than the reverse. Monument construc-tion commenced on the moor during the early and middle parts of the neolithic era – that is, between c.3500 and 2300 BC. People of these times built long cairns (three have so far been identified, although others probably await discovery) that point towards impressive tors; they also used small rocks to create low, loosely constructed walls that enclosed some of the tors, such as Rough Tor and the Cheesewring. This latter is a fantastically weathered rock stack among companions of similar appearance. Both these prominent locales are highly exposed to the elements and do not possess local water sources, so they are unlikely ever to have been used for permanent settlement. 'They were meant to be seen, climbed up to, visited for ceremonial events and then left,' Tilley instead suggests. The significance and power of the places had survived in the minds of the people through the many generations from mesolithic times. Parts of the moor became settled in the late neolithic and Bronze Age, and major ceremonial monuments were erected. These included stone rows and at least sixteen stone circles, examples of which we will visit in Part Three. They were all located close to tors.

In Lapland the Saami also sometimes embellished their usually unaltered natural sacred sites. The alterations were, in some cases, rather subtle. For instance, one type of sacrificial place favoured by the Saami was a cleft boulder – boulders split by lightning were thought to possess special power – and bones of reindeer or other animals would be deposited in the crevice. Sometimes walls of small stones would be built at either end of the cleft. One unusual site that has been discovered consisted of offerings of hooves and some bones laid inside a 'wall' of rocks assembled beneath a large boulder (Zachrisson 1985).

In many places around the globe ancient people have left hints of their use of natural places for religious purposes, so it is no surprise to learn that half the world away in New Mexico, in the American southwest, archaeologists have uncovered unusual sacred places created by the lost Anasazi Indians. Referred to as 'signal shrines', these features, which were minimally marked with stones, consist of hollows or basins carved out of the bedrock on mesa tops, rock and dune pinnacles and other high points in the vast desert landscape surrounding the Anasazi cult-centre of Chaco Canyon. Offerings of beads, turquoise and shells were found secreted in some of the rock-cut basins. The shrine locations yielded sight-lines to 'Great Houses', somewhat poorly understood ceremonial complexes on the desert surface, linked by the enigmatic, straight 'Chacoan roads', which converge on Chaco Canyon and can be up to 9 metres (30 feet) wide. It is thought that the shrines were used in signalling activities, but the link with that and the seemingly religious nature of the places is not properly understood.

Rock Art

Because it is the richest and most significant of natural place embellishments, rock art warrants separate treatment, although there is space here to give it only a relatively cursory look.

Rock art entices us because it is one of the most direct contacts we have with the minds of prehistoric people. The markings taunt us, hovering just beyond our understanding. Early attempts at interpretation linked images of animals (especially in the palaeolithic caves) to ideas of 'hunting magic' and 'sympathetic magic', the notion being that rituals using the imagery held before a hunt would have been seen by the participants to encourage success or to increase the fertility of the species of animals being hunted. Imagery showing humans and animals in various occurrences of rock art have been interpreted as hunting and scenes from daily life – such depictions in South Africa were once even described as 'childish'. A large amount of rock art, both petroglyphs and pictographs, is non-figurative, often formed of dots, grids, zigzags and other abstract, geometric motifs, and this major element of the phenomenon has tended to be downplayed in favour of the more dramatic images of bison, bears or other figurative imagery. These abstract motifs can be found everywhere, in most if not all groups of rock art around the world. A select number of such markings, such as those carved on slabs in the megalithic monuments of Ireland or on rock walls in North America, have been interpreted as relating to astronomy in various ways – variously as sundials, stone calendars and depictions of lunar phases and major naked eye astronomical events, such as supernovae. Some of the markings on portable objects, such as pieces of bone dating to the palae-olithic, were similarly interpreted as astronomically related markings and as lunar calendars in particular (Marshack 1972).

In the last two decades of the twentieth century, revolutionary new interpretations of some rock art, especially these geometric elements, began to be championed. The proponents of the new interpreta-tion included, notably, David Lewis-Williams and Thomas Dowson at Witwatersrand University, Johannesburg. They were studying the rich legacy of Bushman or San rock art of southern Africa, which had been produced from remotest antiquity until virtually living memory. Although most Bushman groups had effectively died out as cultural entities as a consequence of the European colonization, Lewis-Williams and Dowson studied surviving Bushman societies like the !Kung of the Kalahari and undertook detailed analysis of until then largely overlooked ethnological records of early European scholars in

The foundations of Pueblo Alto, a 'Great House' immediately to the north of Chaco Canyon, New Mexico. Ancient Anasazi roads converged here, through what had been a 'gate' in a wall. The mesas in the distance are the type of location in which many rock-cut shrines are to be found.

ROCKING AROUND THE WORLD

Rock art is of two main kinds: engravings or carvings on stone, called petroglyphs, and imagery painted or sprayed through the mouth on to rock surfaces using pigments derived from vegetable and mineral sources. This is called pictographic rock art. There is also an important sub-category of rock art study concerned with markings made on portable surfaces, such as pieces of stone and bone.

Prehistoric and ancient peoples produced rock art in many places on every continent of the world. It appears on the walls of caves and rock shelters ('parietal' rock art), on exposed rock outcrops, on boulders and on cliff-faces. It often pre-dates the appearance of monuments, although in some cultures it continued to be produced concurrently with monument building and even embellished megalithic monuments. In Europe, for example, the famous painted caves of France and

Spain, such as Lascaux, Chauvet and Altamira, contain rock art that is palaeolithic – tens of thousands of years old, long before there were monuments – yet it is also to be found on the much later neolithic megalithic monuments in, say, Ireland and Scotland and other areas of Europe's Atlantic fringe, and reverted to rock surfaces once more in the Bronze Age. But this ancient tradition of rock art represents the work of different cultures, different peoples and, probably, different beliefs and practices. In some places, such as South Africa and Portugal, rock art was produced until recent times, and in Australia the tradition still survives after a fashion.

There are, of course, many differences in styles and purposes in the rock art produced by various cultures around the world, but, as noted in these pages, there are similarities as well.

South Africa. This, combined with interviews of surviving Bushmen elders and a major new, painstaking survey of the rock art itself, caused them to see the imagery in a new light. Put in the simplest of terms, they concluded that much of the rock imagery related in one way or another to shamanic experience (Lewis-Williams and Dowson 1988, 1989). Ecstatic experience was central to Bushman religious life, and to this day the !Kung conduct 'trance dances', in which healers go into altered mind-states in order to treat sick tribal members, visit distant places and spirit otherworlds, meet the ancestors and the gods, make rain and conduct the business of shamans generally. Lewis-Williams and Dowson identified characteristic elements in figurative panels of the rock art that suggested they were, in fact, visionary scenes as would have been observed by the shamans or healers themselves in their altered states of consciousness rather than being trite, everyday records. The abstract, non-figurative patterns, they concluded, were derived from 'form constants', which are specific motifs, such as spirals, concentric rings, zigzags, wavy lines, dots, grids and arabesques, that appear in the vision of people undergoing trance. (The 'tunnel' image so prevalent in modern near-death experience reports, where it heralds a sensation of the mind or spirit leaving the body, is a classic motif of this kind.) Because these mental motifs – properly termed 'entoptic patterns' – are universal, manifesting in the visual cortex of human beings undergoing trance in all times and places, the abstract, geometric rock art imagery should occur outside Bushman rock art – anywhere, in fact, that rock art was produced by people who used some form of institutionalized mind-altering practice (which, surveys show, included most early cultures). And so it does. Research now associates rock art with shamanism in, for example, North America (Whitley 1994), with similar altered mind-states in Ireland (Dronfield 1995) and probably also in France (Bradley 1989; Patton 1990, 1993), and in South America anthropological work over many years has identified surviving tribal people deliberately using entoptic patterns seen in trances induced by plant hallucinogens as the basis of their tribal art (Reichel-Dolmatoff 1978). It is becoming increasingly clear that at least

some rock art is a kind of script of the ancient human spirit. Because that is an area that modern academics often tend not to consider, it is an interpretation that has been largely overlooked until now.

The full range of rock art around the world undoubtedly supports several authentic lines of interpretation, and some rock art is schematic and has narrative functions, not related at all to trance or shamanic rituals. Some interpretations, however, need not be mutually exclusive – for instance, it has been proposed that in certain places some rock art forms may indeed originate in entoptic imagery but were used to symbolize astronomical and meteorological

Bushman painting in the Zimry rock shelter, South Africa. Note the 'entoptic' dots involved with the fine depictions of the animals. (Thomas Dowson)

phenomena (Thackeray and Knox-Shaw 1992). This raises the important point that although the forms of entoptic imagery may be universal, the meanings ascribed to them were not but depended instead on the cultural contexts in which the rock art was produced.

By overviewing some selected rock art locations around the world, we can perhaps obtain an overall sense of the rock art phenomenon for ourselves, the most intriguing, complex and mysterious early sign that survives of ancient mind meeting natural place.

SOUTHERN AFRICA

Rock art in this region occurs as painted imagery on boulder surfaces or, often, on large panels in rock shelters in mountainous regions like the Natal Drakensberg and as petroglyphs, primarily in the interior plateau of southern Africa, on rocky outcrops, stony river beds or simple rocks out on the flat veld. Both types of rock art contain figurative and geometric elements. By carefully relating the garnered Bushman or San beliefs and religious practices to the art, researchers like Lewis-Williams and Dowson perceived that the paintings primarily concerned aspects of Bushman shamanism, as noted

A human-deer hybrid figure sometimes referred to as a "trance buck", displaying flowing lines from the shoulders: an expression of the soul flight of the southern African trance healer or shaman, and the transformation of body image (a sensation often occurring in trance) into one of the key power animals of the Bushman people. (Harald Pager)

above. There were depictions of trance dances, showing characteristic body postures and even the nose-bleeding that commonly afflicts the healers or shamans who attain profound states of trance during the dance ceremonies. Some scenes that had earlier been taken to be of battles are now considered to more likely show visionary scenes of 'arrows' of disease being countered by the healers. Other images are metaphorical, showing bird and fish images, which relate to the 'flying' or 'swimming' sensations that the Bushmen liken to the sensations in trance. There are many depictions of animals, particularly creatures such as the eland, which are thought by the Bushmen to contain concentrations of supernatural potency, which they call n/um and which they believe is raised in the human body during trance dancing. A common sensation felt by people in trance is that their body is changing shape, and there are rock art images showing distorted human figures and human beings that are seemingly turning into power animals, such as the eland. Some of these figures have mysterious lines trailing from their heads and shoulders, and it is thought that this may be expressing the 'out-of-body' feeling that is the characteristic experience in shamanistic trance. The paintings and engravings also display a great range of abstract, 'entoptic' imagery, often superimposed on or juxtaposed with figurative depictions. Some of the painted figures of trance dancers, for instance, have small dots down their backs; researchers suspect that this was a way in which the painters tried to indicate the rise of n/um up the spine. In the petroglyphs the image of, say, a giraffe might have a fine network pattern partially superimposed on it. In some cases, especially with the petroglyphs, abstract imagery can occur in isolation. Dowson has even attempted to link some of these markings to certain entoptic patterns known to occur in specific stages of trance.

The researchers have discovered that the paintings themselves were thought to be sources of power, and it seems that in the past trance dancers would touch or even merely look at the rock art as a way of accruing n/um. The implication of this is that the rock art was seen by the Bushmen not only as marking or embellishing natural places but also actually enhancing their spiritual potency. The Bushmen did not give significance to every feature of the landscape, Dowson observes, but 'importance was certainly attached to some and these were incorporated into their myths and beliefs' (Dowson 1992). We remain puzzled by some seemingly insignificant natural sites that were clearly important to them. A case in point are low hills or simply slight rises in the ground in otherwise featureless terrain. One such place in the Northwest Province of South Africa is a hill less than 9 metres (30 feet) high, which has more than 500 rock art images clustering together at points on its slopes and summit (Ouzman 1998). The hill is bounded by twenty-seven standing stones. But an understanding is developing about some other types of Bushman rock art locale and about the significance of rock surfaces.

Rainmaking was an important aspect of much shamanism in Bushman societies, and certain places were thought to be especially appropriate for this, notably those near waterholes or springs. This was because it was believed that a mythical creature, the 'rain-bull', inhabited such places. The rain-bull was one of the complex metaphors used by the Bushmen in their weather magic: it was 'captured' by the sorcerers and led around the country away from the waterhole to another site where it was 'cut' or 'bled' (meaning the rain was made to fall). Bushmen informants made sketches of the creatures for the earlier ethnological researchers, and these looked remarkably similar to rock art imagery engraved on boulders a short distance from a spring said to remain active

A detail of a panel within the rocks at Harmonie. Note the geometric 'entoptic' elements mixing with the animal outlines. (Thomas Dowson)

even in times of drought. One rather dramatic rainmaking site in the mountainous Eastern Cape Province of South Africa is a cave overhang over which runs a waterfall. Here, the importance of the rock surface itself comes to the fore, and a key factor not only in Bushman rock art but also elsewhere in the world is expressed. At this site there is a rock art panel more than 9 metres (30 feet) long, which contains depictions of four rain-animals along with human beings apparently involved in a rainmaking ritual. The creatures are shown as if emerging from the splash pool of the waterfall. More specifically, the hindmost animal appears to be emerging from a step in the rock face.

This convention is a persistent feature of southern African rock art indicative of San belief that the rock face constituted an interface between this world and the spirit world ... Steps, cracks and the like were construed as pathways which connected the two worlds. These pathways could only be followed by shamans and inhabitants of the spirit world ... rock images are not so much put on to the rock surface as experiences of the spirit world brought out from behind the rock face.

(Ouzman 1998)

Desert varnish darkens the images on this boulder at Rietport, South Africa, indicative of the rock art's age. (Thomas Dowson)

So it was not only the place, but the substance of the rock itself that had significance. It was the interface between this world and the otherworld. This had been perceived earlier by Lewis-Williams and Dowson, who wrote in 1990 that: 'Neuropsychological and ethnographic evidence suggests that San shamans visited the spirit world via a tunnel that, in some instances, started at the walls of rock shelters.' In their paper they note a large number of site examples displaying the relationship between Bushman rock art and fissures, cracks and other variations in rock surfaces. At one site, they observed that black paint had been applied to a groove in a rock face, out of which emerge a man-animal figure and other figures, one bleeding at the nose, the sign of trance. In other cases, painted lines seemingly emerge out of cracks, interact with rock art imagery, then disappear into other fissures.

THE AMERICAS

Prehistoric rock art, in the form of both pictographs and petroglyphs, can be found in many places throughout the Americas. The imagery runs the full gamut, from human and animal figures, semi-human figures, distorted and abstracted human figures, carved human footprints and animal tracks, and human artefacts to a vast range of abstract or geometrical designs. In its various forms American rock art dates from Archaic Indian times, c.3000 BC, to the proto-historic times of recent centuries. In North America there are notable concentrations in Ontario and adjacent parts of the Canadian Shield, in the Mississippi Valley and in western and southwestern USA, including Texas. In Mexico the northern area of the Chihuahuan Desert has rock art sites, and in the far south of the country, in the Yucatán, there are Mayan and pre-Mayan cave paintings and carvings on cliff-faces. The full extent of rock art in South America is not known, although petroglyphic sites have been found even in the Amazon, and ancient rock art is indeed to be expected anywhere that people dreamed, had visions, conducted ritual or wished to record elements of the world around them.

The Canadian Shield has more than 400 rock painting sites on cliff-faces. Bright red ochre images, perhaps two millennia old, depicting animals, humans, canoes and the paraphernalia of 'medicine' ritual, such as drums, rattles and medicine bags, were painted on rock faces close to rivers, rising sheer out of water or even 'in spectacular settings 20 metres [65 feet] up the steep cliff-faces with no visible perches for the painter to stand on', remarks rock art researcher Grace Rajnovich (1994). She also observes that many are on rock faces that have crevices or small caverns 'giving the effect of entrances to the cliff'. The images mark places where the medicine men or shamans sought manitous, spirits who lived in the rock. Gifted shamans had the power to enter the rocks (obviously in spirit, in trance) and exchange tobacco for medicine power. Probably the best known Canadian rock art site is the engraved horizontal limestone outcrop known as the Peterborough Petroglyphs in southern Ontario. Hundreds of figures are carved into the rock, some of them similar in appearance to the cliff-face paintings. American rock art expert Polly Schaafsma states that the Peterborough outcrop is known to have been an Algonkian shamanistic site (1996).

In California the prime rock art sites are those that belonged to the ancient Chumash Indians, who inhabited the present-day Santa Barbara coastal region. Their multicoloured rock paintings occupy hundreds of sandstone caves and rock shelters and display a variety of images, including a great number of abstract and geometric signs and markings, making it look hallucinatory or visionary in nature. Again, the Chumash were a shamanistic people, who employed the potent plant hallucinogen *Datura* (jimson weed).

The rock shelters, which were used for ritual activity, were seen as places of power and were resorted to by Chumash shamans, who were sunwatcher priests, the practitioners of ceremonial astronomy. Further northwest in California, towards the western edge of the Great Basin, there is a major concentration of petroglyphs in the Coso Mountains, with other examples scattered throughout the vast and arid Great Basin region that stretches across Nevada and north into Oregon and east into Utah. This range was considered to be an important rainmaking centre for shamans of the ancient Shoshone, Paiute and Kawaiisu peoples, and they would journey there from great distances. Among the images of shamans, medicine bundles, hunting scenes and elaborate abstract markings, a commonly recurring motif in the Coso rock art is that of bighorn sheep. Ethnological investigation by archaeologist David Whitley has revealed that this image was both a metaphor for rainmaking and represented the spirit helper of the rain shaman. The

Sheep as symbol: a rock engraving of a bighorn sheep from the Coso Mountains, southern California. (David S. Whitley)

shaman would hang a length of bighorn sheep hide from his belt and use a bull-roarer made from the horns of the animal. He would seek a dream, a vision, in which the sheep would appear. It was thought that rain would fall when a mountain sheep was killed, and so a dream expressing this gave the shaman power. It is easy to see how the engravings of 'hunting' scenes and images of bighorn sheep scattered among the Coso rocks could be misunderstood without knowledge of

The engraved image in the upper left 'quadrant' of this broken boulder at McCoy Spring, southern California, depicts a 'rattlesnake shaman'. The figure has emerged from the crack as a rattlesnake – the trance-spirit image of the shaman – and is transforming back into a person on his return from the 'other side' of the rock face. The other imagery on the rock is largely historical graffiti. (David S. Whitley)

this deeper symbolism. Some of the sheep have human feet, indicating that they represent transformed shamans. There are an estimated 100,000 rock art depictions in the Cosos, and they typically occur on open basalt cliffs and boulders, locations considered strong in supernatural power, *poha* (with so many such places in the Coso range, it is clear why it was a focus for shamanic vision-quests). Although the making of Great Basin rock art was continued until recent centuries, its origins are extremely old – experimental dating of desert varnish on the Coso markings have come up with dates as startlingly old as 19,000 years. If confirmed, this would put the rock art in the same age bracket as the palaeolithic cave paintings of Europe (Whitley 1996).

Whitley has uncovered ethnological evidence indicating that cracks and crevices in the rocks were perceived as portals through which shamans could enter the spirit world, and he has noted markings, such as a wavy line, representing a rattlesnake (another common shamanic spirit creature) 'emerging' from a rock crevice and transforming into a human figure, the shaman. This visionary entry into the rock was sometimes expressed in terms of sexual symbolism in shamanic ritual, and rock formations suggestive of the vulva were natural targets for rock art (Whitley 1998).

Field research by Ralph Hartley and Anne Wolley Vawser (1998) in southeastern Utah indicates that rock art there marked other types of place, notably distinctive, highly visible features in the landscape, locations on or close to established trails and at the confluences of creeks and rivers. Landmarks were thus accentuated with rock art, and markings 'accumulated' at some of them over long time periods. This indicates that in addition to the places themselves being viewed with significance, there were also implications for route navigation through the territory. This may have included not only everyday activity, but special religious routes such as the symbolic celebration of ancestral migration routes or pilgrimage journeys to holy places.

From AD c.300 to 1450 peoples of the Anasazi culture group dominated the San Juan Basin, which stretches across the large Four Corners region, where the modern-day states of Utah, Colorado, Arizona and New Mexico meet. Their key sites included, among numerous others, Hovenweep in Utah, Mesa Verde in Colorado and Chaco Canyon in New Mexico, and their rock art is scattered throughout the whole rugged, arid region. Chaco Canyon, which was a major religious centre, contains a range of rock art. Engraved spirals near the top of the distinctive Fajada Butte in Chaco

interact with shadows and slivers of light caused by slabs leaning over them to provide an accurate solar calendar, and similar shadow and light interactions with rock art have been observed at other Anasazi locales, such as Hovenweep. Sunburst-style painted markings on the walls of Chaco Canyon are thought

A rock art panel in Chaco Canyon, New Mexico.

to mark stations used by sunwatcher priests to observe the annual passage of the sun along the canyon rim in order to pronounce the times of important ceremonial gatherings. What is thought to be another astronomical pictogram is to be found on a rock surface at the western end of the canyon, showing three symbols – a hand, a crescent shape and a rayed, star-like image. It is widely assumed that this represents a supernova that was prominent in Earth's skies in AD 1054. On 5 July in that year the moon would have been visible as a crescent in the sky near the exploding star. (Similar rock images exist at two other Anasazi sites in Arizona and at the Abbo monument in New Mexico.) Anasazi rock art also typically

An extremely old rock engraving in the angular anthropomorphic style at Sand Island, Utah.

depicted animals, masks, concentric circles, spirals, zigzag lines, handprints, mythic beings, such as the famous humped-backed flute player (an image of considerable antiquity known to the Hopi as Kokopelli), and angular human figures shown with broad, straight-shoulders, officially known as the San Juan Anthropomorphic Style. There were considerable modifications to the Anasazi style over the long existence of the culture and in various parts of the region. After the demise of the Anasazi culture, the Navajo moved into some of the Arizona and New Mexico territories. They also had a rock art tradition, and examples of this mix with the earlier Anasazi imagery in many places, such as Chaco Canyon.

Although there were also other, distinguishable ancient rock art traditions, such as that of the Hohokam in Arizona, Anasazi influence extended southwards in its heyday through New Mexico and Arizona and into what is now Mexico. After AD c.1300, when the Anasazi culture began to break down, the rock art of the Rio Grande region began to shift to a new tradition, combining numerous influences, and this is generally classified as various forms of Pueblo rock art. At least some of the Pueblo peoples, which include tribes such as the Hopi, Tewa and Zuni, were shamanistic and used mind-altering plants such as jimson weed.

Further west, in the Pecos River area of southwestern Texas and northern Mexico, a distinct rock-painting tradition had developed from c.2000 BC. A central motif of the Pecos River Style consists of monochrome and coloured human-like figures, usually depicted with outstretched arms and with elongated rectangular or ovoid shapes forming the body. The heads are either missing entirely or represented by squarish or other geometrical shapes, or else animal heads are provided. Some of these figures are very large, extending to over 6 metres (20 feet) in height. They are accompanied by a variety of other motifs, including *atlatls*, dart points, wavy lines and geometric imagery. One of the humanoid figures, on a large painted panel within a rock shelter along the Pecos River, has been dubbed the White Shaman by investigators. This is appropriate, because caves and rock shelters of the general Pecos region have yielded archaeological evidence of ancient deposits of mind-altering plants. dating back to as early as c.8000 BC. A study by Carolyn Boyd (1998) has now shown that the imagery in the Pecos rock paintings relates to the peyote-based religion of northern Mexico's Huichol Indians, an ancient people who make an annual pilgrimage to the Wirikuta plateau in San Luis Potosí in order to gather the sacred cactus. The Huichol produce textile images based on their peyote visions, and the related traditions and these images share some of the self-same motifs as those found in the rock art. Moreover, the rock paintings allude to some of the metaphors used in the Huichol peyote religion. For example, the Huichol refer to the peyote cactus as a 'deer', and when they go to Wirikuta they 'hunt' it using a stylized ritual. (Some anthropologists suspect that such ideas are faint echoes of the Great Hunt shamanistic tradition of the palaeo-Indians, the first peoples of the Americas who came from Siberia across a former land bridge over the Bering Straits.) 'Virtually every major aspect of the ritual has its corresponding rock art representation,' Boyd states.

It is clear that a great deal of North American rock art is founded in the visionary mental realities of shamanism.

This is even more the case in Central and South America, where there were very ancient and well-evidenced shamanistic traditions using plant hallucinogens, some of which continue in some areas to this day. The whole issue of altered or visionary mind-states in ancient peoples, whether obtained by the use of plant substances or other methods, is a sub-text to numerous topics being addressed by this book. The visionary component should be borne in mind even when the subject being discussed is venerated natural features, sacred geography or megalithic monuments – topics that seem at first glance to be completely separate to such considerations. While it would be wrong to claim that all ancient societies everywhere in the world were shamanic, it is safe to assume that a great many of them did seek visionary states of consciousness in one form or another. Prehistoric rock art, one of the earliest signs of the ancient mind we can find recorded in the environment, simply underscores this assumption.

AUSTRALIA

Aboriginal rock art in Australia is among the most ancient in the world, perhaps the oldest, and yet, curiously, it is also the newest, because traditional rock painting and engraving survives, albeit to a limited extent. Rock art is found in many parts of the continent, but there are notable ancient examples in northern regions such as Arnhem Land, where there are several hundred sites, and parts of the Kimberley district. The art, variously, takes three basic forms. Painting was done with ochres (reds and yellows), pipe clay (white) and charcoal (black); there was no blue in ancient Aboriginal rock art. Images were etched into rock surfaces by the use of a corrosive fluid, and figures made from moulded beeswax formed low-relief figures on rock surfaces. There are also some stone-hammered rock surfaces, producing sets of shallow, round indentations, pecked dots, grooves and other such markings and manipulation of rock faces. Imagery includes mythic and supernatural figures of many kinds, both human and animal, human-plant imagery, dots, curved lines, circles, hand stencils (especially in southern Queensland), animal tracks, both painted and engraved on smooth rock surfaces, and a distinctive 'X-ray' style of painting that shows the internal organs of animals and fish. Paints were applied directly by hand and by mouth-spraying. The rock art can be found on many kinds of rock surface, such as boulders and cliff-faces, but typically occurs in caves and, especially, curved walls forming the rear of rock shelters. The rock art specifically embellishes landmarks, some of which are easily apparent to non-Aboriginal eyes and others that are much more subtle, noticeable primarily only to Aborigines and appearing as nondescript places to the untutored eye. Many rock art sites are 'stations' on invisible, mythic routes – the so-called 'songlines' or dream journey paths that exist

Indented rock surfaces at an ancient Aboriginal rock art site in the Kimberley district, Northern Territory, Australia.

only in the collective knowledge of the tribal people inhabiting the land. For those who can read them, the rock images tell the stories of the Dreamtime beings who created the songlines and the topography through which they invisibly run. Because the songlines are mapped in the minds of native inhabitants, knowledge of them can readily disappear when tribal traditions become fragmented and the people disperse elsewhere due to external pressures, especially the arrival of Europeans in Australia and their appropriation of the continent. Many of the songlines have now sunk back into the land, as it were, as a consequence of this mighty disruption, and many rock art sites now stand alone as isolated places instead of points on an interconnected mythic network. Not all such knowledge has been lost, however, for traditions survive in some of the more remote areas, and a concerted effort is being made by some Aboriginal communities and scholars to recover information from ethnological records.

The dating of Aboriginal rock art is an ongoing process, using sophisticated techniques such as the radiocarbon dating of pigments or chemical analysis of the natural varnish that builds up on rock surfaces in arid climates. The origins of some instances of rock art in various parts of Australia have now been fairly securely dated to, variously, 10,000 or 12,000 years ago. There are claims that rock art in the Olary region of South Australia is up to 30,000 years old. Two sites have been dated in Arnhem Land by luminescence techniques to c.50,000 BC or older (Chippindale and Taçon 1998). Finding the earliest date for a panel of rock art can be difficult, however, because countless generations of Aborigines going walkabout along their songlines would often repaint the images situated at the places of mythic importance along the route. The images have been kept fairly fresh over vast periods of time because of this tradition of renovation. But when

SPIRITS OF THE WILDERNESS

Details of panels of Aboriginal painting in a Kimberley rock shelter, Northern Territory, Australia.

such repainting was done, the imagery in a panel was often added to or modified. Anthropologist Charles Mountford witnessed this for himself at the low, rocky cave of Jukiuta at the eastern end of Ngama, a rock outcrop situated in central Australia, north of the McDonnell Ranges and Blanche Tower, a twin-peaked hill known as Winbaraku to the Aborigines. On the first occasion Mountford visited this place in 1951 he was unaware that it was situated on a long dream journey route mythically created by the Dreamtime entities of the snake-man Jarapiri and his companions, but in 1959 he was escorted along that route by Aboriginal elders and he was able to map it and photograph the sacred, totemic sites along it, of which Ngama was a key one (Mountford 1968). There are two large panels of painting in the Jukiuta cave, where Jarapiri emerged from the ground in the time-less time of the Dreamtime. One, about 11 metres (35 feet) long, shows a writhing serpent painted with red outlines and filled in with white – old Jarapiri himself.

He is surrounded by small white markings, representing the dog-people of Ngama, and red horseshoe-like shapes, indicating camping places. Two long, closely parallel straight lines depict Jarapiri's spear. The other panel is 7 metres (24 feet) long, with fainter, abstract images that Mountford was told referred to Jarapiri's companions. Mountford observed that distinct changes had been made to the Jarapiri panel: the snake's head had been at the right end of the serpen-tine form in 1951, but now the head had been moved to the left end. Additional designs had been painted on the cave wall above the Jarapiri image, while other parts of the panel had been allowed to fall into disre-pair and were almost obliterated. Mountford noted that photographs taken since 1960 show that 'many additional designs' had subsequently been painted on the cave wall.

Traditional Australian Aboriginal societies are not generally thought of as being shamanistic, yet that great scholar of shamanism, Mircea Eliade, considered that the use of ecstasy in Aboriginal religious, magical and healing contexts was comparable to that found elsewhere, and researcher Kim Sales has gathered a wide range of ethnographic evidence to support that opinion (Sales 1992). There is a deep, ancient but now almost extinct tradition of Aboriginal 'clever men', 'men of high degree' or 'doctors' who practised sorcery, magic and healing, sometimes in the context of shamanism. Such people might enter a trance in order to send their ya-yari or spirit out of their body to travel long distances to gather information, fly through the sky on invisible 'aerial ropes' or dive into waterholes to contact the rainbow serpent (of which Jarapiri is, of course, an aspect). Such activities are similar to those recorded of shamans in other cultures, and the ability to fly up to the heavenworld or dive down into the underworld is a classic expression of the shamanic 'Three World' cosmology (see Part One). Some Aboriginal clever men also developed X-ray vision while in trance, another hallmark of shamanism, and this might well relate to the X-ray style of rock art. Sales has recorded a wide range of entoptic phenomena that can be perceived as being depicted in the geometrical and abstract imagery found in Aboriginal rock art around the continent and has pointed out that ordinary Aborigines in recent times considered the art to have been produced by clever men. Clever men could also see spirits, known as *mimi* in parts of northern Australia. Aboriginal tradition in Arnhem Land records that it was the *mimi* who taught the Aborigines how to paint on the rocks long ago (Chippindale and Taçon 1998). The *mimi* are still present, but they are very thin and so are able to slide into cracks in the rocks – an allusion to the link between the rock art and features on the rock surface that we have already noted in numerous instances elsewhere.

THE PALAEOLITHIC PAINTED CAVES

Caves containing both a few examples and whole 'galleries' of Old Stone Age paintings have been discovered in southern and southwestern France, the French Pyrenees, Spain (especially northern – Cantabrian – Spain), Portugal, Italy and Sicily, with a scatter in eastern Europe and Russia. Recognition of the rock art took a while to happen: decorated bone and stone portable objects associated with finds of Ice Age animal bones and palaeolithic stone tools had been discovered in caves and rock shelters in southwestern France in the mid-nineteenth century, but any imagery noticed on the cave walls was disregarded. Paintings were found in the Spanish cave of Altamira in 1880, and a local man insisted they were of prehistoric origin, but the archaeological establishment rejected the idea. Then, in 1895, rock wall painting of bison were revealed at the La Mouthe cave in the Dordogne when it was being unblocked from fallen material containing palaeolithic deposits. By 1902 the establishment had no alternative but to accept the reality of art dating from such a remote period of prehistory. In the following decades many more cave painting sites were discovered, including the famous Lascaux and Les Trois Frères, each of which contain hundreds of images. (Lascaux alone, discovered in 1940, has 600 paintings and 1500 engravings.) It is a process that continues, with major painted cave discoveries being made in the 1990s at Cosquer and the remarkable Chauvet cave in France. In all, almost 300 palaeolithic painted cave sites are currently known.

The figurative imagery in the caves is principally of animals. Many species are depicted, although overall the most frequently seen creatures are horses and bison. Mammoth and deer are also fairly common, and there are some rhinos and lions, among other beasts. There are only a few mythical animals, an example being a 'unicorn' in Lascaux, and there are some incomplete or unidentified animal depictions. Animals are usually shown in side-view and most frequently in a still or standing pose. The occurrence of human handprints or stencils is widespread throughout palaeolithic cave art, and a curious feature of certain examples of these – often in caves hundreds of miles apart – is that some of the fingers appear incomplete, as if partially amputated. Does this mean that a large section of Ice Age Europe's population was afflicted with some disease or that there was some kind of widespread cult that required finger mutilation or are these marks of an itinerant group of cave art – and perhaps magico-religious – specialists? The caves are silent. Images of human beings are rare, although 'composites' – animal-human figures – have been noted at about fifteen cave sites. Figurative imagery can stand in splendid isolation or overlap earlier work. Non-figurative or geometric markings are the most common imagery in palaeolithic cave art, greatly outnumbering figurative images. These markings – which include the usual array of dots, solid circles, lines, arcs, zigzags, rectangles and so forth, sometimes in complex arrangements – are usually referred to as 'signs' by scholars researching the caves. They can occur in isolation, singly or in groups or clusters, or be associated with figurative imagery, sometimes superimposed on animal forms.

The paintings were made using primarily black (manganese or charcoal) and red (iron oxide) pigments. The colours were applied by fingers or by

A palaeolithic painting of a horse, Pech Merle cave, Quercy, France. Note the dots and handprint imagery and the way the cave artist made use of the shape of the rock wall. (C.M. Dixon/Photo Resources)

spraying from the mouth or through a tube, and it is thought that brushes made from animal hair or applicators, such as softened and frayed sticks or twigs, were also used. While many paintings were created on reasonably accessible rock walls, a large number are in deep, difficult-to-reach sections of cave systems, and some painted panels are so high up on cave walls or even cavern ceilings that scaffolding of some kind must have been used. Holes that might have been made for such supports have been found.

A remarkable feature of cave painting is the way that the contours of a cave wall or stalagmite were often used to enhance the realism of a figure – so a bulge in the rock might be incorporated into a painting to give three-dimensional impact to, say, a bison's shoulder. The use of various dating techniques, including the radiocarbon dating of organic material such as charcoal in pigments taken from the rock surfaces, suggests that the paintings date from between c.30,000 and c.8000 BC. Earlier generations of researchers felt that there had been a stylistic progression from crude earlier painting to more accomplished later examples, but with more examples to study and far better technical resources, not to mention being unfettered by former views that saw humanity rising incrementally from barbarism to civilization, today's archaeologists are satisfied that there is no such progression present in the quality of the cave art. Superb examples exist from the earliest times. In addition to paintings, there are a great number of engravings, as well as high- and low-relief work in clay and even fully three-dimensional representations of animals in clay, not to mention a number of statuettes.

Unlike southern Africa, the Americas and Australia, there is no direct ethnological information to guide researchers as to the meaning of this rock art – the people who made it are long gone and are effectively unknown to us. There are only the images themselves.

Interpretation has therefore been extremely difficult, and theories have come and gone. The first view was that art was simply the doodling of idle or bored hunter-gatherers holed up in their caves. But as the range and richness of cave art unfolded, this view had to be discarded. Then the French scholar and priest Henri Breuil dominated opinion with his idea that the art represented 'hunting magic', but as more and more examples were found in newly discovered caves it was realized that something more complex than this was involved. This was followed by various other theories, but, again, as more caves were uncovered, the thin basis for these was eroded. There is now an 'interpretative void' with regard to European palaeolithic art, suggests the South African trance-art pioneer David Lewis-Williams (1991). He offers the suggestion that the 'signs' are, in fact, entoptic markings resulting from trance states – these mind patterns are universal, being common to the human nervous system and so can be expected to be found anywhere and in any time period that people used trance in their magico-religious rites. They can be found in the ancient rock art of Europe as much as in that of southern Africa or elsewhere. In short, it is something researchers can recognize if they know what they are looking for. Although there is no ethnography – there cannot be – to back up this approach, there is some circumstantial evidence. There are, for example, the 'composite' figures – the human-animal hybrids. As we have already noted, this type of image is absolutely typical of depictions of body-image changes, especially the hallucinatory or visionary transformation into animal forms common to shamanic trance, noted even in the imagery of witches, who took hallucinogenic 'flying ointments' in the Middle Ages, and frequently reported in modern accounts of mind-change experiences with psychoactive drugs. Even the early researchers considered the composite figures to be representations of shamans,

The Lascaux shaman, abstracted from the surrounding rock art imagery, as described in the text.

perhaps wearing masks and animal skins as ritual garb. Yet British rock art expert Paul Bahn questions this interpretation, saying, somewhat weakly, that 'they could simply be people with bestialized faces or humans with animal heads' (Bahn 1996). To anyone familiar with the iconography of shamanism, this seems to be taking scepticism to the point of perversity. In any case, a composite image on the walls of Lascaux gives clear evidence that the association between these types of figure and shamanism is likely: amid surrounding imagery, a male figure with a bird's head is apparently lying down near a bird-headed stick. It appears that the 'bird head' on the man could, in fact, be a mask, and sticks with representations of bird heads at one end were noted by travellers in Siberia in the eighteenth century to be a shaman's 'badge of office'. The use of bird imagery to allude to the ecstatic state of soul-flight experienced in trance is a world-

wide shamanic symbol. The man is supine, suggesting that he is dead, asleep or in trance (shamans in trance were considered to have temporarily died). Further, he has an erection, and erections can commonly occur in trance states just as they do in the dreaming state. Some composite figures in other caves are shown sprouting or wearing antlers: again, antler headgear is part of the uniform of shamans from Eurasia to North America.

Another piece of circumstantial evidence to indicate a religious association with the cave art (and 'religion' for hunter-gatherers almost invariably involved some form of shamanism) is in the Chauvet cave, where the first investigators to enter it found a bear skull that had been placed on a block of fallen stone, forming the appearance of an altar. The skull had remained untouched since the Old Stone Age.

Yet another piece of evidence has come from an unexpected source: experiments with acoustics within some of the painted caves are indicating that the rock walls containing the most imagery produce the strongest echoes. This suggests that sound may have played a significant part in rituals associated with the imagery. Intriguingly, it has been found that percussive sounds (such as drumming and clapping) can produce echoes from the rock art panels that sound like the beating of hooves – perhaps the soundtracks to the silent pictures we now see (Dayton 1992; Bahn 1996).

Another simple fact is that the environment provided by these deep, inky-dark caves is itself profoundly conducive to producing altered states of consciousness, for sensory deprivation is a key method of doing so, let alone the use of additional methods such as drumming, fasting, drugs and flickering flames of torches, lamps or fires. We can perhaps imagine scenes in which the palaeolithic hunter-artist-shamans conducted long ritual sessions in the caves that began with fasting and long periods of total darkness and silence, which were eventually augmented by driving drum beats, resonating so strongly within the caverns that the participants' bodies actually reverberated with the deep rhythms. With a sudden eruption of flickering light from burning torches or stone lamps, the groups would see and hear the bison, reindeer, rhinos and other creatures come alive before them. We probably cannot fully imagine what these people actually experienced in such circumstances and mental states, but it is perhaps not altogether irrelevant to note that tribal peoples in many parts of the world had a powerful belief that in 'former times', a lost golden age, the animals could speak with human beings. This curious but persistent idea might well have originated in broadly comparable ritualistic experiences in remote antiquity.

In addition to cave art of the palaeolithic, archaeologists now also realize there was open-air rock art of the era as well, although it has weathered almost to invisibility while the imagery in the caves remains virtually fresh. In 1994 an outdoor site was discovered in the Côa valley in Portugal that involves a number of clusters of engravings stretching along the valley for several miles. Other sites have been identified in Spain. One of their investigators, Jean Clottes, points out that the functions of the cave and open-air art might have been quite different, as the outdoor imagery would have been much more readily accessible to a larger number of people than those in the subterranean depths, suggesting, possibly, a difference between public ceremony and ritual by an elite group of specialists. 'That change of worlds between outer light and inner darkness, which plays such a great part in many origin myths ... may also be regarded as a metaphor or a substitute for shamanistic experience,' Clottes remarks (1998). Clottes further suggests that there may have been topographic factors affecting where the open-air imagery was produced – the

currently known panels of such art are all seemingly associated with water, for instance, with many facing streams and rivers. There is much yet to learn and understand.

ATLANTIC EUROPE

Those regions of northern and western Europe bordering the Atlantic – Scandinavia, Ireland and the British Isles, the Breton coast of France and the Iberian peninsula – contain a great many examples of rock art that span the whole latter period of prehistory from the neolithic era to the Bronze and Iron Ages. There are certain similarities in the rock art of these regions as well as some marked local differences.

In Scandinavia the span of rock art production runs from the late mesolithic, c.4500 BC, to the early centuries AD, although in Norway there are a few sites that are thought to date as far back as 8000 BC. There seem to be two general traditions of rock art: one associated with societies based on hunting, fishing and gathering, and the other with farming and more settled lifestyles (Sognnes 1998). This can be loosely thought of in terms of northern and southern styles respectively, and while they broadly reflect a transition from hunting to farming through the neolithic to Bronze Age times, this is not neat and tidy, because there were overlaps – in mid-Norway, for instance – when both hunters and farmers produced the rock art contemporaneously for a thousand years or so in the late neolithic–early Bronze Age era. Norway possesses some of the richest assemblies of prehistoric rock art in northern Europe, with concentrations in the far north along the Alta fjord, in the mid-Norwegian area around Trondheim, at Vingen in western Norway and around the Oslo fjord in the south. Sweden also has important sites widespread through its territory, notably in the Bohuslän area of western Sweden, the provinces of Östergötland and Uppland on the southeastern, Baltic, side of the country and a major concentration at Nämforsen in the north. These are all rock engravings, clear and well-executed, and they form the bulk of Scandinavian rock art, although there are also about a hundred rock painting sites in Norway, Sweden and Finland. There is only a relatively limited amount of rock art in Denmark.

The range of Scandinavian rock art motifs includes cup marks (rounded hollows a few inches across, sometimes encircled by one or more rings, when they are called cup-and-ring marks, a type of prehistoric rock marking that is fairly ubiquitous in Scandinavia and common to much of Atlantic European rock art); animals, including deer, bear, elk, fish, whales and birds; human figures; soles of feet, shod and unshod; and ships of various styles and periods. The scale of the motifs can range from rather small to lifesize. There are also many abstract and geometric 'signs', which can occur singly or in clusters.

The paintings are almost always found on cliff-faces, often under an overhang or in a cave; the engravings are usually incised into flat or sloping areas of exposed bedrock. Kalle Sognnes (1998) notes that most rock art of the northern tradition is found 'at conspicuous topographical features', not at the tops of such features but around their lower edges, often facing the sea. The prominent landmarks chosen are located at the border between sea and land. Southern tradition rock art was created at places close to dwelling sites, out of the sight and reach of casual travellers, but in the north the engravings occur at points 'which declare themselves to the hunter's view'. Sognnes further remarks that the depictions of ships in all the rock art were of the same type of vessel, but the northern and southern traditions show them in very different styles and carved in different types of location.

The meaning of the Scandinavian rock art is, like most prehistoric rock art everywhere, open to inter-

Rock carvings at Alta fjord, Norway. The engravings are painted red by the authorities to enhance visibility. (Robert Wallis]

pretation. As with the palaeolithic cave art, ethnographic information is not available for the Scandinavian imagery, except possibly for some of the latest examples dating to the late Iron Age and early historical period. People have seen the

Scandinavian imagery as being, variously, religious or cult iconography, symbols of social or religious systems, markings denoting prehistoric territorial boundaries or a mapping of gender associations with parts of the landscape – and much else besides. Some of these themes are still pursued in various versions, while others have fallen by the wayside. Sognnes argues that northern rock art locations were sanctuaries along important hunting trails and in some cases marked places where 'rites associated with territorial passage' occurred. Eva Walderhaug sees disturbances caused by cultural shifts being reflected in the varying styles of the rock art of western Norway and allows that the abstract signs that occur may have been of entoptic origin, as shamanism would have been present, signalling that, in addition to external developments (such as the change to farming from hunting), internal struggles may have been occurring as elite groups attempted to seize control of hallucinatory/visionary experience. She also notes that in western Norway, as we have seen elsewhere, surface

A late Bronze Age stone setting in the shape of a ship, on the island of Gotland, Sweden. (E.R. Gruber/Fortean Picture Library)

imperfections in rocks were clearly acknowledged by the rock artists. At Ausvik, for example, she points out that a major set of rock art panels are, variously, inscribed in natural hollows, separated by crevices and wide cracks or mineral veins (Walderhaug 1998). We have already seen that such acknowledgement of rock surface imperfections is indicative of the shamanistic metaphor or belief concerning access to a spirit world behind and beyond the rock face.

Currently, the most exciting and far-reaching interpretative ideas concerning Scandinavian rock art are being forged by Richard Bradley, at least with regard to the ship and footprint motifs. The background to his observations on the ship motif is two-fold: first, the western coastlines of Norway and Sweden have risen appreciably since the last Ice Age, to the extent that sacred sites created near the shoreline in, say, the mesolithic and neolithic eras are now situated in relatively inland positions; and, second, profoundly ancient Scandinavian beliefs associated death with the sea. This is disclosed archaeologically in a number of ways. One is that drawings of ships have been found on stones in Bronze Age burial mounds in Sweden, and another is the very ancient Scandinavian tradition of ship burials. Further, canoes have been found in mesolithic and neolithic burial sites, and stones arranged in ship settings have been found beneath Bronze Age mounds. The tradition continued in the form of ship-shaped settings of standing stones surrounding burials through the Iron Age to the Viking and medieval periods. Bradley advises, therefore, that the rock carvings of ships should not necessarily be taken too literally as simple reference to sea transport, but may have been more complex symbols relating to death or, at least, funerary beliefs and practices. He has focused on the rela-

Rock carvings of a ship motif in Bohuslän, Sweden. (Robert Wallis)

tionship between rock art sites and Bronze Age burial cairns in the Bohuslän coastal region of western Sweden. As the sea receded here, it left behind agriculturally rich silts that became the platform for Bronze Age settlement. 'The rock carvings occur in local concentrations along the junction between the areas vacated by the sea and the hills that had always been above the water,' Bradley notes (2000). The burial mounds are positioned along the crests of these hills and higher ground and also on offshore islands. Bradley feels that the rock art sites were primarily designed for a viewer looking uphill from the strand of domesticated silted land where the human population was settled. Rock art sites do not occur on the offshore islands containing cairns. Apart from cup marks, ships form the main motif of the Bohuslän area rock art; tellingly, about 80 per cent of them are arranged on the rock surfaces in a generally horizontal manner. This means that at the upper limits of the Bronze Age domesticated coastal lowland veritable fleets of stone ships echo the lines of the contours of the land in which the rock surfaces are set. In short, they mark where the ancient seashore once existed around the base of the now inland hills, many of which may once have been islands like those currently offshore. 'Where such islands really existed, their edges would be self-evident, but where inland features were accorded the same significance, it was necessary to describe their limits by depicting an area of open water,' Bradley suggests. 'That was achieved most effectively by drawings of ships.'

In this interpretation, then, the ships represent water, the sea, creating a mythological landscape in which the hills became symbolic islands, recalling their former condition. But because the sea was also associated with the realm of the dead and corpses would have to have been carried out to islands by means of boats, the ship symbolism was probably deeper than simply this. That is where Bradley's startling insights into the rock footprints comes in. He noticed that more than three-quarters of the carvings of footprints in the Bohuslän rock art did not follow a horizontal direction like the ships and some other of the motifs, but instead described a vertical course. This meant that the footprints, which generally appear in pairs and are mainly but not exclusively shod, were describing an axis aligned between the lower ground and, ultimately, the sea and higher land where the burial cairns are located, as if following a path up and down the rock surfaces. The footprints are carved at lifesize, which is not the case with humans and animals depicted on the rocks, so they cannot be interpreted as leaving these tracks. No; whoever 'left' these tracks was invisible. 'Are they the dead?' asks Bradley. He refers to the mythology of northern Scandinavia, in which the world of the dead is, of course, underground; this underworld is inverted in relation to our living world and so the dead walk upside down, their soles sometimes touching ours. Bradley thinks that the footwear indicated by the shod versions of the rock art footprints represents hell-shoes, which according to myth had to be worn by the recently deceased to enable them to journey to the otherworld: dead men walking.

This interpretation is given further impetus by findings in Scania, Sweden, at a site called Järrestad 4. Rock carvings are found there on a sloping sheet of exposed rock that overlooks a valley leading down to the modern shoreline. At the upper edge of the rock are two mounds, the survivors of a group of three Bronze Age burial sites. Nearby there had been a burial cist containing the carvings of two ships. More ships are carved on the sloping sheet of rock. At right angles to these are carvings of footprints, shod and unshod, providing a link between the summit of the outcrop and a small bog below. The shod feet, some of them paired, extend across the whole panel of carvings, but the unshod feet tend to occur around the edges of the rock surface. Like the shod feet, the majority lead downhill, with only a few indicating the opposite direction. In the main, the footprints seem to lead down out of the Bronze Age cemetery towards the bog, probably a former pool, and Bradley points out that they follow a course that could ultimately have led to the sea. He cites a poem, 'Shadows in the Water' (1903), by the mystic Thomas Traherne, that contains remarkably relevant imagery:

> By walking Men's reversed Feet
> I chanc'd another world to meet;
> Tho it did not to View exceed
> A Phantom, 'tis a world indeed,
>   Where Skies beneath us shine
>   And Earth by Art Divine
> Another face presents below,
> Where People's feet against Ours go.

With the conservatism natural to the scholar, Bradley warns that it would be wrong to assume that these interpretations automatically explain such motifs throughout Scandinavian rock art, but here in these pages we can be a little freer and speculate. If Bradley's interpretations are upheld, it seems that some aspects (at least) of Scandinavian rock art describe a geography of the dead and map where ancient spirits walked. The rock art sites may have been where funerary rituals were conducted, perhaps each leaving its mark on the rock. But was only funerary activity involved? What about shamanic procedures? After all, the abstract 'signs' hint that trance was involved at these places. Did not the shaman 'die' for a while when in trance? Did he not visit the spirit realms? Was he not a psychopomp who guided the souls of the dying to the otherworld? Were his the

Tracks of the dead? Footprint rock carvings in Bohuslän, Sweden. Note that there are images of both bare feet and shod ones, the latter perhaps representing the hel-shoes of the newly dead. (Robert Wallis)

unshod feet or those leading up towards the cemeteries rather than down to the sea? These are questions that further research may one day enable the carvings to answer for us.

Moving on down the Atlantic shores of Europe, we come to the British Isles. Here rock art is petroglyphic in form and, as in Scandinavia, is mainly confined to natural rock outcrops, boulders and exposed shelves of rock rather than emblazoned on megalithic monuments of which there are relatively few British examples and which are not, in any case, our immediate concern in this part of the book. The carvings are situated principally in northern Britain, with some notable concentrations in southwestern Scotland, in Northumberland in northeastern England and on moorlands in West Yorkshire. Petroglyph panels have also been found in Cumbria, England's Lake District, in the northwest of the country. One of these, discovered in 1999 by amateur rock art investigator Paul Brown, is on what was a major route to and from Pike o' Stickle in Langdale, a stone axe production centre (see above). The rock art in Britain, variously, is usually dated to the late neolithic and early Bronze Age periods. (There was also a distinctive rock art tradition expressed in the carved stones of the Scottish Picts of the later Iron Age and earlier historical – Roman – periods.) Remarkably, this ancient heritage was not consciously noted by scholars until the nineteenth century, and it is only relatively recently that it has become properly accepted as a suitable subject of study by professional archaeologists. As Bradley has commented, British archaeologists 'have been happier at studying settlements and artefacts than working with the natural features of the terrain' (Bradley 1992). Most of the running has been made by amateurs, exemplified by the heroic work of Ronald W.B. Morris in Scotland and Stan Beckensall in Northumbria.

In Ireland the reverse of the pattern in Britain is to be found, with relatively few sites of carved natural rock outcrops and the major examples of rock art appearing on the megalithic monuments, such as Knowth and Newgrange in the Boyne valley, the Loughcrew cairns and elsewhere, sites we will look at in Part Three. Nevertheless, rock art at natural places is to be found, with some important examples in County Kerry in the west and County Cork in the southwest.

The British and Irish natural site rock art is essentially non-figurative, the principal motifs being cup and cup-and-ring marks, to which can be added long single and double lines (sometimes wandering between cup marks), cup markings within rectilinear enclosures, cup marks forming circular and other configurations, spirals, wavy lines, zigzags and chevrons, lozenge shapes, grids and hatchings, U-shaped motifs, flower-like shapes and a range of idiosyncratic designs, such as the famous form on the appropriately named Swastika Stone on Ilkley Moor in Yorkshire. There are the prints of small left hands carved on a boulder at Barnakill, near the Crinan Canal, close to Kilmartin in Argyll, but these are hard to date.

Being so ancient and abstract, the British and Irish rock art naturally poses extreme problems with regard to interpretation. This has not deterred speculation, however, and it has been estimated that around a hundred theories attempting to explain the imagery have been put forward at various times. Among these have been suggestions that the markings represent knife-sharpening holes, moulds for metals, masonic marks and depressions for primitive animal-fat lamps. More extended ideas have associated the rock art with sex-rites and human or animal sacrifice – the linear grooves being seen as 'gutters' for blood to drain away from the cup depressions, which are regarded as reservoirs. There are profound objections to all these notions, although as far as the 'sex-rite' proposal is

Cup and cup-and-ring markings on an exposed sheet of rock at Achnabreck, Argyll, Scotland.

concerned, cup-and-ring mark designs that have a groove coming out of their centres could conceivably be seen as vulvic symbols. There have also been a variety of astronomical interpretations. These have ranged from bizarre notions like that of L.M. Mann in 1915 that the cup-and-ring motifs represent celestial bodies orbiting around a 'supreme central force', to more feasible ideas that the cup and cup-and-ring markings were some kind of solar symbol. Versions of these motifs are found throughout Atlantic Europe, and they must presumably have related to some concept that was widespread throughout the huge region, the sun being as viable a candidate for a common denominator as anything else. There are other possible hints, too, in observations such as that the rock art on the boulders and outcrops on Ilkley Moor, for example, apparently occurs only on the surfaces that receive sunlight – parts that are permanently in shadow are said to be clear of carvings. Nevertheless, none of this is very strong evidence. Alexander Thom, a pioneer of archaeoastronomy, noted in 1967 that a complex carving on a boulder near a cairn in Perthshire marked a stellar alignment

from the cairn, but evidence of this kind is extremely patchy and could easily be coincidental. The more recent 'entoptic approach' lends itself to these abstract markings, and in Part Three we will cite interesting research that has been done with regard to the Irish megalithic petroglyphs that supports this angle on the problem.

The actual meanings of the British and Irish rock markings themselves may remain elusive, but some information might be forthcoming from considering the geography of the rock surfaces that were selected for carving. The more researchers study this aspect, the less random it appears to be. In 1974, for instance, Evan Hadingham noticed that panels of complex motifs occur almost exclusively on horizontal rock outcrops, with a general absence of complicated patterns on other surfaces such as boulders. Hadingham then went on to make the most obvious, simple and yet perhaps informative observation about the geography of the rock art: 'The careful siting of

These cup markings with connecting grooves on a moorland boulder in Yorkshire have been interpreted by some as representing a 'tree of life' symbol.

complex patterns not merely on the nearest available flat rock but on impressive slabs which usually overlook wide-ranging views, should excite the visitor's curiosity.' Beckensall similarly notes that the chosen outcrops represented 'high places with good views' and were often spaced along natural routes. 'Someone was marking the routes,' says Beckensall (1992), 'to define territorial division, hunting grounds, the way to sacred places?' The places were clearly selected. But what's in a view? Well, views work both ways, of course, and a place with a view is likely to be highly visible. As archaeologist James Dyer has commented with regard to Roughting Linn, the most inscribed rock surface in Northumberland, the rock 'is visible for some distance and must always have been a landmark' (Dyer 1981).

We have already noted that overlooks, wide views, are associated with the hunter's vision, as Bradley explains:

Farmers define agricultural territories by enclosing them, but hunter-gatherers define their territories in a very different way, by monitoring paths running between specific places. Those places overlook the surrounding land, and hunter-gatherers define their territories by the views seen from them. For hunter-gatherers, tenure is ... 'one-dimensional' because it is based on places and paths respectively. Among agriculturists it is 'two-dimensional' because it works by delimiting an area of ground.   (Bradley 1994)

Bradley conducted pilot studies of selected rock art concentrations in England and Scotland, where he carefully mapped the spacing and complexity of motifs on the rock surfaces involved. He found various patterns. At Strath Tay in Scotland there was a steady increase in the complexity of the rock carvings – and more cup-and-ring marks – the higher the land they were on. This was the land that would have been used for seasonal occupation by hunters, gatherers and herders. The lowland areas, where rock engravings were more simple, would have been occupied by farmers in year-round settlements. In Northumberland it was found that one set of rock art sites with complex patterns and wide views was within sight of certain ceremonial monuments, which were invisible to another, similar group of carved rocks that afforded exclusive views to other monuments. Many of the complex rock art sites were on ancient routes. Overall, Bradley found indications that the rock art consisted of carefully spaced complex motifs in places where it would be seen relatively briefly by different kinds of people on the move, like hunters or those on the way to attend ceremonials at

Carvings on the Hanging Stones, on the edge of Ilkley Moor. (Brian Larkman)

Handprints on a wall of a cavern in the Lol-Tun cave complex, a Mayan and pre-Mayan ritual site in the Yucatán, Mexico. These are 'negative' stencil prints, created by the artist-shaman expelling pigment through the mouth in an explosive spray over a hand pressed on to the rock. Hand symbols are a recurring motif in rock art around the world, from the Americas to Australia and even the palaeolithic caves of Europe. We cannot be sure what the significance of the image was in such varying contexts, but in North America, at least, what evidence there is tends to indicate that it related to 'supernatural importance or power associations', to cite Polly Schaafsma and M. Jane Young. Something of this nature was probably the case here in ancient Mexico, and doubtless everywhere, for the motif seems always to be associated with places that were clearly sacred, venerated or otherwise of cultural importance.

monuments and simpler where it would be seen on a regular basis by a more limited and stable audience. Studies like this do not tell us the meaning of the signs, but they begin to tell us something about context and the prehistoric audience that viewed the rock art. This, in turn, might eventually lead to revelations as to meaning.

Further south along the Atlantic fringe we come to the Channel Islands and Brittany, northwestern France. This region was once collectively known as Armorica. Here, as in Ireland, the main emphasis of rock art is with regard to megalithic monuments, which we will return to in Part Three.

Finally, we arrive at the Iberian peninsula. In northern Portugal and northwestern Spain there are carved outcrops and painted rock shelters. Lara Bacelar Alves has found that many of these places have been given names, indicating their importance as landmarks to the peasant population of the region and their continuing role in defining the village territories of northern Portugal. Until recently people conducted an annual ritual in which various signs were made on natural outcrops to mark territorial limits. Village elders maintain that this was simply a continuance of the actions of the ancestors, who made the prehistoric rock art. Alves found extant folklore attached to the natural rock art sites that tells of spirits that are trapped in the rocks. This is expressed in the legends in terms of 'beautiful young mooresses' residing in the rocks. They guard treasures and can leave the rocks and mix with the human world only on St John's Day (summer solstice revelries). Alves wonders if these legends and recent customs echo pagan traditions that themselves reach back to a time when a semi-mobile, prehistoric population inhabited the same territory (Alves 1999).

In Galicia in northwestern Spain Bradley has been busy yet again, mapping engraved rocks with Spanish colleagues. The motifs here include simple pecked dots, cup marks, circular motifs and connecting lines, as well as representations of deer, horses and human figures. Again, the study looked at the relationship of carved boulders and rocks to the local topography. An interesting finding was that motifs were aligned and repeated on rocks in various parts of the landscape in such a way that they reflect the passage today of free-ranging horses over the terrain. Deer would once have been likely to follow similar migratory routes through this countryside. So did the marked rocks simply indicate where the horses and deer imaged on their surfaces would have grazed and sheltered during the late summer drought? Possibly; but as we now know, whether it is 'battle scenes' in Bushman rock paintings or ships in Scandinavian petroglyphs, all might not be what it seems in prehistoric rock art. The rock surfaces were emblazoned with symbols and metaphors as well as pigments and engravings.

The ancient mind had been attached to natural place.

Natural Sacred Places

After this consideration of rock art and the other 'early signs' of natural site modification and embellishment, we turn now to look at specific examples of some of the principle types of natural sacred places. Four of the fundamental kinds are presented: caves, mountains, trees and water sites. However, we shall see that even this basic categorization can be difficult to maintain at times, with stalagmites being venerated as stone trees, sacred caves perforating sacred peaks, holy waters occurring inside caves, and other confusions.

RITUAL CAVES
Where they existed, caves were favoured places of natural sanctity for virtually all peoples everywhere. They were not only habitations and shelters, they were also the first cathedrals. It is not difficult to understand their numinous power – we can feel it now whenever we enter one. This is because the cave is archetypal: the entrance to the underworld, the liminal place where light ends and eternal darkness begins. The cave is metaphor: it is the womb of the Earth, yet the gateway to the realm of the dead; it is the threshold between the warmth and sounds of day and the chill silence of a cavernous night; it is the boundary between the living world of humanity and the mysterious, dark realms of the shades and of the shaman; it is the passage between waking consciousness and the dark deeps of the unconscious mind, the place of visions and dreams and of spectral, tortured images glimpsed in the phantasmagoric forms of stalactites and stalagmites. No wonder the shamans and sorcerers of the Ice Age conducted their rituals and vision-quests in such places. Perhaps we can catch the spirit of the palaeolithic paintings by thinking of them as frozen visions left on the walls of prehistory, the collective unconscious of humanity. Small wonder that Australian Aborigines used cave mouths as places of initiation, where they wrestled with the spirits between light and dark, life and death, sight and vision.

Cave cults survive in Mongolia to this day (Humphrey 1995). Certain caves are distinguished by the name of *umai* ('womb'), which is different from the usual word for cave, *agui*, such as is applied to caves used as retreats by Buddhist ascetics. These special caves, seen to harbour female energy through the agency of spirits, occur sporadically along the northern borders of Mongolia, in Buryatia and in the Xorchin region of Inner Mongolia, and they are used as shrines associated with female fertility rituals, which involve women crawling through narrow crevices. The procedures have to be directed by a shaman. The ritual performance is a representation of the female ability to give birth. The Dayan Derke cave in northwestern Mongolia has a series of chambers. There, the woman struggling through the complex is suddenly told by the shaman to look up into the cavernous gloom and report what she sees. If the perceived configuration of rocks and stalactites seen in the half-light resembles a child or animal, it is taken to be a positive indication. The Buddhist llamas disliked these rituals and in a vain attempt to resist the cave-spirits would sometimes resort to putting up phallic wooden effigies facing the caves.

Chinese Buddhists came to make use of caves for their religious activities, to such an extent that, with incredible labour, they even created caves in cliff-faces for the purpose, an example of a modification of a natural place. A prominent example of this are the Caves of the Thousand Buddhas (the Mogao Grottoes) near Dunhuang in Gansu province, northwestern China. They started to be hewn out in AD 366 and

A natural altar dedicated to a female divinity in the Muang On Cave, Chiang Mai, Thailand. (Chris Ashton)

were in use for shelter and meditation for many centuries, by which time there were some 500 caves, ranging in size from grottoes to great caverns. They lie on the ancient Silk Route and within them are 2000 statues and more than 40,000 wall paintings on Buddhist themes. A similar – but greater – complex, the Fenxian Caves, exists at Longmen, near Luoyang. Here, there are 1300 caves hewn out of the living rock, with 100,000 carved images, the greatest being a statue of Vairocana Buddha 17 metres (55 feet) high. It is intriguing to note that in creating such cave complexes, human beings were imitating natural places. It indicates the numinous power the archetype of the cave has on the human mind. This was further exemplified at places such as Sokkuram, Korea, where there are neither caves nor carveable rock cliffs; there the Buddhists built a completely artificial grotto to house a sculpture of the Buddha.

Natural caves were recognized as part of the sacred geography of early Buddhism in India, too, and the early texts mention a number (Law 1979). One, near the ancient town of Rajagaha, in the hills near present-day Gaya, was called Sattapanni and was where the first Buddhist Council was held. Another cave sacred to the early Buddhists, Indasala, is in the same region. Between c.250 BC and AD c.650 Indian Buddhists carved out cave temples and monasteries in the western Deccan region east of Bombay. The most famous of these rock complexes is probably Ajanta, located in a spectacular setting in a bending valley of the Waghora River, which enters the valley in a series of seven waterfalls. Doubtless the powerful, holy aura of this place had been recognized even before Buddhist times. Most of the caves were painted, many showing scenes in the life of the Buddha, and the stone-wrought façades on some of them mimicked elaborate woodwork. Sculptured decoration was rare in the early caves, but became lavish in the later additions. Another famous cave complex, Ellora, is in the same general region, and on the west coast close to Bombay is Kanheri, which remained as an active centre for longer than Ajanta. More than 300 caves were cut out of the rock at this site between the first and tenth centuries AD, and natural caverns were enlarged.

Apart from the palaeolithic rock art caves, ancient Crete and Greece probably had the richest tradition of sacred caves in the European sphere. People have lived on Crete, from the neolithic period and before. It is not clear whether neolithic Cretans selected any of the 2000 limestone caves on the island for sacred purposes, but up to thirty or so of them certainly were so used during the remarkable era of Minoan Crete, which lasted as a recognizable culture in varying phases from c.3000 to c.1450 BC, although the earliest part of that period was transitional from the preceding order of life. One of the major cave sites on the island – or the one that has had the most extensive archaeological excavations – is the Psychro Cave, situated over 900 metres (3000 feet) up on the northern side of the Dicte mountain range, high above the Lasithi plateau. It has a strong claim to be the Dictaean Cave, the birthplace of Zeus in the myths of classical Greece.

The Psychro Cave had been discovered by peasants in 1883, and in the following years a small number of archaeologists, including Sir Arthur Evans, the British archaeologist whose fame is forever tied to Crete, made some perfunctory studies of it, but it was not until 1900 that D.G. Hogarth opened up the site and made the first major study of it. The cave has an upper and a lower chamber. The upper chamber revealed traces of an enclosure, remnants of a stone floor and a rectangular stone altar. Fragments of pottery, figurines, little altars with inscriptions in Linear A script, small 'double axes' (see Part Four), knives,

THE BIRTH OF ZEUS

The Titan Kronos was warned that he would be overthrown by a son, and to prevent this he 'swallowed as each came forth from the womb,' as Hesiod put it. But when Rhea, consort of Kronos, was pregnant with Zeus, she fled to Crete with the help of the Earth-goddess, Gaia, and gave birth. Gaia hid the baby in a cave. Rhea returned and tricked Kronos by giving him a rock wrapped in swaddling clothes for him to crunch on. Amaltheia suckled the child Zeus in the cave and bees brought honey, pigeons brought ambrosia, and an eagle delivered nectar. Armed Kourites outside the cave danced, shouted and clashed their spears against their shields in order that Kronos would not hear the babe's cries from within.

Zeus grew up and did eventually overthrow his father. He also forced the old Titan to vomit up his swallowed siblings. Zeus returned to his birth cave from time to time, and it was there that his son Minos came to consult with him in order to receive the Code of Law that he could give to the Cretans.

bracelets and other votive offerings were found. The entrance to the main, lower chamber was blocked by fallen rock, and this had to be cleared. There was revealed what Hogarth called 'an abysmal chasm' that dropped 60 metres (200 feet) into the subterranean depths. Hogarth described the descent:

Having groped thus far, stand and burn a powerful flashlight. An icy pool spreads from your feet about the bases of fantastic stalactite columns on into the heart of the hill. Hall opens from hall

INTO THE GROTTO OF ZEUS

Down through the entrance of the Psychro Cave and into its 'abysmal chasm', stalactites and stalagmites unfurl endless phantasmagoria before the awed gaze of the visitor. All manner of mythic beings have been glimpsed in the fantastic forms within this great cavern, including the face of Zeus himself.

with fretted roofs and the same black, unruffled floor, doubling the torches you and your guides must bear. An impassable labyrinth before, where rock and water meet; behind and far above a spot of faintly luminous haze.

In and around the stalactites, in every crack and crevice of the rocks, they found votive objects jammed and squeezed. Some of these votive deposits in the deep chamber dated to the middle of the Minoan era, c.2000 BC, while those in the upper chamber were considerably later. Some of the stalactites had been modified and smoothed in places, and it is clear that here as in many of the Minoan cave sanctuaries special attention was given to stalactites and stalagmites, their convoluted, folded, complex shapes resembling figures, faces and animals. 'The forms of Zeus, Artemis, Athena and Hera appear in the semi-darkness, calm and undisturbed,'

Georgios Panagiotakis comments (1988), '... justifiably the stalactites became part of the objects of devotion.' The water in the lake in the deep chamber of the Psychro Cave would also have been vested with special properties because of its mysterious subterranean sources, and many deposits had been cast into it.

Other sacred Minoan caves in Crete include Kamares, beneath one of the twin peaks of sacred Mount Ida (Psiloritis), Skoteino, Chosto Nero and Louktas, among many others. There is subtle archaeological evidence that several cave sanctuaries in addition to the Psychro Cave had been modified by architectural additions. Stone walls marked off especially sacred parts of a cave, and artificial spaces were created for worshippers in front of a cave's mouth. In at least one case it is thought that a temple was constructed in front of a cave. Natural rocks were used as altars, but sometimes constructed altars were used.

One archaeologist noted that in some places piles of rubble had been collected and arranged into 'rude animal shapes', as if augmenting the simulacra glimpsed in the rock walls and the hanging stone drapery of the stalactites and stalagmites.

Greatly influenced by Minoan culture, the ancient Greeks also worshipped in caves. Their importance to Greek spiritual thought is highlighted by the fact that Eleusis, the great temple of the Mysteries of ancient Greece, was built around a small hill containing a shallow cave. The *Mystai* (those to be initiated into the Mysteries) walked all day in procession from Athens, stopping at shrines along the way. They arrived at the precinct of Eleusis after dark. They drank a potion, thought by many scholars to have been a hallucinogen of some kind, and then proceeded through the temple complex to the Telesterion, where the final revelation, the *epopteia*, would take place, the nature of which is one of the great secrets of the

The distinctive saddle peak of ancient Mount Ida (today known as Psiloritis). The Kamares Cave is the dark, round spot some distance below the right-hand peak in this view. This is the sacred mountain to which the central court of the Phaistos Palace aligns (see Part Four).

Entrance to Hades. The remains of the Grotto and Temple of Pluto in the precinct of the temple of the Mysteries, Eleusis, Greece.

past. One of the temple shrines they visited on the way to the Telesterion was the Plutonion (the Grotto of Pluto), which was built into the cave, and there conducted secret rites. The cave was literally understood as being the Gates of Hades, the entrance to the underworld. A temple had stood within the cave prior to the building of the Plutonion, so it was clearly a sacred spot from the remotest times.

Westwards, in the Americas, the importance of the cave as a natural sacred place was also recognized. A belief among some Eskimos overtly linked caves with shamanism, for it was said that a shamanic initiate had to go at night to a cliff-face containing caves and walk towards it in the dark. If he is to become a shaman, he will enter a cave; if not, he will crash into the rock. If he enters a cave, it closes behind him for a period of time; when it opens again he must seize the moment and exit or remain entombed forever. Clearly, this tradition relates to the idea we noted earlier of shamans entering rock surfaces through cracks when in trance. As Eliade observes: 'Caves play an important part in the initiation of North American shamans.'

We will also recall that hallucinogens were found in Texan caves that were used thousands of years ago. The most dramatic remains of cave use left in North America are the rock shelter dwellings of the lost Anasazi people. The most famous site where these can still be seen is Mesa Verde, Colorado, but other such locations exist, such as Canyon de Chelly, Arizona, and Butler Wash and Arch Canyon, Utah. While these rock overhangs and caves provided useful protection and shelter for dwelling, as they did in Europe and elsewhere, they also contained kivas – circular ceremonial and ritual structures – and some also display rock carvings. It is important that we do not project our own modern ideas about the division between secular and sacred.

An unknown people built the great ceremonial city of Teotihuacán 2000 years ago in the Valley of Mexico, not far from present-day Mexico City. It contains many temples and plazas and ceremonial roads, as well as two giant terraced pyramids, dedicated to the sun and the moon by the Aztecs, who thought the gods had been born at Teotihuacán. In 1971 the entrance to a cave was discovered beneath the Pyramid of the Sun. Steps led down to a long, natural subterranean passage that gave entrance to a four-lobed cave chamber. It was found that the passage had been modified in the first century AD by narrowing it in places and lowering the ceiling here and there with slabs, making it more constricted and sinuous than in its natural state. The reason for this must have been so that those entering would have repeatedly to alternate between standing, crouching and kneeling. Clearly, the modifications were designed to facilitate some ritual procedure. The cave chamber was certainly used ritually, because offerings of shell, bone and ceramic were found, as well as evidence of the use of fire and water (Millon 1993). It so happened that the cave passage aligned to the setting point of the Pleiades constellation. The Pyramid of the Sun (see frontispiece) was built over the cave that had previously been in use for an unknown period and exactly oriented on the Pleiades line of the cave passage. Then the orientation of the entire street grid of the huge ceremonial city was set out from this alignment.

Further south, in what is today Mexico's Yucatán peninsula and beyond, was the domain of the ancient Maya. Caves were vitally important sacred places to these people. They are still held in veneration by some present-day Maya, although most of the ceremonies that used to be held in caves have transferred to churches. In Chiapas private ceremonies are still held at Sacamche'en (White Cave), for divination and healing, continuing practices there that may well go back to ancient Mayan times. The Maya there say that caves have curative and magical properties and that el *dueño de la tierra* (the Master of the Earth), lives in them and that thunder, rain and lightning can issue from them (Sanmiguel 1994). To the classic Maya (AD c.300–c.900) caves were entrances to the underworld, as were all natural openings. They were also the abode of the gods and ancestors, and within living memory it was a practice of the Maya to bury afterbirths in sacred caves (Freidel et al. 1993). The importance of the cave to the ancient Maya is shown by how they incorporated it into their architecture: a chamber inside a pyramid represented the cave within the mountain. Furthermore, some Mayan structures were built over caverns, the so-called High Priest's Grave at Chichén Itzá being a notable case in point.

The Yucatán is limestone and has underground water systems that have created many caverns, and, in their search for water – for drinking or for ritual purposes – the Maya had, during their long civilization, effectively explored them all. Some were used as sources of drinking water, others for, variously, refuge (although this was a minor use), burials and cremations, the discarding of used ceremonial equipment and, of course, religious rites. Stone and wooden idols have been found in the ritual caves, as well as a limited amount of wall paintings and hieroglyphs. Censers and votive pottery were also deposited, among other objects. Stalactites and stalagmites were worshipped, and in some cases they were worked by human hand to emphasize the suggestive forms inherent in them. Bosses of rock on the walls of caverns were sometimes carved into masks or skulls, again often enhancements of simulacra. This also happened with weirdly shaped lumps of rock lying in the caves. Parts of certain ritual caves were modified by platforms and the artificial narrowing of passages, doorways and walls. Some of the caves seem to have been

dedicated to various deities, such as the jaguar-god, the gods of rain, death and maize and the Mayan moon-goddess.

One of the better known examples of a Mayan ritual cave is Lol-Tun (Stone Flower) in the Yucatán, so named because of the flower-shaped petroglyphs at the site. Edward Thompson was the first to excavate at the site in 1890, and he was followed in 1895 by Henry Mercer, who excavated thirteen of the twenty-nine Mayan caves he visited. On an exterior rock face near the entrance there is a larger-than-lifesize relief

Anasazi caves at Butler Wash, Utah. The thirteenth-century AD ruins inside the large cave show it to have been used primarily for ceremonial purposes, because, in addition to habitation and storage quarters, the cave also contained four kivas (subterranean or semi-subterranean ritual chambers) – three of them round in the Mesa Verde Anasazi style, one of them square in the Kayenta Anasazi style. The dark markings on the rocks have been caused by water run-off.

THE CAVE OF STONE FLOWERS

Above: When they are struck, these two giant, fused, stalactites–stalagmites issue deep tones that resonate within the cave. This would certainly have been used by the Maya, and it is thought that many ancient peoples around the world who resorted to sacred caves used the acoustic effects sometimes offered by stalactites.

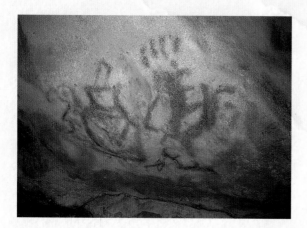

Above: Mayan paintings on a protruding boss of rock. These were produced using a mouth-spray technique, and this is one of several panels of paintings in Lol-Tun.

carving of a man in profile, colloquially known as the Lol-Tun Warrior. It is probably the most ancient such carving in the whole of the Maya lowlands and is thought to date to the pre-classic Mayan era (c.300 BC–AD c.250) – hence it is rather weathered and faint. The cave system itself consists of a series of cathedral-like chambers, which Mercer considered to be 'awe-inspiring', connected by relatively spacious passages. At one end of the system is a cavern whose roof has partially collapsed, allowing dramatic beams of sunlight to enter. A carving on the wall of a mask or face may be of the rain-god, as the cavern drips with water, and strangely shaped rocks and stalactites can be glimpsed looking vaguely like human figures or animals. Mercer noted a massive stalagmite shaped like 'a crouching cat', and there is indeed such a shape. 'At several places masses of stalagmite had been crudely chiselled to represent human shapes,' Mercer further observed (1975). It seems that the ancient Maya had interacted with features in the caves much as had the Minoans. At various points along the cave walls are paintings – simple outlines, images and handprints, carvings of spirals, geometric and flower-like shapes and a crudely carved effigy known as the Lol-Tun Head, discovered in 1960. Excavations in the cave system have shown that it was used from early times: animal bones, including, interestingly, those of mammoth, have been recovered, as well as stone tools, and these are dated to c.2200 BC. The earliest pottery fragments found at Lol-Tun date to c.700 BC.

Balankanché (Hidden Throne), near Chichén Itzá, also in the Yucatán, is smaller and less well known, yet it is the most spectacularly dramatic of any Mayan cave yet explored. Its entrance had long been known to the local Maya, but it was blocked by a rock fall. Mayan legends persisted that there was something remarkable hidden inside. In 1959 a guide at Chichén Itzá cleared a way through and, proceeding with great difficulty over a period of two hours, encountered offerings just as they had been left by the ancient Maya. The full cave system has apparently still not been fully explored, but what can be accessed is utterly remarkable. A passage takes the visitor past various small chambers and side passages, some with incense burners and pots placed many centuries ago as offerings beneath rows of stalactites. It finally leads into a great circular cavern, about 15 metres (50 feet) high, with a curiously domed floor rising about 6 metres (20 feet) in the centre. There, linking the cavern's ceiling and the dome's crest, is a giant stalagmite in the remarkable likeness of a great tree – a stone *axis mundi* wrought by nature – surrounded by offerings that have lain undisturbed for a thousand years. The 'trunk' is actually formed by the fusing of a stalactite and a stalagmite and the impression of 'foliage' is formed by countless small, spiky stalactites. The 'tree' is surrounded by innumerable offerings, including stone and wooden figures, spiked or knobbed pottery incense burners, some with appliqué decoration showing the image of Tlaloc (the Mexican rain-god), stoneware, charms, many small pieces of jade (probably from what was once a mosaic), miniature corn grinders, tiny pots and spindle whorls. The total effect is overwhelming. Some of the deposits have been removed to museums, but the remaining ones are in situ, just as the ancient worshippers left them. Radiocarbon dating of charcoal from a censer and a hearth yielded a date of AD c.860, give or take a century, suggesting that the use of the cave, at least at that point, had been when the Maya were coming under strong Mexican influence, thus explaining the image of Tlaloc. From this chamber, as powerful in its raw way as any Gothic cathedral, two passageways branch out, one leading down to water.

The startling likeness of the central formation to a tree would not have been lost on the worshippers at

The awesome cave system of Balankché has several small caverns, like 'side chapels', with offering vessels and copal censers laid on the ground, often before curtains of stalactites, that are passed before the main chamber with the amazing 'stone tree' is reached. This extraordinary formation would unquestionably have symbolized Ya' axche Cab, the Central Tree, for the Maya.

Balankanché, and indeed the Maya did have a World Tree concept: they imaged it in the form of a great ceiba tree, linking heaven and Earth, with its roots penetrating to the underworld. Balankanché must surely have been an especially powerful place for them – so much so that its memory could persist in local Mayan lore for a millennium.

SACRED PEAKS

If the cave is the deepest, most resonant archetype conjured by a natural sacred place, then the mountain must closely follow. We know its attributes: stillness and permanence. That is why the mountain provided the image of a Cosmic Mountain – the World Centre, the *axis mundi* – for many cultures. It is a water-bearer: the source of rivers, streams and the maker of rainclouds, thunder and lightning. Snowy peaks reach to the sky, soaring into the rarefied realms of the heavens. Visible from afar, mountains are remote and unsullied by the world below. The physical image of the mountain can create all these associations and feelings within us. The mountain is the perfect place to imagine as the habitation of gods; it is obvious why the ancient Greeks placed their pantheon on Mount Olympus, and it is equally clear why the Zoroastrian mystics of ancient Iran conceptually cloaked the physical mountain geography of their country with the transcendent inner geography of the paradisal lands they saw in their visionary trances – the 'mountain of the dawns', as Corbin (1990) notes, for is not the high snowy peak the first to gleam in the rays of the rising sun? The mountain is a perfect symbol of transcendence and so provides a most appropriate environment for the yogin, the meditating monk, the ascetic or simply those wishing to calm their ruffled souls by looking out over all the petty scenery of human life to see grander vistas. The mountain can also be the volcano, wreaking havoc

on the human world: an angry god to be placated, to be sacrificed to. The human race has used mountains as spiritual tools for all these purposes and more. Nor does it have to be some high, pyramidal Himalayan summit – for it is, in the end, a symbol. Hilltops can work just as effectively in their own context.

Specific mountains are chosen as special and sacred for a variety of reasons: they may be the dominant feature on the skyline or in a district – a landmark, in other words; they may happen to lie in a cosmologically significant direction; they may have dangerous properties, like volcanoes, holding the life of a society or even a civilization in the balance; or they may have some distinctive visual characteristic – such as appearing to be very regular and pyramidal, having an usual shape, such as having a cleft peak, or resembling an animal or human figure or profile. Further, they may be the only source of water in an arid area.

Let's take a quick world tour to spy on a selection of the planet's most sacred peaks.

Pre-Columbian Native Americans had many kinds of sacred peak. Some cliff-faces on mountains sacred to the ancient Algonkins of the Canadian Shield were painted with panels of red ochre washes to denote the power of the mountain itself – *manitous* or spirits lived in the very rock of the place. In Montana, close to the Canadian border, stands the Blackfoot holy mountain of Ninaistakis. Even in that part of the Rockies it is a landmark, high enough to catch the first and last of the sunlight each day. Moreover, it can make sounds ('sing') when the wind blows through fissures in its summit rocks, it has simulacra on one of its cliff-faces that illustrate a Blackfoot legend, the shape of the peak looks like a Blackfoot chief's ceremonial headdress, and it is the abode of a great spirit. Consequently, it is a place of powerful dreams and vision, and in the mountains all around it are the subtle features denoting vision-questing beds

– cleared areas of rock, placed slabs or rings of low stones. The sacred aspect of Simloki (Soldier Mountain) in northern California was its shadow. The Ajumawi Indians there considered this to be a spirit in its own right, and at certain times of the year braves would try to outrun its movement across the valley floor in order to gain medicine power. Mount Shasta, also in northern California, was (and is) sacred to the Wintu Indians, who believe that their souls fly there after death.

Avikwa'ame (Spirit Mountain) in Grapevine Canyon, Laughlin, Nevada, was sacred to the Yuman people because of a legend known as the Shaman's Tale, which is essentially a creation myth. The Yuman shaman would travel to this mountain in order to 'dream' this creation myth – that is, he would enter a trance and experience visions, in which he would witness the events and supernatural beings involved. A rock at the foot of the mountain has a panel of shamanic rock art, and this place is where the great creator spirit, Mastamho, lived. Variations in the natural varnish coating the petroglyphs suggest that this site was in use for possibly thousands of years (Whitley 1996).

The Pueblo Indians of southern Arizona and New Mexico share a strong directional cosmology – they are all at Centre Place and the Directions have powers. As 'Centre Place' varies according to where the tribal pueblo is situated, selected directional mountains can vary somewhat, but the Pueblo world in general is reasonably well confined to an overall territory bounded by the Sandia Mountains on the east and the San Francisco Mountains, home of the Kachina, on the west (Tyler 1964).

The Indians of Mesoamerica sought out the mountain gods primarily to ensure a supply of water. The Aztecs in the Valley of Mexico conducted rituals for this on Mount Tlaloc, near present-day Mexico City

The shamanic rock on Spirit Mountain, Nevada, which represents the 'house' of the mythic being, Mastamho. (David S. Whitley)

(see Part Three). Another important sacred peak in the Valley of Mexico is that of the volcano Popocatépetl. To this day, Indians still make pilgrimages up its slopes in order to make offerings. Popocatépetl is a primary source of rainclouds and water for the surrounding region. Chalcatzingo to its south is a rocky hill that was sacred to the Olmec, the oldest civilization known of in Mesoamerica. On a rock face facing the volcano there is a petroglyph showing an ancestral figure seated within a cave from which mist issues, forming rainclouds. A sculpture was found near the base of Popocatépetl depicting the Aztec god of flowers, Xochipilli: engravings on the effigy have been shown to depict a range of mind-altering plants, including a mushroom that apparently grows only on the slopes of the great volcano. This would doubtless have been taken as a sign of its special powers. But Popocatépetl

Popocatépetl, Mexico, which was sacred to the Aztecs and to civilizations before them. Indeed, the volcano is venerated by local Mexican Indians to this day.

not only has its beneficent aspect of providing the waters of life, it has from time to time also wrought destruction in the Valley of Mexico with its eruptions. After a long slumber, it is rumbling again.

Across the Atlantic certain peaks in Ireland were likewise considered to be sacred. The most famous is that of Croagh Patrick, which has been the focus of Christian pilgrimage since at least the Middle Ages and which is increasingly being seen as a recycling of earlier pagan practice. This is recorded in the legend of St Patrick, who cast out the serpents from Ireland while on spiritual retreat on the mountain in the fifth century. Croagh Patrick is situated on Ireland's west coast, near Westport. The power of the mountain is best appreciated from some miles inland, when its almost perfectly symmetrical pyramidal profile can best be seen. It is a relatively isolated peak and must always have been a singular landmark that would have been freighted with meaning by early people.

In Scotland there is another isolated sacred eminence, a rocky hill called Dunadd. It is situated in Argyll in western Scotland, north of the town of Lochgilphead. That, at least, is its modern geographical location. More importantly, it is situated at the southern extremity of Kilmartin Glen, which has been a sacred landscape from neolithic and Bronze Age times, and there are several special arrangements of prehistoric cairns and standing stones and a plethora of rock carvings. The rocky knoll was occupied in neolithic times, and among other artefacts a stone ball was recovered from it. These neolithic stone balls are very mysterious objects and have been studied by architect and geometer Keith Critchlow (1979), who found them to display sophisticated geometrical knowledge. The best attested phase of Dunadd, however, concerns the early historical era. Artefacts dating to between the seventh and ninth centuries AD have been unearthed, and these, linked with very old literature sources such as the *Annals of Ulster*, show Dunadd to have been the capital of the Dal Riata, a clan of the Scotti, who came from Ireland and who ultimately gave their name to Scotland. Some of the rock surfaces on Dunadd bear carvings, including a remarkable image of a boar and some ogham script. Most intriguing, however, is a carved footprint (shod) on one of the rock summits of the knoll. This and a nearby rock-hewn basin are thought to relate to the kind of inauguration ceremony of Celtic High Kings known of during the Iron Age. This was a ritualistic affair of sacral kingship, probably incorporating themes from even greater antiquity that required the king and the land symbolically to become as one. Dunadd had clearly been a recognized 'peak' for thousands of years, and its use as a Celtic royal centre and fort indicates that the nature of the prehistoric ritual landscape of Kilmartin was still being recognized.

Next, the Mediterranean, where mountains had been considered sacred in Crete from unknown antiquity, with worship taking place on a considerable number of selected peaks (the full extent of this is unknown). The Minoans continued this ancient practice, in some cases building sanctuaries on the previously unadorned sacred summits, probably at the time they were building their ceremonial palaces, such as Knossos. As Alan Peatfield (1994) has pointed out, Crete is a land of mountains, and any culture that evolves in such a landscape is going to have an appropriate ritual response to it and for the Minoans 'that response was the cult of peak sanctuaries'. Some scholars feel that the Minoan goddess was Mistress of the Animals and Peak Sanctuaries, for that is how she is portrayed in seals found at Knossos.

The peak sanctuaries were often placed near the summit where the widest vistas were obtainable, rather than always on the very top of a mountain (Bradley 2000). View was clearly important, and it

Minoan seal showing "Goddess of the Mountains" symbolism.

Lord of all he surveys: the inaugural footprint for the sacral king on the summit of Dunadd, Kilmartin Glen, Scotland.

transpires that the Minoan peak sanctuaries were intervisible. They were sometimes placed on peaks that related to the palaces below, but sometimes they were situated in remote locations. All the sanctuaries were wild and elemental places, however, even the best researched example, that on Mount Juktas overlooking Knossos. (To be in this place during an electrical storm, as this writer has endured, is to appreciate this most keenly.) Twenty-five Minoan peak sanctuaries are currently known to scholars, but there may well be more yet to be discovered. The forms of Minoan peak sanctuaries were defined by the existing natural situation, such as the shape and extent of the rock outcrop on the mountain; they did not come as pre-packaged concepts like today's shopping malls. Before the Minoan adaptations with walls and structures, there were only the wild and natural places themselves, with minimal additions. A wide variety of offerings has been found in the sanctuaries, with some differences between those near palaces and those in more removed locations. Rural sanctuaries contained a range of pottery, ceramic models of livestock and other votive items and also a considerable

CLOSE TO THE GODS

The view northwards towards the Aegean from the top of Mount Juktas, Crete. The Minoan peak sanctuary is built into and on to the rocky summit at right.

The remains of the peak sanctuary's walling are keyed into the natural rocks.

Part of the fissure that cleaves through the summit rock in the heart of the peak sanctuary, into which offerings were deposited.

The remains of the altar on the summit of Mount Juktas, within the precinct of the sanctuary.

number of pebbles from the surrounding district. This seems to have been an example of the 'pieces of places' phenomenon we have already encountered and to which we shall return in Part Three. The sanctuaries on mountains closer to the palaces tended to have a wider range of offerings, but metal objects were less common than in the sacred caves. Offerings were often placed around specific stones or in fissures and rock clefts. At the Juktas sanctuary, for instance, the Minoan structure surrounds a natural, distinctive fissure running through the summit rock, and offerings were put into that.

Moving on rapidly eastwards, we can note that there were many sacred peaks in the Middle East, such as Mount Sinai in Egypt, the Horeb of the Old Testament, where Moses received the Ten Commandments from God and which has been the focus of a Christian pilgrimage circuit from early historical times. In Jerusalem Mount Moriah (Temple Mount) curiously became the focus of three great religions, Judaism, Christianity and Islam, and it is of importance to them still.

The Himalayas are a very different environment, both geographically and culturally. The Tibetan-speaking Khumbo of northeastern Nepal have a deep association with their holy mountains. The deities that inhabit them preside not only over Khumbo territory, but also over the social and symbolic aspects of the society. So people by birth 'belong' to certain mountains; a child's soul is automatically related to a sacred mountain depending on which clan it is born into (Walter 1995). Mount Kailas, which is also part of a Himalayan range, is the physical embodiment of the Hindu mythical Mount Meru, a World Mountain version of the *axis mundi* known as Mount Sumeru in Buddhist cosmology.

Buddhism, of course, adopted the sacred mountain motif from earlier cultures as they did with caves – it

The northern face of Mount Kailas in the Himalayas. (William Eddy)

is an archetypal image belonging to all peoples from all times. For example, the Chinese neo-shamanic Taoists sought supernatural power or spiritual enlightenment in the mountains, and Mount Tientai was a sacred place for them. The Buddhists took over this tradition and in the sixth century AD built a temple there, which became a Buddhist holy mountain. Other long-revered peaks that became sacred to Chinese Buddhism include Wu'Tai Shan and Omei Shan. In a similar manner, when Buddhism came to Japan in the sixth century AD it adapted to a vigorous tradition of pilgrimage to sacred mountains and worship of the gods and spirits belonging to them that was exercised by the already ancient animistic folk religion that came to be known as Shintoism. By the eighth century Buddhism had developed a Nature Wisdom School, which sought Enlightenment by being close to nature in the mountains. Eventually, these movements merged into the Order of Mountain Ascetics (*Shugendo*), which, although being ostensibly Buddhist, retained Shinto elements and became a hugely popular movement in following centuries. It even got to the point where models of mountains were made for people who could not make it to the actual peaks. In Japan there are still numerous groups devoted to sacred mountains, and pilgrimage continues to be conducted to places like Mount Fuji, which was first the abode of a fire-god and later of a Shinto goddess (Kitagawa 1992).

Uluru (Ayers Rock), near the centre of the Australian continent: the holy mountain of the Aborigines. (John Miles)

Finally, we should mention the Aboriginal 'holy mountain' of Uluru, Ayers Rock, in central Australia. Just as Mount Fuji is an emblem of Japan, so the image of Uluru has become a symbol of the Aborigines around the world. Unfortunately, this has made it a target for many tourists, with the attendant problems that an intensive tourist trade brings to sensitive and sacred places. Tourism vies with the subtlety of this place. Every part of this giant dome of rock is 'mapped' in the Aboriginal mind; every part relates to the beings and events of Aboriginal myth, which for traditional Aborigines is experienced directly. Indeed, there does now exist an actual, drawn map of the complex contours of the spiritual terrain lying invisibly over this sacred mount.

VENERATED TREES

Although perhaps less obvious to us today because of their relative transience (as compared with geological features), trees have been as much a focus of natural sanctity as have caves or mountains. They have been so much a part of our spiritual environment over the ages that they, too, have taken on archetypal properties. The tree, whether in its native state or as a pole or post, is the *axis mundi par excellence*, as we noted in Part One, and in one form or another it was often associated with shamanic practice. The drums of Siberian shamans were said to be made from a branch of the World Tree, which stood 'at the golden navel of the Earth'. Trees also make sound when the wind blows through their foliage, so they were resorted to for oracular purposes, such as at Dodona. And the gnarled and venerable appearance of an aged tree or the solemnity of a forest has always invoked the sense of the sacred in human beings.

In pagan Celtic Ireland a sacred tree was known as a bile, and there were said to be one such sacred tree for each of the country's four provinces, with the fifth on the slopes of Uisneach, the central sacred hill of old Ireland, beside the natural rock known as the Stone of Divisions, the navel or *axis mundi* of the land. Myth had it that the great goddess-queen of Connacht, Medb, had her own sacred tree, *bile Meidbe*. The Druids, we recall, worshipped in sacred groves, and the oak was especially sacred to them. The oak was said to attract lightning and so was favoured by the gods. We can be sure that such veneration of trees went back far into European prehistory, but because trees eventually perish we cannot see them still as we can, say, mountains. What modern archaeology in Britain, using not only excavational methods but also electronic, geophysical detection techniques, has begun to reveal, however, is the extent to which timber was used in prehistoric sacred sites, and we now know that Stone Age people were also 'Wood Age' people, building timber circles as well as stone ones and even what appear to have been great timber temples. A few such former sites, like Woodhenge, near Stonehenge, were long known about, but the extent of this practice was not realized until fairly recently. Now, around fifty such sites have been detected in Britain. Among the more dramatic finds has been the discovery that the largest stone circle at the Stanton Drew group in Somerset once had a timber structure with 500 posts in nine concentric rings standing on its site. This mighty edifice would have been around 90 metres (300 feet) in diameter and is estimated to have stood about 9 metres (30 feet) high. Again, air photos over part of the Avebury complex revealed dark marks on the ground at West Kennet Farm, which, on investigation, proved to be the remains of what had been a massive timber building 180 metres (600 feet) across, spanning the Kennet stream. Posthole evidence revealed that great oak posts up to 9 metres (30 feet) high had formed a dense palisade. It was estimated that some 20,000 linear

metres (66,000 feet) of timber had been used. Animal deposits had been placed at the bases of some of the posts, presumably foundation offerings.

Ironically, the world's most famous stone circle, Stonehenge, may prove the point about the use of wood in the Stone Age. There, before the erection of the giant outer ring of sarsen stones that most of us associate with the monument, a timber avenue had led from the southern entrance to a complex timber circle in the centre of the ditch and bank enclosure (the actual henge). Moreover, the way the later monument, Stonehenge itself, had been built is revealing: techniques were used on the stone that belonged to woodwork. Mortise and tenon methods secured the great stone lintels on the giant uprights, and some of the other stones had been prepared for tongue and groove joints. As archaeologist Alex Gibson has put it: 'Stonehenge represents the zenith of a timber circle building tradition' (Gibson 1999). It seems that building in stone took over from a long period of building with timber.

What this discovery of a timber temple tradition in neolithic times indicated was that wood, notably oak, was deemed appropriate material for a sacred place. But this did not exactly prove that trees as such were similarly regarded. That is, not until 1999 and the discovery of what came to be nicknamed 'Sea Henge'. This was a timber circle with a central timber feature that was located in what is now the shoreline at Holme-next-the-Sea in Norfolk, on the eroding eastern coast of England. Washed by the tides, the sands had shifted to reveal the site. (Although this was a discovery for the archaeologists, it had apparently been revealed previously at times in years past and so had been known to some locals for a long time.) To find a partially extant prehistoric timber circle was so unique that English Heritage felt the site had to be saved from the sands and burrowing beetles and so it

The great sacred tree stump, bile, of the 'Sea Henge' timber monument on the Norfolk coast being hoisted out of the sands. (Alun Bull/English Heritage)

was removed for preservation to a safe site, Flag Fen. This procedure caused much controversy, as many local people and others felt it should have been measured, photographed and studied, but left *in situ* to meet its natural fate over time. When the central feature was plucked from the sands – with considerable engineering difficulty – it was found to have been the great stump of a giant oak tree that had been placed upside down into the ground with its roots in the air. (This recalls the – much later – Saami tradition of making wooden idols from tree stumps with their roots uppermost.) The relic lent itself to extraordinarily precise dating, because radiocarbon methods used on it could be cross-checked with dating by means of the annular tree rings in the mighty oak itself. It was found that it had been felled – or had fallen down – between April and June in the year 2050 BC. The surrounding timber circle had been made from oaks felled one year later, in 2049 BC. Part of a honeysuckle rope was found around the great central oak stump. So now the timber circle tradition could be related directly to a tree, specifically to an oak tree. The great central stump had surely been a *bile*. The timber ring

indicated ritual activity associated with the sacred tree. What Sea Henge reveals is an early sign of the shift from natural sacred trees to an altered, monumentalized version expressed in the timber temple tradition of the neolithic period, equivalent to the early signs we have seen of such a development with caves and mountain peaks.

Despite the megalithic-building activities of neolithic societies, aspects of the timber tradition seem to have survived through to the Celtic Iron Age, the age of the Druids. For example, at the hilltop site of Navan Fort in Armagh, Northern Ireland, the foundations of a gigantic timber structure were unearthed by archaeologists. The building had been circular and about 40 metres (130 feet) across. It had consisted of concentric rings of massive timbers and had probably been roofed over. It was dated to c.100 BC and stood on evidence of earlier, Bronze Age and possibly neolithic, occupation of the hill. There had also been Iron Age earthworks and structures on the hill since c.700 BC. Of particular interest is that in the centre of the circular building there had been a massive oaken pole that had stood about 11 metres (36 feet) high, presumably poking through a roof aperture if the building had been covered. As scholar Anne Ross has remarked, this must have been the focal point not only of the temple itself, but for the entire countryside around – a sacred landmark. She goes on:

> The fact that the oak tree from which it was fashioned was already 200 years old at the time of its felling is itself of great interest and suggests that it may well have been one of the sacred trees, bile, of Ireland which are so well-attested down the ages, a structure of such sanctity requiring that the central post should in itself be sacred.
>
> (Ross 1986)

The association with oaks evinced by the Iron Age Druids would seem therefore to have been a clear echo of the neolithic timber tradition and, in turn, along with evidence like Sea Henge, to reflect a deeper reflex concerning sacred trees from the earliest times, quite possibly reaching back to the mesolithic or beyond. The Celts also invested trees other than oak with significance and could consider certain stands of trees and even whole forests to be sacred. But it was not just the Celts who acted in this way. We know from the classical writers that in the same general era Greeks, too, venerated trees. Like the Celts, they associated certain trees with certain deities. They had sacred groves, some of them associated with sacred mountains and with various forms of divination. Pausanias, writing in the second century AD, gave an account of a festival near Palatia, the preparations for which involved people laying out pieces of meat in an oak wood where the tree trunks were the thickest in the whole region. They watched as flocks of crows came flying down and perched on the branches. They closely observed from which tree the crow that first pounced on the meat fluttered down. They felled that oak and made an effigy from it that was decked out then placed in a wagon to be carried in a procession to the top of a sacred mountain, where a ceremony was conducted that involved the burning of the effigy and animal sacrifices. The similarities between Celtic and Greek traditions of tree veneration point to a broadly common, archaic source lodged back in the animism and shamanism of prehistoric Europe.

In Minoan Crete, long before classical Greece, there is evidence of there having been a major tree cult. The pioneering Minoan scholar, Arthur Evans, noticed scenes on gold rings showing individual trees surrounded by a wall like a sacred *temenos* (precinct), sometimes surmounted with Horns of Consecration or in association with temples or apparent deities. Evans

made a number of lateral connections from this finding. He was aware, as any visitor to Knossos is aware, that columns are a major architectural feature of the Minoans, and that columns that taper slightly towards their bases are a Minoan hallmark. But Evans deduced that this went deeper than mere architectural device, for in the palace-temples of Crete there were the remnants of what had been enclosed, dark chambers containing free-standing pillars where rituals had taken place. These 'pillar crypts', Evans reasoned, were mimicking the caves where ritual also occurred. The pillars were stylized representations of the stalactites and stalagmites, which were also worshipped, as we have noted. The tree and the stalagmite were the natural models for the Minoan column, Evans argued. (We recall that similar correspondences were made by the ancient Maya, who venerated a tree-like stalagmite at Balankanché.) In turn, he suggested that the pillar, a phallic form, symbolized fertility. This was certainly supported by a finding inside the Cave of Eileithyia

A depiction of a sacred tree within an enclosure found on a steatite bead uncovered at Ligortino, Crete. (Arthur Evans 1901)

The (now unroofed) pillar crypt at the Minoan palace of Mallia, Crete.

Within the inner enclosure, a small rectangular space, there rises a solitary stalagmite, the upthrusting presence of universal fertility. The phallus. Here it is, an uncarved rock, unmistakably present in the 'holy of holies' of a feminine shrine. Here is pillar worship in its most primitive and naturalistic form. Moreover, there are obvious connections between the cult of the pillar and that of the sacred tree. The Minoans surrounded the latter with walls and placed boughs on domestic altars.   (Cotterell 1979)

Cotterell concluded that Evans was correct in finding tree and stalagmite worship inseparable and relating that to the pillar crypts and a 'column cult'.

So there was tree veneration in the European sphere back through the Iron, Bronze and Stone Ages. Vestiges of it passed down into the succeeding centuries of the historical era in Europe, and we pick up its echoes in a variety of ways, some stronger, some fainter. The Samoyed (Nenets) of northern Russia, for instance, had a major tree sanctuary at a place known as Kozmin Copse, a narrow strip of forest that lay across their annual migratory route. Researchers have found offerings fixed to the trunks of well over 200 trees on both sides of the trackway cutting through the strip of forest. The offerings included bells, metal discs, bronze and copper items (both metals were considered to have supernatural properties), rings and even buttons. Most were fixed to birch trees, regarded as a sacred tree throughout Eurasia, possibly because it shares a symbiotic relationship with the hallucinogenic fly agaric mushroom, which was used for trance purposes by many Eurasian shamans. Other selected trees were fir, aspen and rowan. Contemporary ethnological material records that Samoyed shamans *(tadibeis)* were 'duty bound' to hew a tree from this specific place to make their drums: an ancient, ancient

at Amnisos, located at a point along the northern coast of Crete a few miles east of present-day Heraklion and in Minoan times the port for Knossos, but now silted up. This cave's name recalls that in Minoan times it was used as a sanctuary dedicated to the nymph or goddess, Eileithyia, who was the protector of women in childbirth. Inside is the natural prototype of the pillar cult: a quite regular, pillar-like stalagmite surrounded by a low enclosure wall. As Arthur Cotterell has described it:

association. Throughout Europe and over many centuries, people made offerings at trees, decking the boughs with ribbons or rags, hammering nails into the trunk and performing countless other votive practices.

Apart from obvious direct survivals like these, there are more folkloric vestiges, such as the Celtic belief, especially in Ireland, that the thorn tree was the abode of fairies or other spirits, especially if the tree was solitary, twisted, next to a rock or spring or, most particularly, standing at a crossroads, for spirits meet there. The cult of the Glastonbury Thorn was part of this whole belief pattern but given a Christian gloss. Then there are the special trees found or formerly found at certain locations. A boundary clause in a charter of AD 845 mentions 'the ash tree which the ignorant call holy' at Taunton in Somerset – a faint echo, perhaps, of the mighty Yggradsil. Such trees preceded the boundaries they came to mark because of their importance to local people and their permanence due to great antiquity or – often – because special trees were replanted to replace ones that died. Some boundary trees were known as 'Gospel Oaks' and were specifically associated with Rogation Day, an April festival that involved a procession led by a priest. The participants carried crosses and foliage. The land and crops were blessed and the

An aged yew tree in the churchyard at Compton Dundon, Somerset. (Simant Bostock)

boundaries of the village marked. The Gospel Oak would be a 'station' on the way, where the priest would stop and read the scriptures. This festival is known to have been directly adapted from a much more ancient pagan observance of similar purpose, called Robigalia in Gaul. Again, yew trees were planted in churchyards as a Christian adoption of pagan sanctity.

Trees were, of course, venerated widely elsewhere in the world than Europe. The Lakota Sioux Indians would seek a tree and cut it down with ritual, trim and paint it, treat it as if it were a human being and raise it as the pole at the centre of their sun-dance ritual. The pole was recognized as representing the centre of the world for the duration of the ceremony. The ceremonial version of the tree, the pole, was used by a number of American Indian tribes; the Omaha, in particular, had a pole held in great reverence. There were also Native American legends about trees that glowed and that marked the meeting-point of the Four Directions. The Maya, we have noted, had the concept of a World Tree, *wakah-chan* ('raised up sky'), imaged in the real world by the northern Yucatán Maya as the ceiba tree; in other parts, the Maya imaged it as a maize tree. It was symbolically represented by a visual device that the Spanish thought was a 'foliated cross', which it does indeed resemble. Ancient carvings of this device occur at, for instance, Palenque. Modern 'Maya Crosses', which are mildly Christianized versions of the ancient World Tree symbol, are decorated with mirrors and dressed in clothing or flowers and pine boughs. They are considered to be living beings, much as the Lakota regarded their pole.

In Fiji the war deity Ravuravu is – or was – believed to reside in a tall tavola tree, and its wood is used for making the great slit drums with which in olden times one group challenged another to war (Toren 1995). In parts of eastern Bengal there is a tree-cult dedicated to the tantric goddess Durga-Kali, who is said to live in the roots of specific trees (Eliade 1988). The village of

Tamdungsa, in the Tamang territory of the north-western Kathmandu valley, Nepal, has two groves, one occupied by the deity Shyihbda and the other by the divinity Shyingmardung. To cut any of the trees or otherwise defile the groves would be to invite calamity on the village. In the highlands of Madagascar certain types of sacred place are marked by three kinds of tree that are said to be unable to grow anywhere else but in these sacred sites.

And so forth: there is a whole global forest of sanctity.

A sacred Bo Tree, Chiang Mai, with Chinese New Year spirit shrines. The tree stands on the inside bank of the eastern moat of the old city. (Chris Ashton)

HOLY WATERS

Without water, the water of life, physical life cannot be maintained. So fundamental is this fact that it is only to be expected that water became metaphorically associated with spiritual life, as persists in the ideas of baptism in Christianity or the sacred bathing of Hinduism. Like caves, peaks and trees, water has taken on an archetypal resonance. It has many ways of being in the world, and many of these lend themselves to spiritual interpretation. Like trees, natural forms of water are ubiquitous, but where a people has disappeared and left no record or where water sources and courses have dried up, the sacred places associated with those waters become lost to us. Fortunately, plenty still survive so that we are able to identify a range of examples.

In North America the Cheyenne believed that springs were openings through which animal spirits could enter or leave the Earth and become materialized. The Mescalero Apache considered springs to be a source of power – *diyi'*, a supernatural potency – because the water has just emerged from within the Earth. The power is carried into the physical word through the agency of the water. Spring and streams are therefore classed as 'living' water, but lakes and ponds are considered 'dead' in terms of *diyi'*.

In Mesoamerica the Maya of the Yucatán, where surface water is scarce, were dependent on underground water, and we have noted that seeking it was part of their purpose in exploring the caves of the limestone peninsula. But it was not just water for drinking that concerned them; water also figured as a spiritual requirement. They considered water from particular caves to be especially spiritually potent, for it was uncontaminated 'virgin water' (*zuhuy ha*), arising from the depths of the ground, from the underworld. Numerous stone water containers or troughs are found in many Maya caves deployed to catch drops of water from cavern roofs and, especially, from

stalactites. The fragments of countless pottery water jars have been found in caves, clearly accumulated from periodic ceremonial breakage. They are often found in association with pools and lagoons of water that are in deep parts of caves, difficult of access. This is the case even where there are streams and other water sources much closer to the surface, so these ceramic vessels were clearly not associated with the collection of drinking water. Such underground lakes of water are also often associated with offerings, and rock surfaces, blackened by the fumes from copal incense, testify that the collection of virgin water was accompanied by ritual activity. Virgin water is still used today by the Maya in rainmaking rites and is also used in Quintana Roo for baptismal purposes (Thompson 1975). The water has to be collected from subterranean sources where women never go, and after collection it is not allowed to fall on the ground.

Sacred cenotes (natural sinkholes through the limestone crust) were also a feature of Maya water veneration. Again, as with caves, some of these features were used as mundane sources of freshwater, but others were set aside as special. In particular, the Sacred Cenote at Chichén Itzá was a major pilgrimage and sacrificial site for the ancient Maya for many centuries and was still active when the Spanish arrived. Dedicated to Kukulcan, the Feathered Serpent,

Virgin water: a subterranean lagoon in the deepest reaches of the Balankanché cave system, Yucatán, Mexico.

This remarkable Celtic holy and healing well, in, appropriately enough, Holywell, Cornwall, consists of endlessly replenished pools of freshwater located in a sea cave accessible only at low tides. Pilgrims' steps have been cut in the rocks at the cave mouth.

The Sacred Cenote, Chichén Itzá. Sacrificial victims were thrown from the temple platform on the right.

the cenote is fairly circular, about 60 metres (200 feet) across, with the water surface some 21 metres (70 feet) below the rim. Offerings were thrown into the water, both objects and human beings. The waters of the cenote have been explored by dredging, diving and suction, and many artefacts and skeletons have been recovered. The remains of forty-two people have been identified, most of them of children. Only eight were of women, contrary to lurid accounts of virgins being sacrificed. The human sacrifices were really in aid of divination: they were cast in at sunrise with their hands and feet unbound and if they survived until noon, they were hauled up and questioned for anything they had learned from the divinity within the water. It has also been suggested that the surface of the cenote's water was used like a dark mirror for divination. The objects deposited were many and varied, including items made from gold, copper, jade and rubber – some of them from distant places like Colombia in South America. The most common objects were copper and gold bells, but there were also balls of incense, ceremonial axes and small idols.

Some of the artefacts had depictions of the Feathered Serpent inscribed on them.

A noteworthy religious use of water in South America was – and perhaps still is – the resort to sacred waterfalls by the Shuar (Jivaro) Indians of Ecuador. Starting at the age of about six years, the Shuar male is taken to a sacred waterfall – always the highest one within a few days' travel – to seek a vision, an arutam. Such places are believed to be the gathering points for ancestral souls, which wander around as breezes, scattering the spray from the waterfall (Harner 1984). It is these souls that vouchsafe a vision and the spiritual power that comes with it. The vision-seeker walks naked and shivering back and forth all day between the cascade of water and the rock face with the aid of a balsawood staff, chanting '*tau, tau, tau*' continually. At night, the vision-quester, who is fasting, drinks potent tobacco water and awaits the appearance of the vision. This whole process can be repeated for up to five days until the vision appears. If this still does not happen, a hallucinogen (*Datura*) is consumed. The vision will generally take the form of a pair of jaguars or anacondas appearing out of the forest, a floating human head or a ball of fire. The quester then has to approach the somewhat frightening vision and touch it, upon which it explosively disappears. When the person returns home and falls asleep, he dreams of the ancestral soul who manifested the vision and the power of that spirit enters his body.

The ancient Greeks placed their oracle sites and their healing centres dedicated to Aesculapius at water sources or, more likely, such places probably developed from springs and wells that had already been seen as sacred places from an even remoter antiquity. Before undertaking an oracular session, the Pythia (prophetess) at Delphi would bathe in the Castalian spring at the foot of the slope on which the temple complex was built and would then drink the waters from the Kassotis spring that ran beneath the Temple of Apollo where the sessions took place. At that other major oracle centre, Dodona, a sacred spring gushed forth from beneath the root of the great oak that stood there. It seems that the sounds made by the wind blowing in the leaves of the sacred oak tree and by the murmurings of the spring water were both used for oracular interpretation. This association between springs and trees, especially sacred groves, seems to have been a deliberate and strong one in ancient Greece (Birge 1994). The 300 or so Aesculapian healing centres in Greece were also located at water sources, having their own wells and reservoirs for ritual use. The well at Epidaurus, the main Aesculapion, is known to have been ancient before the temple-spa complex was created. The Minoans in Crete also had sacred springs, as might be expected, probably the best known being the water shrine in the Caravanserai at Knossos.

Water sites were among the most important ancient sacred places in Madagascar (Radimilahy 1994). Springs there were reputed to be haunted by the spirits of the ancestors, the *vazimba*; canoes containing the remains of ancient monarchs were immersed in designated sacred lakes; and the ancient kings would engage in the ancestral religious tradition of 'enchanted' bathing in certain rivers and along specified parts of the coast of the great island (such as on the northwestern shoreline).

A reflex of holy waters, especially venerated lakes, is the sacred island. To take two cultural examples, at opposite ends of the Earth, we can first return to the Saami, who had many such islands and islets. An eighteenth-century account refers to a reindeer-hunting episode in the waters around an islet in the freshwater lake of Leunje Jauvre, in Varanger, Norway. After the kill the hunters made an offering of the rein-

deer's antlers on the islet. Archaeologists have found a circular sacrificial site at this place. Another example of a Saami island site is Ukonsaari in Lake Enare in northern Finland. It is shaped 'like a giant tortoise' and was sacred to the thunder-god. The young Arthur Evans, who visited the place in the years before his great Cretan adventure, found a shallow cave or cleft in the rocks that was crammed with bones, showing it to be a sacrificial site.

Half the world away, the ancient people of the Andes had a major holy lake – Titicaca. This mysterious saltwater expanse, stranded high in the Andes, was the key cosmogenic site for the ancient peoples of the Andes, for it was here that the great creator god Viracocha emerged from the waters. The ancient nearby ceremonial city of Tiahuanaco has a great pyramid, the Akapana, surrounded by a moat so as to emulate the sacred Island of the Sun in Lake Titicaca – and Tiahuanaco shrines are to be found on the island itself. The mythic power of the Island of the Sun was appropriated by the later and geographically distant Inca who claimed it as their place of origin.

Lake Titicaca and the Island of the Sun, Bolivia. (John Miles)

spirit rocks, sacred stones

Building the sacred – Moving a stone's throw away – Mystery markings – Inhabited rocks – Light fantastic – Pointing it out – Light and shade – Sexy stones

'It was the manipulation of large stones that signalled the true beginnings of monumentalization... the turning of place into monument was so fundamental that its resonance has reverberated through all the succeeding ages of mankind.'

A cup-marked standing stone with the moon, Nether Largie, Kilmartin, Scotland.

Something strange and almost inexplicable happened at various times and places in the long morning of human prehistory: people began to build their own sacred places. No longer content with resorting to the natural features of the Earth in order to express and experience their ideas of the holy, they felt inspired to create their own. It was a process that had been foreshadowed by the sort of embellishments of natural places described in Part Two and was already under way with the building of timber and earthen structures. But it was the manipulation of large (mega) stones (liths) that signalled the true beginnings of monumentalization. Indeed, it is thought that some megalithic monuments were basically copies of earlier timber ones, as has already been mentioned with regard to Stonehenge. Stone lasts effectively for eternity; it is the structure of the ground beneath human feet, it is the stuff of mountains and of caves.

Monumentalization using stone was a cautious and gradual process in many cases – the insertion of a few slabs of rock into the earth to make a modest tomb or the erection of a rough, moderately sized rock – but over time the stones got larger and were sometimes dressed (shaped and smoothed), and they were assembled to make structures – tombs and megalithic temples. Even then, the natural sacred places were often still revered, and the stone monuments were, in a sense, adjuncts of them. But they were also extensions into the human world of what the old places had represented, extensions into the realm of culture and away from the natural domain. As the ages passed, those two worlds, natural and cultural, became ever more distant from each other, until eventually a constructed sacred place did not need to have any reference to a former natural sacred place at all.

The decision to create artificial sacred places was an early indication of the fabulous ability of humanity to transcend its environment. It was, literally, the

TURNING TIMBER TO STONE

Above: Rounded tenons can be clearly seen on the tops of the two giant Stonehenge uprights in this picture that are no longer supporting lintels.

Below: A vertical groove can be seen on the left side of the standing bluestone in the foreground, as if for a tongue-and-groove fixing.

monumentalization in stone of those engineering traits in us that we admire because they can improve the human lot, and fear because, taken to excess, they can destroy us and the natural world around us. The creation of sacred places was but an early step on the same road that we continue to tread with our creation and mastery of complex technologies, our awesome manufacturing ability and our ever-more sophisticated manipulation of the natural world, such as in genetic engineering. The decision made by human beings at various times and locations in the neolithic era to 'alter the Earth', as Richard Bradley has termed it, the turning of place into monument, was so fundamental that its resonance has reverberated through all the succeeding ages of mankind. Some people see the birth of monumentalization as being expressive of the Fall of humanity from a natural state; others see it as the start along a road of progress.

Megalithic sites have been found in many parts of the world, produced by diverse cultures. Discounting the sophisticated temples of antiquity in the Old and New Worlds, the sort of places we readily recognize as architectural structures, and focusing on what the nineteenth-century traveller and antiquarian, James Fergusson, called 'rude stone monuments', we can note that various kinds of megalithic monuments have been found in the Mediterranean area – in southern Italy, on islands such as Minorca, Corsica, Sardinia and, especially, Malta, as well as in Morocco and Algeria. Elsewhere in the African continent there are notable areas of megaliths: hundreds of stone circles in the Gambia on the west coast; sites in Ghana and Nigeria; tall standing stones and cists (small stone 'boxes' for burials or cremations set in the ground or in earthen mounds) in central Africa; and hundreds of standing stones in Ethiopia, where there is, notably, a monstrous monolith, 30 metres (100 feet) tall, in the north of the country, with plain and engraved stand-

The ruins of the Ggantija megalithic temple, Gozo, Malta. (Malta National Tourist Office)

ing stones in the south, including the Soddo region, and dolmens in the east. Stones and dolmens were also erected in recent centuries in Madagascar.

Moving on, lands around the Black Sea possess prehistoric stone monuments, such as the chambered burial mounds of Bulgaria and the rectangular slab-tombs of the Caucasus region, many with portholes or 'spirit holes' in their frontal stones. In the Near East, in a zone at the eastern end of the Mediterranean extending through Syria, Lebanon, Israel and Jordan, stone monuments date back to the fourth and third millennia BC and include simple dolmen structures. Far to the south, in the Arabian peninsula, the Yemen can boast rows and rings of standing stones and platforms surmounted by megalithic chambers, while Bahrain in the Persian Gulf has prehistoric tombs in the form of stone 'chests' up to 12 metres (40 feet) high and divided internally into various areas.

In Asia parts of the Himalayan region, Pakistan and India are scattered with megaliths. This is especially so for the Deccan, southern India, where there are literally thousands of mounds or former mounds with porthole-stones covering the entrances of passages leading to square or cruciform megalithic burial

A dolmen at Pullicondah, near Madras, India, according to a drawing in James Fergusson's Rude Stone Monuments of 1872.

chambers. These sites appear to date to the first and second millennia BC, the age of the Vedas. The Far East also has a share of megaliths, with rectangular megalithic chambers in some southeastern regions of China. These can be substantial structures – the capstone of one in Manchuria, Che-pin-shan ('stone table mountain'), for instance, weighs around 70 tons. Similarly, in Korea a chamber dated to the first millennium BC is covered by a stone more than 7.5 metres (25 feet) long. In the latter centuries BC and the first millennium AD megalithic building also took place in Japan, one of the best known examples probably being the concentric circles of standing stones on the summit of the giant Tatetsuki mound at Okayama. Isolated occurrences of generally more recent megalithic sites occur in parts of southeast Asia and Oceania, including Malaysia, Borneo and some Pacific islands.

Although several civilizations in the Americas built in stone – including the great Mayan temples – megalithic features of the types we are considering are rare. One example that can be mentioned, however, is the isolated group of megaliths in the San Augustín region of Colombia. There, sculpted stone uprights or steles are accompanied by dolmen-like structures, remarkably like those in western Europe.

It is in western Europe, indeed, where we end our whistle-stop megalithic world tour. This large region, especially northern Europe, such as northern Germany and Poland and the Atlantic lands from the Iberian peninsula north to Scandinavia, harbours the richest range of megaliths in the world and seemingly the oldest too. Material from megalithic tombs in southern Portugal yields radiocarbon dates of the fifth millennium BC, and some of the chambered mounds in Brittany, northwestern France, have provided similarly extremely ancient dates – in fact, two small, simple chambered sites have been dated to the early sixth millennium, to c.5800 BC, the late mesolithic.

One of the oldest megalithic sites: Creevykeel, Ireland.

Even a complex megalithic structure like the Barnenez monument, at Plouézoch in Finistère, containing multiple chambers and a passage, has a late fifth-millennium BC date. Fourth-millennium BC sites are quite numerous in Iberia and northern and western France. Long barrows with megalithic tombs in them similarly date to the early or middle fourth millennium BC in Denmark, as do court cairns like Creevykeel in western Ireland. And all these dates may yet be pushed further back: people started turning places to monuments with stone long, long ago in Europe.

Such is the plethora of megalithic monuments in the world that almost countless books and papers have been written about them and will continue to be written. All that needs to be done in the limited space available here is briefly to touch on some of their key aspects, with an emphasis on those that most concern the central thesis of this work – the shift from natural to artificial sacred place.

Casting the First Stones

It has already been observed that certain natural boulders and rock outcrops became venerated at places throughout the world, often because of some peculiar or distinctive quality about their appearance or location. So, for instance, the Arctic Samoyed (Nenets) of Russia, whom we met in Part Two, would make pilgrimages to an isolated and conspicuous natural boulder on the tundra of the Barent Sea's Kanin Nos Peninsula and leave offerings around it, very much as it was noted the Saami of Lapland treated selected natural rocks. It was not seemingly a great move from this sort of veneration to taking special stones away from their natural location and placing them in human-devised contexts or placing such a context around them *in situ*.

BLUESTONES ON PARADE

Above: Part of the outer ring of the bluestones, encircled by the outer ring of larger, lintelled sarsen megaliths.

Below: The shorter upright stones here are part of the bluestone inner horseshoe setting.

'PIECES OF PLACES'

This apparently simple yet crucially significant behaviour can perhaps be seen in the presence of the famed bluestones at Stonehenge. These are the smaller stones to be seen in inner settings at the monument today, the taller, lintelled stones of the outermost ring and the trilithons that most people associate with Stonehenge being local sarsen stone. Richard Bradley has pointed out that the bluestones seem to have formed the first megalithic setting on the site. While the local stone remained in position once re-erected, the bluestones were erected, taken down and re-erected at least three times. 'Thus the bluestones could have been considered as the oldest material in the monument, as well as the most exotic,' Bradley observes (2000). All these stones came from the Preseli Hills and their immediate vicinity, a small but visually dramatic area in southwestern Wales. How they travelled the 210 kilometres (130 miles) from there to Salisbury Plain where Stonehenge stands, whether by human effort or by glacial action, has remained a topic of debate for many years. That particular matter does not concern us here, but the source of the bluestones does. Although they came from the same region, they are of different rock types from differing deposits, and these were segregated at Stonehenge: as they stand today, the outer ring of the bluestone setting (inside the sarsen outer ring) represents all the range of non-local (Welsh) stones at the site, the inner horseshoe setting of bluestones (inside the horseshoe of massive sarsen trilithons) is of spotted dolerite, while the Altar Stone at the apex of the bluestone setting and on the axial line of the monument, is of green sandstone. (Bradley notes that this largely represents the relationship of the deposits in Preseli, with spotted dolerite towards the centre and a more scattered distribution of rock types around.) These Welsh rocks were therefore deliberately handled and considered and appear to have been treated with specific importance and, presumably, veneration. For at least 500 years this was the case, as they were arranged and re-arranged and enclosed in rings of local stone. By then they must not only have represented or embodied the sanctity of an important distant place, they must also have been symbolic of past time. Preseli stone was also used in the manufacture of axes that circulated over wide distances, and it has already been argued that some axes were holy artefacts and used for ceremonial purposes and for offerings – and, indeed, axe images are carved on stones at Stonehenge itself, we have noted. They were venerated relics, 'pieces of places' as Bradley puts it. Were the bluestones also just such sacred relics from a distant, sacred landscape – perhaps a region retaining origin myths?

The answer is likely to be in the affirmative, because the Preseli region was clearly a holy, ritual landscape (see below) and the practice of bringing materials from distant locales to use in monuments was widespread in the neolithic period. One classic example of this is the quartz facing on the great passage mound by the Boyne River in Ireland, Newgrange, much of which had been brought from the distant Wicklow Mountains. Another example is material in West Kennet long barrow at Avebury, where gaps between the large stones were filled with limestone from the Calne district 11 kilometres (7 miles) to the west and oolitic limestone was imported from outcrops 32 kilometres (20 miles) further than that to the west. There was no shortage of local packing material, so these inclusions had to have been deliberate.

So the first steps towards megalith building may in many cases have been based on the removal and ceremonial usage of sacred materials from venerated natural places.

MAGIC MARKINGS

The bluestones of Stonehenge have a distinctive hue that gives rise to their name. This colouring shows most noticeably when the stone is wet, and it is possible that this is reflected in a legend attached to Stonehenge that states that when the monument's stones are washed with water, the liquid takes on healing virtues. This colouring property of the rock raises another factor seemingly influencing the selection of stones for use in megalithic monuments, namely the occurrence of unusual visual markings and textures. We have already seen (Part Two) that cracks in rocks could be regarded as significant, and veins of quartz, colouring and other factors also seem to have been prized. For instance, virtually all the stones of the Callanish main site and some others of the Callanish group on the Isle of Lewis, Scotland, contain crystals of one kind or another – quartz, feldspar or hornblende. We would probably be wrong to assume that

The range of rock art motifs typical of the Irish passage tombs or temples is well expressed here, in kerbstone 52 at Newgrange. The vertical line in this case is thought to relate to the midwinter sunrise alignment that so famously occurs at Newgrange – the kerbstone stands directly on the sunrise line through the monument.

RAINBOW CIRCLE

It has been widely noticed by visitors to the Easter Aquorthies recumbent stone circle in Aberdeenshire, Scotland, that it is made up of stones of distinctly different hues and textures. Look at these examples of its stones and see ones that are variously white, pinkish, dark and quartz-veined, light green, dark green and jasper red. Clearly the stones were deliberately selected by the circle builders. And it does not end just with the hues, as we will learn a few pages later on.

the megalith builders simply wanted pretty, decorative material as we might today; it is far more likely that such visual characteristics of stones were seen as denoting special properties, such as supernatural power or holiness, that they would want to embed within their monuments. There was still a respect for the natural status of things, for the gifts of Mother Earth.

Some markings must have appeared to neolithic people as images wrought by the spirits or ancient gods – a case in point is to be found at the entrance to Stoney Littleton long barrow, near Bath, Somerset, England. This site has a curved forecourt in which is set the entrance to the monument's passage. The limestone of the forecourt's walls sets off the blue lias stones that form the lintel and jambs of the entrance. On the lower part of the western jamb there is a conspicuous ammonite cast, more than 30 centimetres (12 inches) in diameter. There can be no doubt that its inclusion and positioning was deliberate: it literally fossilizes a human decision made thousands of years ago.

The fossil at the entrance to the Stoney Littleton long barrow, near Bath, England.

The Stoney Littleton fossil is a natural marking, but neolithic people also decided to make their own markings on the stones forming their monuments. The rock art we saw in the preceding part of this book was on natural rock surfaces, but broadly similar kinds of images were engraved on standing stones, too. What was the relationship between these two traditions of rock art? Did one precede the other or were they concurrent? And what were the differences? From his study of the problem, Evan Hadingham concluded that, with a few possible exceptions, the carvings on the natural rocks did not depict complex patterns such as chevrons, lozenge shapes and interlinking spirals, such as are found in the great Irish passage graves like Newgrange, Knowth or the Loughcrew cairns, while by the same token there are relatively few cup-and-ring markings on monuments compared with their profusion on natural rock surfaces. There are cup markings on megaliths, however, such as on the Clava cairns in Scotland. And the representation of axeheads that appear on some megaliths are not found on natural surfaces – as exemplified in Kilmartin Glen, where

Distinct cup marks on an upright in one of the Clava cairns, Scotland.

The stone seen here at the far end of the passage in the Table des Marchands, Brittany, has symmetrical rows of hook-like motifs carved on it. The stone is thought to have been a solitary idol stone before being incorporated into the megalithic monument structure. (Simant Bostock)

there is both megalithic and natural rock surface engraving. Hadingham also found that, again with a few exceptions, 'no examples of passage grave art are known anywhere near the thickest cup-and-ring concentrations in West Cork and Kerry'. Hadingham outlined the problem:

> The carvings on the outcrops and boulders seem to have called for a narrower selection of symbols than the ornament in the tombs. Did the cups and rings of Kerry and Kircudbright develop from the art tradition of cemeteries like Loughcrew or did they precede and perhaps give rise to it?
>
> (Hadingham 1974)

Of course, some of the markings might have been added to some monuments a long time after construction, but because of the positioning of many markings this is unlikely and is definitely not the case with structures like Newgrange and Knowth.

Hadingham also pointed out that most of the great stone circles in Britain – Avebury, Callanish, the Ring of Brogar in Orkney – do not have carvings, which he felt indicated that 'the traditions of the carvers were not identical to those of the megalith builders'. There is a paucity of carvings on British megalithic monuments in general, in fact, and many of those that do have carvings, such as those in western Scotland, Cumbria and North Wales, were probably influenced by the much more vigorous Irish tradition of megalithic rock art. Some cup marks have been found, however, in the furthest southwesterly tip of Britain, in Cornwall. A stone covered in cup marks was discovered in the Tregiffian neolithic tomb, near Lamorna, and in drought conditions in the 1980s ten cup-marked stones were found in the Stithians reservoir. Some had only a small number of markings, but one had forty-eight (Straffon 1994). But again, these could have been the result of Irish influence: Irish monks crossed the water to Cornwall as part of their Celtic Christian mission, and so the influence of an older faith could similarly have arrived on the peninsula in much earlier times.

French megalithic monuments were also often carved, although the imagery here is generally somewhat different. In the Table des Marchands passage grave in Brittany the end stone of the chamber is carved with rows of hook-like shapes, often referred to by researchers as shepherds' crooks. This stone is sandstone and is visually distinct from the granite rocks in the rest of the structure, and it is thought that it was originally a free-standing monolith or 'idol' on to which the rest of the chamber had been built. At this site, as elsewhere, there are wavy 'serpent' lines and other imagery. At some sites there are breast forms carved in the rock surfaces (see below). The most astounding carvings, however, are those found

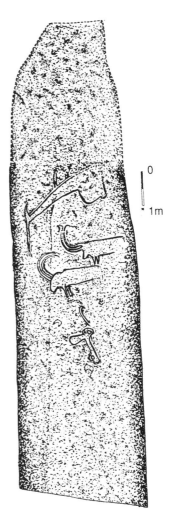

The giant monolith, now broken up and forming the capstones of Gavrinis and two other monuments in Brittany, is shown here complete, so that the carvings on it can be seen as a whole.

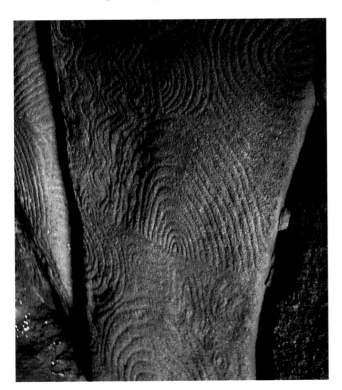

One of the many carved stones in the chambered cairn of Gavrinis, Brittany.

inside the Gavrinis chambered cairn, also in Brittany. Here the whole interior is covered with flowing linear markings reminiscent of giant fingerprints as much as anything else. Within this visual activity there are depictions of axeheads (see Part Two).

But there is a distinctive mystery about the rock art of Brittany, and it was triggered by the discovery that the huge capstone of Gavrinis had carvings of a wholly different nature on its other side – that is, the side facing upwards, which was covered by the material forming the mound raised over the passage and chamber. On this side – and therefore hidden from view within the chamber – are large carvings of horned beasts, hafted axes and other objects. These representational images contrast sharply with the abstract imagery on display within the chamber and passage. By tracking the fragments of the representational images on the 'wrong' side of the capstone, archaeologists found that it had once been a single, gigantic standing stone, 13.5 metres (45 feet) tall, other parts of which had been used as capstones in two other monuments, one of them the Table des Marchands, where a hafted axe is visible on the underside of the capstone. Re-used parts of stones in other monuments have also been found. Obviously, something culturally momentous had happened in Brittany in the early neolithic era that caused such a drastic change of art style. What could it be? Two lines of research converge to give a convincing answer, and this leads us to attempts at the interpretation of megalithic rock art in Atlantic Europe.

As with the rock carvings and paintings on natural rock surfaces, nobody alive today knows for sure the meaning of megalithic art, but there are some hints. As we noted earlier, some of the imagery in certain instances of rock art on natural surfaces was interpreted as deriving from trance experiences in a shamanic context. Jeremy Dronfield, an archaeologist at Cambridge University, developed an ingenious line of enquiry to see if this interpretation could hold with regard to megalithic art (Dronfield 1995). Using computer techniques, he made detailed measurements of motifs in the passage tomb art of Ireland and of motifs from sites such as Knowth, Newgrange, Dowth, Knockmany, Sess Kilgreen and several of the Loughcrew cairns. These were compared with equally precisely measured entoptic imagery recorded in drawings produced by both traditional people using sacramental hallucinogens and volunteer subjects in modern tests studying the effects of certain hallu-

cinogenic substances – including cannabis, LSD, mescaline and psilocybin ('magic mushrooms') – plus a variety of electrically stimulated entoptic patterns mimicking those produced by migraine, cocaine intoxication and light flicker. Both sets were, in turn, checked against a control set of randomly generated patterns. Dronfield found that none of the megalithic art imagery matched the control set and that there were no matches for cannabis or the pseudo-cocaine entoptic patterns – all of which was to be expected. But he did find matches for psilocybin and other hallucinogens found in fungi, in imagery produced in the mind's eye by means of flickering light on the retina, and the typical flickering 'fortification' entoptic pattern experienced by migraine sufferers. In some sites – Knowth, Newgrange and Cairn L at Loughcrew – these matches overlapped; in others they did not. Mind-altering mushrooms are readily found in the Irish countryside, and their use or the use of similar fungi was part of a northern Eurasian tradition of ancient shamanism. The migraine patterns point to specific medical conditions, which were often associated with those who became shamans in tribal cultures and which may have been prized rather than considered pathological. The flickering light evidence is of particular interest: the Irish monuments, such as Newgrange and Knowth, were planned so that sunlight flooded down their passages on calendrically significant days and manual flickering with fingers or ritual objects fleetingly interrupting such 'laser beams' of sunlight falling on closed eyelids within the chambers would produce the same effects as powerful stroboscopes. Combined with sensory deprivation and, possibly, fasting, not to mention the ingestion of mind-altering substances, this would lead to profound experiences of trance-induced mental imagery.

With regard to French sites, such as Gavrinis, research by Andrew Sherratt of Oxford's Ashmolean

Museum indicates that c.4000 BC a new culture arrived on the Breton scene. This is marked by the appearance in the archaeological record of decorated brazier-like ceramic vessels. Sherratt argues that these may have been for the production of opium fumes (Sherratt 1991). The progress of opium usage across the face of Europe can be plotted to some extent; so old was its use, in fact, that no uncultivated form of the opium poppy can now be found. The appearance of these braziers broadly coincided with the change in the nature of megalithic monuments in the area and the accompanying change in art style. A whole batch of these apparent braziers was found at Er Lannic, the wave-lapped double stone circle on an islet close to Gavrinis, that had been a centre of ceremonial axe production (see Part Two). Did the drastic change in art style relate to a new religion based on opium dreams? In short, is the rock art in Gavrinis the first record of psychedelic art in Europe? The evidence seems persuasive, especially taking Dronfield's findings into account. But even if this is so, we are dealing only with the source of some of the abstract and geometric imagery found in megalithic art – the symbolic meaning granted to neurologically derived imagery is cultural and now probably largely beyond our knowing.

Regarding other attempts at interpreting – probably non-psychedelic – megalithic art, the outlook is not encouraging and amounts to little more than wild guesses. One of the better lines of reasoning suggests that cup marks relate to the sun and perhaps other astronomical bodies. Prehistorian Aubrey Burl is among those who have noted, for instance, that the position of the markings in the Clava cairns might indicate sun symbolism, as the cairns share an axis possibly denoting midwinter sunset. More supportive of this idea, however, he notes (1976) that cup marks at recumbent stone circles in Aberdeenshire, Scotland, specifically cluster on stones facing that orientation.

PATTERNS IN THE MIND'S EYE

Rock art motifs from some of the Irish monuments studied by Jeremy Dronfield, who was testing for imagery that seemingly originated in altered states of consciousness of various kinds: *Above*: kerbstone, Knowth *Below*: entrance passage, Cairn T, Loughcrew.

This possible solar association of cup marks has also been argued for by several other investigators.

SPIRITS IN THE ROCK

We saw in Parts One and Two that the Saami chose naturally shaped rocks that suggested human or animal forms, and other examples of such simulacra were given. This was part of a deep belief held by many early peoples that spirits inhabited rocks. It has already been mentioned, for instance, that spirits were thought to be able to emerge from rocks through cracks and that entranced shamans could similarly

Spirit stones in Wisconsin, USA. (State Historical Society of Wisconsin)

pass into and out of the supernatural realms within rock by means of cracks and fissures. Further, folklore in Britain and elsewhere widely credits ancient stones with the attributes of living beings, with legends referring to stones moving, dancing and displaying other forms of animation.

There are examples of 'spirit rocks' in addition to the Saami *seite* stones. In Wisconsin, for instance, and doubtless in other parts of North America certain rocks were considered to possess 'spirit' and were so identified. These were either naturally shaped rocks, not necessarily suggesting human or animal figures but distinctive nonetheless, or, in some cases, rocks worked by human hand. Very little of the tradition seems to be recorded, other than for a few old photographs.

Another example involves a Scottish site. In a remote and lonely corner of upper Glen Lyon is a small stone 'shrine' at which pagan Celtic observance has been maintained in an unbroken line from at least the Iron Age. It is a tiny house – Tigh nam Bodach (the Hag's House) – and although no one now lives in this remote part of the glen (they did so up to a couple of centuries ago), the lone shepherd taking his animals up to pasture every May (Beltane) takes a set of curiously shaped stones out of the house. Every early November (Samhain), they are put back inside and sealed up snug for the winter. The stones are very strange, water-worn objects. They represent a goddess – the Cailliche or Old Woman – and her husband and daughter. Three other stones have been added in relatively recent times because 'her family has grown'. In legend the goddess, who was pregnant, entered the glen along with her husband during a terrible snowstorm; the people of glen made them a home. She bore the child and stayed in the glen, blessing the people there as long as the ritual observances were made each year. Although some of the stones show signs of having been worked, the Cailliche stone itself, about 45 centimetres (18 inches) tall, is naturally anthropomorphic, although there are faint traces of a face on her 'head' and possibly of a torc around her neck (Clarke 1994). Just one part of the nearby stream – the Cailliche Burn – shapes stones in this distinctive dumb-bell form.

A third ethnological example of spirits in stone are the Bhume stones of eastern Nepal. These belong to tribal rites of the non-literate Thulung people, and observances regarding the stones are beginning to die out. Bhume sites consist of sacred stones in various contexts – perhaps on a mound or alongside a sacred tree inside a walled enclosure. The stones are related to a Thulung culture hero, Mapa Raja, and are believed to be inspired by his spirit. Researcher Nicholas Allen has identified nine Bhume sites, and from what he was been able to deduce from the now scant oral tradition the stones represent Mapa Raja's fingers and toes, for the legend tells that the culture hero was on a journey, but he was leprous and his digits fell off at certain points (Allen 1981).

When we confront the stones of a megalithic site, there is only silence concerning the myths that inspired them, but it is important to be very attentive, because the 'spirits in the stones' may still be visible to the careful observer. Researcher Cosimo Favaloro had cause to be spending the night near the Aberdeenshire recumbent stone circle of Easter Aquorthies. So it was that he observed a woman visit the site in the dead of night. He cautiously approached her, and it turned out she lived fairly locally. She would on certain occasions visit the site and had names for specific stones in the ring, each of which was a specific character. Favaloro was unable to determine how old such ideas about the stones were. When morning came, Favaloro stood within the circle and looked closely at the stones the woman had identified. Sure enough, now he was alerted to them, he could actually perceive the figures the woman had

The water-shaped stones depicting the goddess and her family in Glen Lyon, Scotland. (David Clarke)

been describing – their forms were indeed subtly visible in the shapes and surface formations of the stones (Favaloro, in a personal communication). Perhaps they are similarly visible in other cases, too, if one has the eyes to see. The stones of Avebury have occasioned comment and speculation, because some of them suggest animal and human shapes. On the one hand, cynics say that it is just accidental weathering that gives some of the mighty Avebury stones their intriguing shapes; on the other hand, Stuart Piggot and Alexander Keiller, who restored some of the Avebury complex in the 1930s, wrote in a 1936 issue of *Antiquity*: 'There can be no question that the stones were dressed to conform to certain required shapes and to this end were selected as near to the required form as possible.' It has to be admitted that it can be all too easy to read meaning into what are simply fortuitous forms, yet it is also important not to be overly dismissive, especially now that we are getting some inkling of how the ancient mind worked. Stones contained spirits, and unusual and suggestively shaped stones caught the ancient eye in this regard. If we can readily see unusual and suggestive forms in some of the Avebury megaliths, so could the neolithic

SPIRIT ROCKS OF AVEBURY

Just three of the numerous strangely shaped megaliths to be found at the Avebury complex in Wiltshire, England.

builders of the monument. Whether or not stones have been dressed, some of them were surely selected and used because of their shapes. It is unquestionably important to guard against wanton flights of fancy, seeing faces and forms in every nook and cranny of the great stones, and it is important that we do not simply project wishful imagery on the stones to bear out some pet theory, but careful and neutral observation could allow authentic insight to emerge from the stone rather than having ideas imposed on it. It is possible to handle subjectivity in an objective way.

With care, we can perhaps still catch genuine glimpses of the old gods and spirits of the neolithic pantheon.

Stones of Light

Quartz is the most common mineral on Earth, but that does not detract from its magical, hypnotic qualities. It was widely associated with shamanism, where it was accredited with supernatural power. Pieces of clear rock crystal were vital parts of some Australian Aboriginal initiation rituals – they were 'solidified light' (Eliade 1964), and we can readily see that it exerted a similar fascination for the megalith builders. Duloe, a stone

circle in Cornwall, is made up entirely of massive pillars of white quartz; another stone circle in that county, Boscawen-un, has a massive block of white quartz in the southwestern section of its great ring of stones. At a point about halfway down the passage of Gavrinis there is a solitary block of quartz. Aubrey Burl has noted that this marks where two astronomical alignments, one solar and the other lunar, intersect within

One of the 3-metre (10-foot) tall rock crystal standing stones at Duloe, Cornwall. The whole circle is made up of such crystal stones, and clearly they were deliberately selected by the circle's builders.

The restored quartz façade at Newgrange Co. Meath, Ireland

the monument. He sees the white, undecorated surface of this quartz slab being illuminated by the light of the rising sun and moon (Burl 1985). Ten stone circles of a group in southwestern Ireland have quartz rocks placed in their centres. In Ireland it has already been mentioned that the quartz covering of Newgrange was brought from a considerable distance, and quartz was used at many other sites there as well. In 1865, when Eugene Conwell was investigating Cairn T at Loughcrew, for example, he noted that 'going all round the base of the cairn, was piled up a layer, rising from three to four feet in height and about two feet in thickness, of broken lumps of sparkling native Irish quartz'. Another investigator in 1895 remarked that the most noticeable thing at the Loughcrew cairns was 'the quantity of small fragments of white quartz scattered through the soil everywhere'. We will see in Part Four that Stefan Bergh, who has been conducting a thoroughgoing study of the monuments in northern Sligo, northwestern Ireland, considers that a mountain source of quartz was marked by a monument. Quartz figures at numerous Irish megalithic sites, either as part of the main structure or taking the form of separate structures adjacent to the entrance areas, as is the case at Knowth and Carrowkeel.

Quartz not only appears in the structure of many megalithic monuments, but it was also used as an offering in many instances. Bergh comments:

> Both the physical and symbolical placement of the quartz within the monument, becomes evident when comparing the smaller and larger monuments. In the dolmens and other small monuments quartz is frequently found as single lumps or as a few angular fragments, placed together with the bones in the deposits. The power of the quartz has been intended to work for the deceased, possibly as a link to the gods or representing the light of the other-world.
>
> (Bergh 1995)

He feels that quartz was first used as an offering or deposit and later became incorporated into the main structures of monuments as part of major ritual symbolism.

In the British Isles quartz has been found as a deposit at a number of sites. In the Nympsfield long cairn in southwest England, for example, three quartz

Castle Frazer recumbent stone circle, Scotland. A recumbent circle is one that has a stone lying altar-like on its perimeter, as is clearly visible here.

pebbles were found with a perforated sea shell accompanying the bones of the ancient dead, and in Scotland a group of monuments probably associated with the people who built the Clava cairns revealed scatters of quartz. Examples of Scottish megalithic sites with quartz scatters include the Castle Frazer recumbent circle in Aberdeenshire and Croft Moraig in Perthshire, where many quartz pebbles were discovered within the circle. The Corrimony passage tomb in Glen Urquart, Inverness, had broken quartz scattered around the perimeter of the cairn during its construction. There are also examples in Wales.

QUARTZ AND ROCK ART

It is being increasingly noted by researchers in various locations that quartz also occurs in relation to rock art. For instance, rock art in Norway is 'in many cases framed by very distinct quartz ores visible in the rock surface' (Walderhaug 1998). Recent perceptions of associations between the mineral and shamanic rock art in southeastern California have led to some serious scientific investigations that have produced revealing insights. The trigger to this

research was a small site known as Sally's Rockshelter in the central area of the Mojave Desert. Inside the natural shelter is a single panel of engravings, but the team of rock art researchers also noticed that quartz cobbles had been inserted into crevices between the rocks and that there was a scatter of quartz flakes on the floor. There was also a deposit of fragments in a depression in a huge boulder forming part of the site. The quartz had to have been imported into the shelter, as there were no quartz-bearing rocks in the vicinity. The rock art was securely associated with a shamanic tradition belonging to Numic-speaking people of the region for thousands of years: the shelter was one of many vision-questing sites used by tribal shamans found in this part of California and across the Great Basin region (see Part Two). The rock art at Sally's Rockshelter was estimated to be a thousand years old at most and probably less than half that. While quartz was used to make rock carvings because of its hardness, the quartz at the site had clearly been deliberately deposited, and ethnological information indicates that even quartz used for making rock carvings was always carefully selected for its supernatural potency.

The finding of the quartz at the site prompted the researchers to make a more extensive investigation of its occurrence at other sites within the region. In all, they studied thirty-five rock art sites in non-quartz locales. The sites were microscopically examined using electron microscopy and various forms of spectrometry. Evidence of quartz being brought to the sites was found in 63 per cent of the cases. The age of the rock engravings with embedded quartz was established by various methods, including cation ratio dating, an experimental technique that makes use of the rock varnish that coats the rock engravings. The researchers found that some of the sites went back at least 10,000 years – that is, into palaeo-Indian times.

The shamanic rock art tradition had continued until the early part of the twentieth century, so there is a real foundation to the researchers' claim that Mojave shamanism 'is the oldest continuously practised religious tradition so far identified in the world' (Whitley *et al.* 1999).

The ritual association of quartz and shamanism (and therefore rock art) in the region is extensively established both in the archaeological record and in the region's ethnological literature. Archaeologically, this is shown at sites such as Corn Springs in the California Desert, where a quartz vein in a rock surface has been incorporated into an engraved motif. At Balch Camp in the southern Sierra Nevada pictographs have been painted over a quartz vein, which has itself been partly painted. And quartz deposits have been noticed laid before other rock art panels in the vast region. In the ethnological record are items such as that concerning Bob Rabbit, the last known Numic rain-shaman in the Mojave Desert region. He used quartz crystals as part of his ceremonial paraphernalia, as did Avenari, a Las Vegas Band rain-shaman, especially crystals obtained from places struck by lightning.

The ethnology also prompted an important realization in the investigators regarding the two different types of quartz deposit at Sally's Rockshelter. The quartz that had been pressed into the rock crevices was in the form of unworked cobbles, but the flakes on the floor and in the boulder depression resulted from quartz that had been shattered. It was discovered that oral accounts gathered from the Yuman Indians of the region described a vision-quest procedure in which rock crystals were broken up in order to release their energy so that it could enter the body of the shaman. One informant was able to identify certain vision-quest locations from the scatter of quartz flakes at them. The investigators realized that

LIGHTNING STONES

A piece of white quartz emitting light milliseconds after friction with another piece of quartz.

In 1880 Pierre and Jacques Curie discovered that certain crystals, especially quartz, produced voltage when subjected to pressure or friction. This is referred to as piezoelectricity. This ability of quartz to transform mechanical effort into electrical charge became a key factor in the development of twentieth-century technology and is crucial to the functioning of many high-tech instruments, especially in the radio, telephone and television industries. In crystals such as quartz the generation of piezoelectricity produces light as a side-effect because it provides the energy to release electrons trapped due to natural radiation in the crystal's lattice structure. As they return to their normal, base state, they give off photons. This effect is called triboluminescence.

this indicated the ritual incorporation of another, intriguing property of quartz: when two pieces are rubbed or banged together, they produce flashes of light – two fist-sized lumps of the crystal rubbed vigorously together are quite sufficient to illumine a medium-sized room. No wonder the stones were known by Indians and other tribal peoples around the world as 'lightning stones'. The light was, of course, understood as a manifestation of supernatural power. To this day Amazonian shamans use pieces of quartz shaken inside special rattles perforated with small holes to produce 'magic fire'.

Remembering the Old Places

The word 'monument' derives from Latin roots referring to memory. Monuments memorialize all kinds of things – events, people, achievements. As we stand

One of the several stones at the Castlerigg stone circle, near Keswick, Cumbria, that appears to mimic the skyline. (John Glover)

before the gaunt megaliths of prehistory we do not know precisely what they were intended to memorialize – in that sense, they are for us today monuments to a kind of amnesia – but we can be sure that the first things which the old stones remembered was 'place'. If we realize that at specific monuments, we can begin to restore our deep-time memory at those sites. Here, we look at just a few of the ways in which stone monuments can refer to the landscape around them.

SIGNPOSTS OF STONE

The simplest but most subtle way is when standing stones act, literally, like signposts. This can be a treacherous phenomenon, however, easily subject to delusional interpretation, and it generally demands a 'judgement call' on the part of the researcher.

One form of such 'signposting' seems to be by means of the shape of the stones involved. Classic examples of this are to be found at the Castlerigg stone circle in Cumbria, northwestern England. Individually or when seen as pairs across the circle the outlines of certain stones closely match the configuration of the skyline beyond them. Artist and photographer John Glover was the first to recognize this at the site, and one of his pictures is shown here for the reader to make a judgement. If this was a deliberate effect – and it is difficult to imagine that the circle builders, so sensitive to natural forms, did not consciously register it – what was special about the parts of the landscape being indicated? A thorough check has not been conducted. It is possible that it would reveal some archaeological indications, but it could equally be the case that the significance of the locales was cultural and has been lost with the people who erected the circle. Perhaps the Castlerigg stones simply indicate places where visions occurred or that were haunted by spirits or where important but now long-forgotten events happened.

Archaeologists in the Brecon Beacons National Park in Wales have noted similar skyline 'coincidences'. They consider that a standing stone in the village of Bwlch may have been shaped to represent the profile of the Sugar Loaf mountain to the southeast. Again, they point out that the top of the Maen Llwyd monolith deep in the Brecon mountains 'may have been shaped to represent the skyline to the southeast'. The axis of the stone also aligns to what appears to be an artificial notch near Mynydd Llysiau (Brecon Beacons National Park Committee 1983).

Many standing stones are of the 'playing card' variety (thin edge, broad sides), and they offer axial possibilities that can be interpreted in a signposting context – certainly the archaeoastronomer Alexander Thom took this to be self-evident. While some of these seem

The further of the foreground pair of stones in Kilmartin Glen, Scotland, is twisted slightly, apparently so as to align to a more distant outlying standing stone, visible across the fence and towards the trees in the distance. The purpose of the alignment is unknown.

to orient to directions with astronomical significance – for example, the flat central stone in the Ballachroy group (see Part Four) – others point to nowhere in particular or, at least, to no place we can recognize today as being significant (if, indeed, they are signposting at all). A case in point is the slab-like Maen Llia monolith, 3.6 metres (12 feet) tall, between Heol Senni and Ystradfellte in Wales, which is oriented almost perfectly north–south and points down the valley, from the far end of which it forms a distinctive skyline marker. In this case, the stone could be marking some prehistoric route, but it stands by the Llia stream and seems to have been a sacred place whatever functional purposes it may also have served. Another enigmatic 'playing card' stone stands at the northern end of a rough line of standing stones in Scotland's Kilmartin Glen. We will visit this group again shortly, but for our purposes here it is noteworthy that the monolith aligns 'nicely' (as Aubrey

Burl puts it) to another standing stone more than 90 metres (300 feet) to the northwest. This alignment has no astronomical significance, and so, as one archaeoastronomer, J.E. Wood, drily remarked, it is possible to conclude only 'that it had some other purpose'. A possible explanation for an axial stone north of Kilmichael Glassery near Kilmartin is that it points to one end of a nearby natural rock outcrop containing carvings.

It would be a gamble, but challenging nonetheless, to run a research trial in which exploratory archaeological investigations were conducted at apparently insignificant places indicated by some of these silent stone signposts.

CIRCLING AROUND

Megalithic monuments can make more specific references to natural features in their vicinity, as Christopher Tilley demonstrated during a series of field observations at various locations. One study area was the Preseli Hills of southwestern Wales, whence came the Stonehenge bluestones, as has been

We can only guess why prehistoric people considered Carn Ingli sacred, but it might be worth noting that local people today are able to see a reclining human figure in the overall form of the whole ridge, as they can in some of the other Preseli peaks. If they can see such simulacra, so, presumably, could the monument builders. There is also another intriguing property about Carn Ingli: it is a natural magnetic anomaly spot. Compass needles spin wildly at places on it, and at the peak the needles of two compasses will actually point in opposite directions (Devereux 2000). No archaeologist today is prepared to consider this as significant, but this may be short-sighted, since there is now abundant experimental and clinical evidence to indicate that changes in weak ambient magnetic fields can affect parts of the brain causing sensations of dissociation ('ecstasy', 'out-of-body experiences') and hallucinations or visions of various kinds.

Pentre Ifan dolmen, Preseli, Wales, with the peak of Carn Ingli in background.

discussed above. Tilley looked at the megalithic burial chambers in the area and specifically included early neolithic sites. These were mainly simple and fairly small stone structures, with just two large and complex monuments, Pentre Ifan and Garn Turne. Tilley was looking for any recurring patterns with regard to their relationships to natural places and with regard to mesolithic 'find-spots' – sites where mobile groups of hunter-gatherers stopped for lengths of time or returned periodically, leaving traces such as accumulations of flaked flints, simple beads, animal bones and so forth. Regarding the latter association, Tilley found that his neolithic sites were situated in 'exactly the same general areas' as the mesolithic find-spots, suggesting a continuity in the identification of places favoured by the earlier hunter-gatherers. Regarding relationships to the terrain, one of the patterns Tilley noticed was that the monuments were sited close to distinctive rock outcrops, specifically those that had either a recognizably linear form or a circular shape. Made of the same rock as the outcrops, the monuments were barely visible at any distance and had minimal intervisibility between themselves. The natural rock features, by contrast, are highly visible landmarks. 'The outcrops key the monuments into the landscape, drawing attention to their location and making them special places,' Tilley observes (1994).

One of the groups of megaliths Tilley studied on Preseli was in the Nevern valley, at the eastern end of the hill range. The dominant natural feature here is the high, craggy ridge of Carn Ingli. Tilley discerned that this seemed to provide the 'central symbolic focal point' for the neolithic monuments in this area: while none of them was intervisible with another, all commanded vistas of Carn Ingli. One of these monuments is Pentre Ifan, a large and impressive dolmen, the remains of a chambered structure. It is so situated that the profile of Carn Ingli dominates the skyline to its west. The dolmen's capstone slopes at the same angle as that of the ridge of Carn Ingli, and the original entrance to the monument would have required anyone accessing the interior to have faced the rocky crag. Carn Ingli was clearly a significant site to the megalith builders, and the memory of the sanctity of this natural place seems to have survived into historical times, for the name means Hill of Angels and refers to the use of the peak by the sixth-century holy man, St Brynach, who retreated there to fast and have visions of angels.

Tilley has also made studies of other areas, such as Bodmin Moor in Cornwall (1996), the Black Mountains

The stones of the Fernacre stone circle, Bodmin Moor, Cornwall, are dwarfed by the bulk of Rough Tor, the natural sacred place to which the monument appears to refer.

on the Wales–England border (1994) and part of southern Sweden (1993b). In Part Two we noted his observations regarding the rocky outcrops or tors on Bodmin Moor and how some of these had been frequented by mesolithic people and the subtle embellishments made to them later on. In addition, he has remarked on the stone circles on the moor.

The Hurlers stone circle, Bodmin Moor, Cornwall, with the weathered tors of the Cheesewring group visible in the distance.

There are sixteen of these, and Tilley considers that a 'special relationship' exists between the circles and individual tors: every one of the monuments is situated in the immediate vicinity of, or even directly at the base of, a tor, as is the case with the Hurlers, Fernacre, Leskernick Hill North and the Stripple Stones circles. With the exception of only three monuments, all are located to the south of their respective tors. Tilley points out that there had to have been a deliberate desire to have prominent tors visible from the circles, because in some cases a shift in position of a monument by only 30 metres (37 yards) or so would have hidden the related tor from view. He also thinks that there were processional routes between the circles and notes that when one approaches the Stripple Stones circle from the Trippet Stones almost 1.5 kilometres (1 mile) away, Rough Tor beyond the circle starts to come into view only at close quarters as one enters the monument and can be seen fully only when one reaches the centre of the circle.

In the Black Mountains Tilley has observed that the axes of long cairns run either parallel to the courses of rivers and their valleys or else align on prominent spurs on the ridges of the Black Mountains. In Sweden he studied selected areas, including Västergötland. The monuments – passage tombs – in this region account for more than half the megalithic sites in Sweden, and they are distributed across a limestone and sandstone plateau that is punctuated by blocks of granite mountains running in a general north–south trend. More than half of the Västergötland passage tombs have visibility to Alleberg, the highest and most distinctive of the granite mountains. It is a place strongly associated with folklore: Alleberg, home of underground rivers and secret caves, is where the gods sleep, awaiting the call to awake and save the motherland, and it is inhabited by mountain trolls. The passage tombs mimic the landscape around them: they are arranged in north–south rows and are oriented along the same axis, while the stones used to construct the tombs, involving marked differences in colour, reflect the structure of the landscape – the upright structures are of sandstone and limestone, while the capstones are of granite, reflecting the low–high dichotomy of the terrain, and the passages in the tombs are such that anyone entering through them is moving towards the mountains.

This kind of appraisal of the landscape setting of monuments is now becoming a more frequent activity in archaeology. The monuments are directing our attention to the otherwise invisible sacred geography that existed in the landscape before their construction, as well as revealing later modifications and developments of that geography by the monument builders. Piece by piece, it might yet prove possible for us to recover a whole Stone Age map of the soul.

Sky and Stones

So much has been written about the astronomical aspects of standing stones and other megalithic monuments that there is little point in attempting to do a wide-ranging review here, and it would, in any case, be outside the brief of this book. It is an important aspect of the ancient stones, however, so what we can do here is to look at just a few examples. The landscape element is implicit, because most megalithic astronomical alignments involve the natural setting of a site whether in terms of the height of the skyline around it or because of skyline features, such as mountain peaks or notches, that act as distant foresights for alignments indicated by standing stones. So, for example, the pioneering archaeoastronomer Alexander Thom claimed that some of the astronomical alignments detected at Stonehenge involved distant topographical features.

CYCLES OF HEAVEN

Although stellar and planetary orientations are sometimes proposed by researchers, most of the postulated megalithic alignments involve key rising or setting points of the sun or moon. The sun's major dates are repeated each year: the solstices (21 June, when the sun rises the furthest northeast and sets the furthest northwest it ever reaches, and 21 December, when it rises and sets at its most southerly points on the eastern and western horizons respectively) and the equinoxes (21 March and 21 September, when the sun rises in the east). In summer the sun rises higher in the sky than it does in winter.

In ancient calendars other solar dates were also important and subdivided the year into more than these four segments. The pagan Celts, for instance, had two halves to their year, marked by their New Year festival, Samhain, 1 November (appropriated by the Church as All Saints' Day or All Hallows, with November Eve still being remembered popularly as Halloween), and Beltane, 1 May in the modern calendar.

The pagan Irish also celebrated Imbolc (1 February) and Lughnasa (1 August, appropriated by the Church as Lammas), giving an eightfold division of the solar year. Archaeoastronomers check megalithic alignments for any of these sixteen rise/set horizon directions.

The lunar cycle presents a much more complex picture – even Sir Isaac Newton admitted that trying to account for the moon's movements was the one thing that made his head ache. Basically, because of its orbit around the Earth, the moon goes through similar north–south swings in its risings and settings and high–low arcs across the sky as does the sun, but it does so each month, waxing and waning as it goes. Its risings and settings switch from one extreme to the other in a fortnight. But unlike the sun, the moon does not return to quite the same northerly and southerly rise and set points on the horizon every year. Rather, these positions creep further north and south over a total period of 18.6 years, sometimes known as the Metonic Cycle. The point where the moon reaches its most northerly point in this cycle is called the major lunar standstill; the point furthest south that it reaches, just over nine years later, is termed the minor lunar standstill. These extreme positions vary on the horizon according to the latitude from which they are being viewed, and the arc of the horizon between them becomes wider the further north the latitude is. The standstills are, in effect, the moon's solstices. Archaeoastronomers, therefore, like to check megalithic alignments for orientations to the northernmost and southernmost lunar rise and set horizon points.

The height of the skyline local to a monument affects the observation of both sun and moon from it, and the azimuth or compass bearing of their rise and set positions on any given date would be different for, say, a hilly skyline from a distant, flat one.

So the position of a sacred site – how far north or south it is and the height and distance of the skyline around it – can be unique from an astronomical point of view.

The winter solstice sunset shining down the passage of Maeshowe, Orkney, Scotland. (Charles Tait)

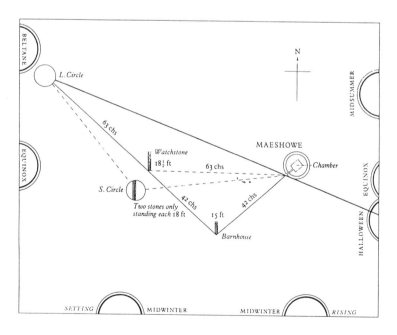

Magnus Spence's scheme of landscape geometry involving the standing stones in the Maeshowe area of Orkney. A "chain" equals 66 feet. [Magnus Spence 1894]

An instance of ancient astronomy linked to possible landscape arrangement of sites occurs in Orkney, where the passage of the carefully constructed neolithic passage tomb of Maeshowe aligns to sunset at the winter solstice. On a clear midwinter eve the sun floods golden light down the passage, but the alignment has more interesting aspects than even that dramatic sight. The line of the passage and thus the solstitial line extends into the landscape to a standing stone about 800 metres (about a half mile) away. This is the Barnstone, and in 1846 Orkney schoolmaster Magnus Spence presented a survey of the local Orkney sites that showed the Barnstone standing in line with another monolith, the Watchstone, the same distance as Maeshowe away, and beyond that the Ring of Brogar. According to Spence's plan, the Watchstone was the same distance from Brogar as it was from Maeshow. These alignments, plus others involving the nearby Stones of Stenness circle, between them aligned to sunrises or set points, variously, on both of the solstices, each of the equinoxes, plus the old Celtic calendrical days of Beltane (May Day) and Samhain, which Spence marked as Halloween. Archaeologist Colin Richards has conducted a modern study of the relationships between the same Orkney monuments (1996).

The Barnstone, with the Stones of Stenness in the background. (Charles Tait)

Looking from the southwestern end of the Nether Largie Stones alignment. The pair of stones in the foreground aligns to the most northerly major standstill moonset; the alignment as a whole indicates another important lunar direction (see text for details).

The floor of Kilmartin Glen in Scotland contains a great 'linear cemetery', consisting of passage tombs, that aligns to a distant peak. This is described in Part Four, but the valley also has an important (and probably earlier) alignment, formed of standing stones and other megalithic features, that is part of its remarkable prehistoric ritual landscape. Known as the Nether Largie Stones (formerly the Kilmartin Stones), the group falls into a broad line running approximately northeast to southwest, echoing the thrust of the valley. Two tall pairs of stones stand at each end of the group, and between there are two settings of short slabs and stones with a tall standing stone rising out of one of them pretty much in the middle of the overall alignment. Thom thought that this alignment represented an important lunar observatory. The southernmost pair of stones forms an alignment between themselves running south-southeast to north-northwest, and this orients quite accurately to the most northerly moonset at the major lunar standstill (see box). Burl has noted that the northerly and southerly end pairs of the group align with the tall middle stone to indicate the most southerly moonset at the major standstill. It is thought highly unlikely that these alignments are accidental. A further intriguing twist is that all of the pairs of stones have cup marks on them, while the centre monolith has over forty cup marks (some of which can be seen in the photograph on the introductory page to this part of the book). Because of the angle of the

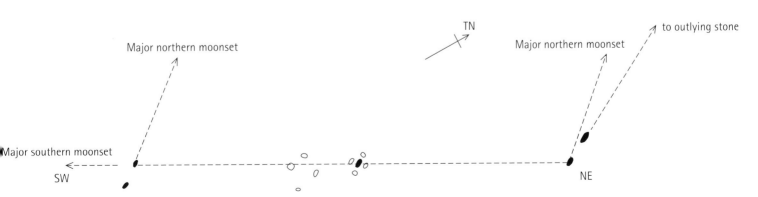

Plan of the Nether Largie Stones showing the main alignments associated with the group.

stones, all these necessarily echo the direction of the long moonset alignment, so a number of commentators have suggested that these markings may represent lunar symbolism.

As a third – and remarkable – example of megalithic astronomical showmanship we can consider a sunrise phenomenon at Cairn L on the Loughcrew Hills in Ireland. There are numerous astronomical events associated with a number of the passage cairns that straggle along the spine of the hills, but Cairn L can boast arguably the most dramatic one. On the November sunrise a beam of sunlight enters through the passage of the cairn and spotlights a free-standing white monolith inside the chamber. The time of year, the angle of the passage and the shape of the near skyline over which the sun rises conspire to 'sculpt' the sunbeam into a laser-like shaft of light to achieve this remarkable and accurate effect (Brennan 1983). For some moments, apparently, the white stone shines out alone in the surrounding gloom of the chamber (Martin Brennan personal communication).

The free-standing white monolith in the chamber of Cairn L, Loughcrew, Ireland, is the target of a sunbeam.

SHADOW PLAY

The archaeoastronomers have, on the whole, neglected shadows, which may have been just as important as the rising and setting sun and moon positions to the megalith builders. For instance, Martin Brennan, who was studying the astronomy and rock carvings of monuments in the Boyne valley, felt that certain standing stones around Newgrange threw shadows at certain times of the year that pointed like fingers to rock art motifs on some of the great monument's kerbstones. Again, perhaps the famed Heel Stone marker of midsummer sunrise at Stonehenge was actually meant to be seen in the other direction – that is, not from the centre of the monument, as is assumed, but from the other, sunward side of the outlying monolith. Amateur archaeological sleuth Terence Meaden thinks precisely this, and he suggests that the Heel Stone's shadow thrown towards the monument at the summer solstice sunrise represents the phallus of the Sky God penetrating the enclosed space of Stonehenge, which he feels represented the womb of the Earth-goddess (Meaden 1992). The event certainly occurs, but Meaden's assumption that it was a deliberate effect and his interpretations of the myths being enacted are, of course, speculation.

An even more dramatic event, for which no prehistoric myths have yet been postulated, occurs at the Castlerigg stone circle in Cumbria. Photographer John Glover noticed that at midsummer sunset the tallest stone in the circle throws an incredibly long shadow right across the valley. It is inconceivable that the circle builders would have been unaware of this startling effect – this 'shadow path', as Glover termed it, is as much a part of the site as the solar alignments Thom found there and even the stones themselves. But if it was deliberate, what is the finger of shadow pointing out in the surrounding landscape?

Archaeoastronomers used to argue that ancient

The sun rises over the Heel Stone at Stonehenge – but should it be viewed from the other side?

Mr and Mrs Stones

It does not take anyone looking at megaliths for any length of time to appreciate that single standing stones – monoliths – can be seen to embody phallic symbolism. It would not have taken the neolithic people long to make the connection either, after they started erecting their own stones instead of resorting to natural outcrops or the phallic stalagmites in the womb-like caves (see Part Two). The stone phallus would be apparent to anyone putting up stones anywhere. Some of the Mesoamerican peoples certainly saw their stones in this way and were not subtle about it. In various places in the Yucatán large and small stones, specifically shaped into phalli, have been found. Not a great deal is known about the cult behind them, but it appears that it was introduced

The Castlerigg midsummer 'shadow path'. (John Glover)

astronomy was the birth of science as we know it, and they claimed tremendous exactitude on the part of the megalith builders. While some alignments do seem to be very accurate, there are many more that are general in their orientation. Although a keen knowledge of naked eye astronomy would certainly have been involved, it is now thought safer to assume that the astronomical aspects of the megaliths should be viewed as having been ceremonial and more cosmo-logical than 'scientific' in the sense that we understand that term. Astrology rather than astronomy.

A tall phallus stone near the Balankanché Cave, in the Yucatán, Mexico. It originally stood a few miles from this location.

shaped stone rising pillar-like from the ground was a universal image of fertility and fecundity.

ENTER THE LADIES

The irony is that there is an ambiguity to the form – it can also look like a figure – and there is no doubt that in parts of neolithic Europe, especially in Brittany and the Channel Islands, some of the standing stones were transformed into idols, such as was the case with the end slab in the Table des Marchands, discussed earlier. Most, if not all, of them represented a female figure – presumably an Earth mother or other fertility goddess. In some of the Breton passage tombs there are breast carvings on some of the chamber slabs. In Prajou-Menhir, for example, in the Côte du Nord, a side slab has two pairs of breasts carved in a

into Mayan culture from the Veracruz area of the Gulf of Mexico towards the close of classic period, perhaps around AD 1000. Uxmal and Chichén Itzá seem to have become two centres of the cult in the northern Yucatán. In Brittany it was the custom until the turn of the twentieth century for women to gather at suggestive-looking menhirs like that at Plonéour Lanvern in Finistère and dance around them. In Ireland the Lia Fail, the Stone of Destiny, is a phallic menhir that stands on the Hill of Tara. Tara was where the pagan Celtic High Kings of Ireland were inaugurated, and the Lia Fail would presumably relate to the king's relationship with the land, for he had to mate symbolically with the goddess of sovereignty. In the inauguration ritual the king had to touch the stone, which was said to cry out if he was the rightful king.

Stone phalli appeared in cultures in Africa, the Middle East, in India and doubtless in many other places around the world. The solitary, smoothed or

The Lia Fail amid the ritual landscape of the Hill of Tara, Ireland.

La Gran'mère du Castel statue-menhir, Guernsey, Channel Islands.
(Anthony Weir/Fortean Picture Library)

Vulva stone, Avebury.

cartouche-like depression. Many of these megalithic idols were minimalistically decorated with breasts and U-shaped motifs probably representing torcs or necklaces, while others were more extensively sculpted – 'statue-menhirs'. Sometimes, the minimalism of representing a highly stylized, abstracted human form could consist of the merest modification of a stone's natural shape, known as the *écusson* in Breton archaeology. It is even thought that stones of simply a diamond- or lozenge-shape could have been goddess idols. Some of the stones at Avebury are like this, and at places on the Kennet Avenue diamond-shaped

stones and pillar-shaped stones can be found facing one another, and this has been interpreted by some as representing female and male respectively. It is another one of those judgement calls whether these interpretations are correct at Avebury, but there is an unquestionable 'female' stone within the great circle of the Avebury henge, for it has natural fissures and features that present vulvic symbolism so powerfully that it cannot be denied.

In the stone-wrought mythic imagery of the neolithic period, as in life in all times, it took two to tango.

geographies of the ancient soul

Setting the scene – Landscapes of the mind – Seeing the ancestors – Topographical peek-a-boo – Death in the north – Triangulating a myth – The Lammas glory – More twin peaks – Primordial mound – Lands of enlightenment – Deserts of the dead – Ways of the soul

'Shamanic sacred landscapes were marked directly on the ground in various ways ... however stylized and structured they may have become in some cultures, their origins lie in the experiences of altered states of consciousness... They represent the direct mapping of mindscapes.'

Tie Creek boulder mosaics, Manitoba.

We tend to think about ancient sacred monuments in isolation. We put mental (and therefore visual) frames around them and approach them in the same way we might inspect an antique vase standing alone on a bare tabletop. At great and important monuments governmental or national organizations put up entrance booths and turnstiles. So we go to see Stonehenge or the pyramids at Giza or whatever as if we were going to see a movie: box office archaeology. This tendency to think about sacred places as sites, as specific locations in isolation, is not only displayed by the general public but it has also greatly afflicted archaeology itself down the generations – the British archaeologist Peter Fowler has called it the 'single site syndrome'. For many decades archaeologists digging away at a site would look up only occasionally, figuratively speaking, to see where they were. It has been a little like that syndrome many of us must be familiar with: we can walk down a street month after month and suddenly realize that our eyes have never really looked up at anything above the ground floor of the buildings lining the street. For this reason, because of this sin of omission, any relationships between an ancient monument and other monuments in the area around it or between an ancient monument and the natural features of the local landscape have tended to go 'by the board'. They have either not been noticed, or they have been noticed but rarely given a second thought. (And the second thought is often the important one.) With an unconscious intellectual and perceptual imperialism, we have imposed our modern compartmentalized ways of thinking and seeing on the physical relics left by ancient minds that thought in often very different ways from us, as was discussed in Part One. Fortunately, this problem, although still present in archaeology to an extent, is at last beginning to disappear. In the final decades of the twentieth century, an increasing number of

SEEING THE WHOLE

The need to study monuments in their landscape setting was noted in archaeology at least as far back as 1970, when Peter Fowler was conducting an archaeological survey of Dorset. He observed that some groups of prehistoric burial mounds (barrows) appeared to have been deliberately sited so that 'a complex system of intervisibility is created'. In fairness, it should also be recorded that this concern with intervisibility was also an early practice of 'fringe' antiquarians such as 'ley hunters', who in journals such as *The Ley Hunter* complained that authorities charged with looking after ancient monuments ought to ensure that no recent developments in their vicinity should be allowed to obscure the views from them (see Woodley 1989). And in 1974 the ancient mysteries writer, John Michell, a *bête noir* of establishment archaeologists, reported on his survey of the Land's End district of Cornwall, in which he studied intervisibility between the isolated monoliths and other ancient markers in that region. Although his choice of some of the markers was later criticized, the principle of observing the landscape setting of monuments was as clearly established as in any archaeological study, and at least some of the alignments he found were as valid as in such literature.

archaeologists started to look more closely at the setting of sacred monuments, and the more they did this, the more they saw relationships. Sacred sites began to be seen in a wider perspective.

This more holistic approach has become better focused in recent years. Some archaeologists are looking ever closer at the settings of monuments in the landscape, searching for factors such as intervisibility (or the lack of it) between monuments or the relationship of monuments to natural topographical features, as we have discussed at various points throughout this book. As this approach progresses, it is being found that we can get a little closer to how the ancient mind ticked; we are learning that it is actually possible to begin to glimpse through the eyes of the ancients. It all depends on the type of mental conditioning an investigator brings to an ancient place – sight to site, as it were. This is the 'cognitive' element in archaeological investigation, and it is becoming more acceptable to explore it, so much so that books by archaeologists can now appear with titles like *Landscape of the Monuments* (Bergh 1995) or even *The Phenomenology of Landscape* (Tilley 1994). This is, in turn, as we have been noting, leading to a need to pay yet more attention to natural places, to see what we can find out about the concept of sacred place before there were monuments as such at all.

This developing strand of archaeological enquiry is analogous to the shift that took place in physics from the idea of hard-and-fast particles to the concept of fields. If the sites are the 'particles', the cognitive exploration of their settings, their relationship to their environments, is the 'field'. Identifying the nature of these 'fields' is, in effect, to disclose the fossilized presence of ancient consciousness left in the landscape along with the physical remains.

We can recall what we have noted previously in this book: earlier peoples tended to exteriorize their consciousness, to lodge it in the land, which held their tribal memory, their myths and their sacred texts and was their temple. Their spiritual consciousness was sacred geography. Their landscape was 'cognized', to use the jargon of some modern scholars. It was a mindscape that could take a number of basic forms, usually

resulting from different cultural, religious, social or geographical circumstances. The main types are:

- Mythologized landscapes, in which natural features are used to express tribal cosmogenic or spiritual belief systems, with no or only minimally constructed features. An example would be the Dreamtime landscapes of the Australian Aborigines.

- Monuments, temples or other constructed places of burial, ritual, ceremony or worship located with regard to topographical features that had existing ancient associations of spiritual or mythic significance. This seems to have been the case on Bodmin Moor (see Part Three), and we will encounter other instances of this type in following pages, such as the placing of Minoan palaces in relation to sacred hills and mountains.

- Monuments placed in various visual relationships with other sacred sites. Examples would include the Barnstone-Maeshowe instance in Orkney cited in Part Three or the intervisible Minoan peak sanctuaries and neolithic Irish monuments discussed later.

- Monuments that relate to landscape features of sacred significance and sometimes to other monuments as well, while at the same time orienting to astronomical bodies. Examples of this might include the ancient sacred city of Vijayanagara in India, where a major axial component orients on the Pole Star along a sightline that includes a sacred hill, Matanga, surmounted by the Virabhadra temple (Malville 1993; Cornelius and Devereux 1996); and stupas in the Kathmandu valley in Nepal, which are either directly oriented themselves or align one to another towards the moon's rising points on dates related to the religious calendar, while marking places of ancient significance (Herdick 1993).

✂ Spirit world or mythic geographies that are mapped, on a large scale, directly on the land using various forms of ground-marking methods. There are several kinds of these terrestrial 'maps', each performing seemingly different, though possibly related, functions. Examples of such 'shamanic landscapes' (as the present writer has dubbed them) would include the Nazca lines in Peru, giant effigy mounds in north-central United States or the boulder mosaics of Manitoba, which we will go on to study later.

While these types of sacred geography can and often do occur quite distinctly and separately, there are locations where some of their characteristics merge or where variations on one or other of these themes occur. Very little in prehistory is as neat and tidy as our modern minds would like! In the following pages we explore a range of sacred geographies that has been revealed as the result of the work of several investigators, including the present writer. Many of the examples may be unfamiliar to the reader, and some are, in fact, being published for the first time. Sacred geography is the crucial context of the sacred place; indeed, it is its ultimate ramification, and its on-the-ground investigation represents a new frontier of research into the ancient mind. This could be called 'fieldwork in the ancient consciousness fields', to use a metaphor employed earlier – exploring the larger sense of sacred place fashioned on the land by ancient ways of thinking and perceiving.

Stone Age Sacred Geography

The spiritual beliefs and religious ideologies of neolithic and Bronze Age peoples in Europe are almost closed books to us. There is no direct access to the societies that gave rise to the monuments of prehistory as there are in some other cultures, such as those of the American Indians, so there are no ethnological studies tucked away in a library anywhere that can give any leads. The only 'texts' we have are the monuments themselves and the landscapes around them. Confronting the bare stones of megalithic sites or the remains of prehistoric earthen monuments is a daunting way to have to start an enquiry into the potential sacred geography that might given them a context and so lead us closer to ancient thinking. It really is a question of attempting to see through ancient eyes and linking that to whatever relevant archaeological data have been gleaned. In doing this in various ways we are in some cases getting just a hint of how certain monument-builders related to the landscape, and in other instances it is actually extending insights into the religious ideas of these people.

The examples we look at here reflect this range, from minor observations extending the context of a monument to useful insights into a former way of thinking and seeing that has passed from the land. But it is merely a beginning, and all that follows – whether preliminary or more developed – should be seen as work in progress.

TOMBS WITH A VIEW

Let us start in the megalithic wonderland of Ireland. It has the mighty megalithic monuments of the Boyne valley, including Newgrange and Knowth, of course, but also scattered around the country are more than

Knocknarea, Co. Sligo, Ireland, with the great mound of Queen Maeve's Cairn or Tomb visible on its flat summit. (Simant Bostock)

1400 other megalithic monuments, which are much less well known to the general public. Some of the oldest are the various types of tomb that were built between c.4000 and c.3000 BC. The main forms of these are known as court, portal, wedge and passage tombs, names that refer to architectural characteristics. The Swedish archaeologist Stefan Bergh has made a magnificent regional study of the Cúil Irra peninsula, which projects into Sligo Bay in the northern part of Ireland's Atlantic coast. He has focused primarily on the passage tombs there. As the name suggests, this type of monument contains a passage, formed by upright stones, which leads to a fairly central chamber arrangement. Newgrange is the classic example of this type, but the Cúil Irra region has the greatest concentration of them in Ireland. Passage tombs come in various sizes and forms, but basically there is a cairn – a mound of megalithic and earthen structure covered by small or moderately sized stones. They are

major structures that required skill and a great investment of labour to build. As Bergh (1995) points out, they were too elaborate and too unnecessary for a simple burial, and 'tomb' is hardly an appropriate term for them. In early neolithic and mesolithic times there were monuments that were simply graves, but these 'tombs' were much more. They were related to the dead, certainly, but it is a more complex matter. They contained layers of bones belonging to numbers of individuals; many of the bones were burned, but not all. It also seems that some bones, such as the cranium and long bones, were passed around other monuments – a circulation of ancestral relics, perhaps similar to the way in which a saint's relics were used in medieval times. There is no doubt, however, that passage tombs were associated with the remains of the dead in some context or other, for they were designed so that repeated access could be made, either to deposit the bones of various members of a clan as they died or to conduct ceremonial or ritual activity in association with the ancestral remains. The passage tomb could have served four basic functions – burial site, ceremonial site, territorial marker and symbol of authority – and, as Bergh has observed, all four of these functions could be combined in the one site. The last two possibilities rely principally on the fact that, unlike the other kinds of tomb, passage tombs appear to have been placed with regard to their visibility. In effect, they made the dead visible in the landscape, as Bergh has put it.

Bergh selected the Cúil Irra peninsula region for his study to see what could be learned about the placing of the passage tombs there. The dominant natural feature of the peninsula is the large, distinctive and isolated hill of Knocknarea situated near its end. It is a striking landmark, with its steep flanks and flat summit, on which are placed several passage tombs. The most visible of these is the massive cairn known as Queen Maeve's Cairn or Tomb (Miosgán Meadhbha), named after Medb, the goddess-sovereign of Connacht. When one stands on Knocknarea the natural definition of the region is plain to see: there are mountain ranges in three directions and the sea in the fourth. The King's Mountain massif and its dramatic cliff of Benbulbin, Sligo's fairy mountain, form a visual boundary to the northeast, while to the southwest are the igneous Ox Mountains. Straggling ends of this range, the rounded forms of Slieve Daeane and Killery Mountain, together with Lough Gill, form a tacit limit to the southeast and east. In the distance to the south, outside what Bergh defined as his primary study area, are the Bricklieve Mountains.

Bergh decided to treat the passage tombs not as burial places but as 'places with burials'. There were

passage tombs on the Ox Mountains, on Slieve Daeane and Carns Hill, and in the very centre of the peninsula, closest to Knocknarea, was the famous megalithic 'cemetery' of Carrowmore, the largest of its kind in Ireland. This concentration of small, ruined passage tombs and dolmens is carefully and precisely placed on a low plateau. The megalithic remains of Carrowmore are dominated by Knocknarea to the west, yet it is not to Knocknarea that the bulk of the monuments align. On the contrary, they face inwards to the centre of the small plateau and towards an area that shows crop marks from the air, indicating a possible former enclosure of some kind. This now subtle feature, Bergh finally came to conclude, had been the true sacred centre of the region. There was reason to believe that Cúil Irra had been a ritual zone 'well before the first megaliths were built in the area'. The landscape was already sacred.

In this relatively early phase it appears that the whole community might have buried its dead in the modest passage tombs – an egalitarian society. Moreover, there was no major effort to make the Carrowmore monuments highly visible over the whole region. But as time went by, the passage graves grew grander and more visible as solitary or small group features, and it seems that there may have been more restrictions on who used them, contrary to the apparent situation at Carrowmore. In what Bergh has concluded was probably the last phase, a small number of really major passage tombs was constructed that visually dominated the Cúil Irra area. These tombs lorded it over the sacred land, and the greatest of them was Queen Maeve's Cairn. 'No other megalithic monument in Ireland dominates visually such a large region as does Miosgán Meadhbha,' Bergh observes. He has determined that the great cairn had 'directed visibility' to the east, notably from Carrowmore. But in addition, its symbolic façade

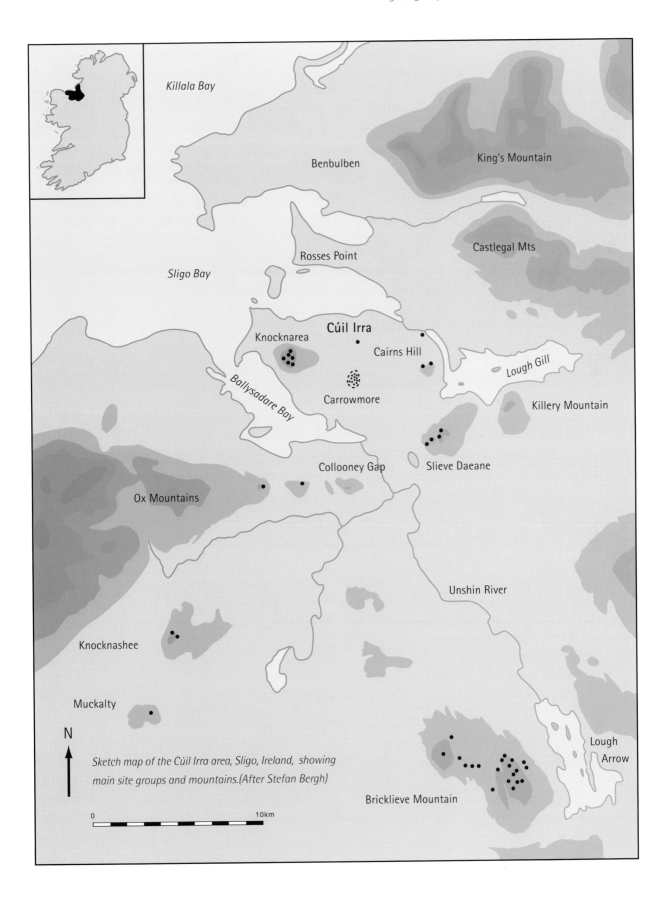

Sketch map of the Cúil Irra area, Sligo, Ireland, showing main site groups and mountains.(After Stefan Bergh)

Some of the Carrowkeel cairns on the Bricklieve Mountains. Co. Sligo, Ireland (Simant Bostock)

faced towards the centre of the peninsula marked by Carrowmore: it was still acknowledging the heart of the landscape's sanctity.

Queen Maeve's Cairn is visible at long distances from many directions and dramatically so to the east; so much so that Bergh felt that Knocknarea might have

Sketch of horizon north and north-west from the Carrowkeel complex on the Bricklieve Mountains: the placing of the cairns on the Ox Mountains (to the left) and other high ridges is such that they appear on the exact skyline as seen from Carrowkeel. Note that Knocknarea and its domi-nant cairn is also visible. (After Stefan Bergh)

had visual contact with even the cairns on the Loughcrew range more than 80 kilometres (50 miles) eastwards: a large, now-fallen quartz block on those hills, if erected, would shine out in the setting sun so brilliantly, Bergh reasons, that it would probably be visible from Knocknarea. The hilltop also has visual contact with the Bricklieve Mountains to the south outside the primary Cúil Irra area, where another passage grave complex, Carrowkeel, is situated. In turn, these monuments share a general tendency to align northwards, towards Cúil Irra. The passage monuments in the Ox Mountains were rather patchily distributed among the peaks, and Bergh had difficulty under-standing this until he realized that they were visible as skyline features from the Carowkeel group – the ridges

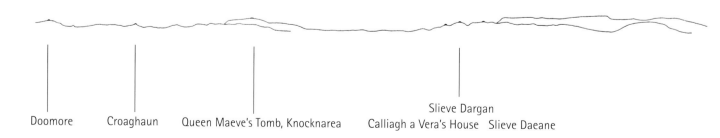

Doomore   Croaghaun   Queen Maeve's Tomb, Knocknarea   Slieve Dargan
Calliagh a Vera's House   Slieve Daeane

beyond the visible skyline formed by the Ox Mountains from there were not populated with the monuments. On the Cúil Irra peninsula itself the massive passage tomb on Carns Hill West has limited visibility, but it is visible from the centre of the peninsula, just like Queen Maeve's Cairn. Bergh went on to discover subtle factors about visibility, alignment and placing concerning a considerable number of the monuments of the region, including determining that one rectangular monument on the summit of Croaghaun in the Ox Mountains had not been placed because of anything to do with visibility, but was marking the local quartz-veined mountain, as white quartz was 'a rock of central importance' to the rituals in the passage tomb tradition as a whole in Ireland (and see Part Three).

Apart from revealing a neolithic (and probably earlier) focus on a particular central area of the Cúil Irra peninsula, Bergh's work demonstrated that the passage tombs of the region had been carefully placed so that they permitted directed and organized views of specific places and other, selected monuments and, more particularly, so that they were visible from specific locations. The whole landscape had been manipulated in the later phase of monument placing in the area, suggesting a shift from one form of religious ideology to a later variant that involved a more dominant element of social and political power and, perhaps, elitism in ritual matters.

> The visibility of the monuments becomes an important and active feature. They are built to be seen and understood by the surrounding world in a way not recognized among the earlier monuments. This ambition means that the landscape becomes an active instrument of influence... Earlier, the landscape directed the setting of the monuments, but now the landscape, or at least the people's comprehension of it, is directed by the monuments. The landscape becomes a part of the monuments and they thereby form instruments to signal power and authority in a considerably more competitive social milieu. (Bergh 1995)

The Swedish investigator additionally noted an intriguing and clearly deliberate orientation, particularly with regard to Queen Maeve's Cairn. A large, flat limestone slab is placed virtually due north of the cairn's perimeter, and a substantial gneiss boulder is placed due south. These two rocks form a north–south axis that cuts directly through the centre of the cairn. Furthermore, two of the three monuments placed south of the cairn on Knocknarea also fall on this north–south line, this meridian. In addition, there are six semicircular 'structures' placed around the base of Queen Maeve's Cairn, which, Bergh states, 'represent an intentional layout', in that four of them mark the inter-cardinal directions, while the other two are placed on either side of, and close to, the south point. The great passage tomb of Knowth, the larger companion to Newgrange, has similar structures flanking its entrance. Bergh therefore predicts that if there is a passage in Queen Maeve's Cairn (it has not yet been excavated), its entrance will be between these two southerly structures, directly in front – north – of the gneiss boulder marking due south. This preoccupation with the cardinal directions is not directly associated with the visual relationships between monuments that Bergh plotted in the landscape of the Cúil Irra region; rather, it would seem to relate to cosmological concerns and, perhaps, a deep-rooted symbolism associated with death. Was north, for instance, symbolic of the dead, the realm of the ancestral spirits?

All in all, Bergh uncovered a great deal about the region and its monuments and several insights into the social and religious life there thousand of years ago that might reasonably have been considered

SIGHTING THE SITES

Studies similar to, if less comprehensive than, Stefan Bergh's work in Cúil Irra had been conducted earlier on the Orkney group of islands off the northern coast of Scotland. These, too, are well endowed with megalithic monuments. In 1979 Colin Renfrew studied the thirteen monuments on the island of Rousay, and he concluded that the land visible from each monument represented a clan territory, each with its – in turn – visible monument. The megalithic monuments were, therefore, interpreted as being territorial markers for distinct groups on the island. In 1983 David Fraser reported on his study of Bronze Age cairns in the Orkney group. He found cairns on different islands to be sometimes visible one to another as well as being intervisible within individual islands. 'Intervisibility is not a simple reflection of proximity', he observed, 'and is influenced by subtle changes in the landscape'. He found sightlines up to 17.7 kilometres (11 miles) long and concluded that cairns that showed evidence of being special in one way or another tended to be located in visually dominant places.

Brailes Hill, Warwickshire, from the southeast.

irrecoverable. They, in turn, provide starting points for further enquiries. And he did it by careful, accurate observation, not by excavation.

A similar situation to Knocknarea and the monuments on the Cúil Irra peninsula exists in regard to a hill in southern Warwickshire, England, if in a more muted archaeological context. The feature in question, Brailes Hill, is a broad ridge of a hill, topped with a neolithic long barrow, which in turn has been highlighted in presumably relatively recent times because a copse of trees has been placed around it. The hill does not seem at first glance to be particularly distinctive, yet it is visible for many miles in several directions. It is a true landmark, especially noticeable to those who live in the region and are familiar with the lie of the land. Clearly, those who placed the neolithic mound on the hill's summit had closely studied the undulations of the countryside around. And more than that, it seems, for Brailes Hill shares a very specific relationship to the King's Men stone circle, part of the Rollright group of stones situated about 8 kilometres (5 miles) south of the hill and 32 kilometres (20 miles) northwest of Oxford. The King's Men stone circle is placed on a ridge running east–west; more exactly, the circle is situated just very slightly south of the crest of the ridge. This placing is remarkable, for Brailes Hill is quite easily visible from the northern side of the circle, but just exactly so from the southern (and original entrance) side of the 30-metre (100-foot) diameter ring of stones. (This is difficult to check now, as a country road – an ancient ridgeway – runs along the crest of the ridge and passes close by the stones, and hedges on either side of it block the view northwards from the King's Men except in the depth of winter

An airview of the King's Men stone circle, Rollright. North is towards the top left-hand corner of the picture. The circle sits just to the south of the top of a ridge, which is marked by the country road, an ancient ridge-way. The view to Brailes Hill is across that road.

when their foliage is scanty.) Any appreciable distance further south and Brailes Hill would not have been visible from the ancient entrance to the King's Men. It now appears to 'stand' on the crest of the ridge from that position, and it slips into invisibility behind it if only a few yards are taken back down the southern slope of the ridge from the monument.

This is not the full extent of the matter. Surveyor Roy Cooper discovered that Brailes Hill is located accurately true north of the King's Men circle – or, to put that more logically, the circle appears to have been built on an exact meridian line running south from Brailes Hill (Cooper 1979). Considering the precision of the visual relationship between the monument and the hill, this is unlikely to have been accidental. Further, Cooper found that the meridian can be

continued south to pass through the site of a former stone circle, a standing stone, hilltop earthworks and on to White Horse Hill, the hilltop in Berkshire that is emblazoned with the famous Uffington White Horse hill figure, now found to date to the Bronze Age. This might just possibly be mere coincidence, but the relationship between Brailes Hill and the King's Men at least appears to have been deliberate. The hill seems to have had significance for the builders of the Rollright site, as it had to those who built the long barrow on it. Perhaps the King's Men circle was positioned to acknowledge the long barrow on the hill's

NE

Glebe cairn – ●

● – Nether Largie North
● – Nether Largie Mid

● – Nether Largie South

● – Ri Cruin cairn

● – Rowanfield cist

Diagrammatic plan of the Kilmartin 'linear cemetery'.

works visible on the western horizon as a landmark over 30 kilometres (20 miles) away when viewed from Brailes. No extant path links the two hills, and it is highly unlikely that a funeral path ever existed between them over such a distance. Rather, the folktale seems to embody some inchoate memory jumbling the themes of death and a connection of another kind between the two places. Local folkloric material like this might on occasion contain seeds of information transmitted from extreme antiquity – this might not be such an incredible idea now that DNA research is beginning to indicate that the inhabitants of some rural places in Britain carry mitochondrial DNA that can be traced back to prehistoric skeletons found in their districts (Barham et al. 1999). It indicates that some strands of the population have been more settled in their local landscapes for much longer than had formerly been assumed.

Yet another circumstantial link between death, a prominent hill and the direction of north is displayed by the 'linear cemetery' in the prehistoric ritual land-

summit, or perhaps the circle was built before the barrow was constructed there, suggesting that the hill was viewed as having intrinsic sacred qualities. Whichever is the case, we find the same deliberate obsession with the north–south axis as existed at the Queen Maeve's Cairn on Knocknarea and possibly the same sort of symbolic association between death and the direction of north.

In this regard, it is interesting to note that in the village of Brailes, situated beneath the hill, there was a tradition that the dead of Brailes used to be taken by a path to Bredon Hill to be buried. This was an oral tradition (Woodward 1988 and personal communication) until it was committed to writing by a folklorist (Bloom 1976). Bredon Hill is a distinctive, isolated topographical feature containing prehistoric earth-

The cairn of Nether Largie South, Kilmartin Glen, Scotland, is positioned about halfway along the 'linear cemetery' running through the valley. Many finds were uncovered within this chambered monument, including neolithic pottery and, according to the excavating archaeologist, 'great numbers of broken quartz pebbles'.

Looking northeast along the line of the 'linear cemetery' from Nether Largie Mid to Nether Largie North and Glebe cairns, towards the pyramidal peak of Dun Chonallaich in the far distance.

scape of Kilmartin Glen, Argyll, Scotland, a location with a rich and varied collection of monuments that we have visited more than once already in the pages of this book. The linear cemetery is one element of the ritual landscape, and it is made up of a set of Bronze Age burial cairns arranged in a fairly exact line, running roughly from southwest to northeast along the valley floor. The alignment begins in the south at two ruined sites, Bruach an Druimein, where nine cists were found along with a jet necklace, and the Rowanfield-Crinian Moss cists, which like the other site might originally have been a cairn. Next, there is the much better preserved Ri Cruin Cairn (see Part Two), then the main, giant cairns of Nether Largie South, Mid and North, followed on the line by Glebe Cairn (Butter 1999; Carr 1998). The alignment, which is about 3 kilometres (2 miles) long, is considered to have its 'focus' at the Nether Largie South Cairn

(RCAHMS 1999). The cairns forming the 'linear cemetery' are presumed to have contained the burials of Bronze Age chieftains or kings, hinted at in the name of Ri Cruin (the King's Circle or the King's Assembly). Obviously, the people buried in the cairns must have been important to the society that constructed the monuments, and it is reasonable to assume that they were great leaders of some sort, but we should bear in mind that the role of such leaders could also have incorporated religious functions, making them priest-kings or shaman-chieftains. This is especially so as a strong tradition of sacral kingship existed in Scotland during pagan Celtic times, which might itself have been a modified continuation of an earlier and perhaps more primary form of the same kind of leadership.

The axis of this 'royal line' can be extended northwards to pass through Dun na Nighinn, a rock ridge supporting an Iron Age fort, and Dun Chonallaich, a rocky massif also surmounted by the (now vandalized) walls of an Iron Age fort. This rock peak is of particular interest because from the floor of Kilmartin Glen it appears as a very regular pyramid shape. It is visible all along the 'royal line' from at least as far back to the south as Ri Cruin. Standing looking along the line of the Nether Largie cairns it is difficult to feel that these great monuments were aligned towards this dominant skyline feature by chance.

MOUNTAINS OF THE MOTHER

The approach of studying monuments in their landscape settings can sometimes be given an extra spin, so that we can actually be led to see the types of idea that informed Stone Age mythology. This is nothing less than an archaeology of ancient dreams.

One vivid example of this takes us to the southwestern coastal area of Scotland, to the Kintyre Peninsula and two of the islands of the Inner Hebrides, Islay and Jura, which are located a little under 30 kilo-

metres (20 miles) offshore. We begin at the site of Ballochroy, a row of three standings stones on a ridge above the western shoreline of the Kintyre peninsula. The middle stone is of the 'playing card' variety, its thin edge oriented out to sea and thus to Jura. Specifically, anyone looking along the broad, flat face of the stone has their eye directed to Ben Corra, in the mountain range known as the Paps of Jura. One of the great pioneers of archaeoastronomy, Alexander Thom, was able to prove that this alignment indicated the sunset on the summer solstice (Thom 1967). On that day the sun viewed from Ballochroy seems to set into the Paps. We noted in Part One that the name 'paps' in Celtic lands indicates breasts, and this is

The snow-dusted Paps of Jura from the east, caught in a late winter dawn light.

because the Paps of Jura are rounded and considerably breast-shaped in appearance, two of them particularly so. It was further noted that such names can persist for long periods. So we could infer from this evidence that the people who constructed and used Ballochroy saw the Jura mountains as expressive of the Earth Mother and at midsummer the sun settled down into her breast. But would we be right in making this assumption? Could it not just be a coincidence involving a range of mountains, a megalithic site and a name relic? In this case, we can be sure that we are indeed picking up on a piece of authentic mythic information from the Stone Age, because this myth can be triangulated.

To do this, we have to travel to the Isle of Islay, the adjacent southern neighbour of Jura. There, we go to a sacred lake, Loch Finlaggan. How do we know it was sacred? First of all, because near its shores stands a substantial monolith. Second, because viewed from the lake two peaks of the Paps of Jura range project dramatically and in isolation above an intervening ridge to the northeast: it is hard adequately to express the visual impact they deliver to an observer on the spot. Third, because of the work of archaeologists on Channel Four Television's Time Team series in the environs of the northeastern end of the loch (Channel Four 1995). One of the first things they did was to

The summer solstice sun setting behind the Paps of Jura, viewed from the Ballochroy stones. (John Glover)

excavate the top of a hillock known as Cnoc Seanndda. This hillock happens to be situated in line between two islets in the loch and the Paps of Jura. The archaeologists uncovered flint cores and blades, evidence of mesolithic activity dating to 7000 years or so ago. Then they found stones indicating that there was also a collapsed burial chamber built into the hillock. Bones were also uncovered indicating that animals had been ritualistically buried there – perhaps as foundation sacrifices. Another telling piece of work was conducted with the help of geophysics experts, whom the archaeologists brought on site and who used geomagnetometers to find a series of pits or stone holes associated with the standing stone, suggesting a stone row. The team concluded that there had been 'a ritualistic prehistoric landscape' around Cnoc Seanndda, with the stone chamber as it centre and a stone row aligned with the islets in the loch in one direction and the Paps of Jura in the other.

It was almost certainly no accident, therefore, that long afterwards the loch and its islets were selected as the administrative centre of the 'Lords of the Isles'. Meetings of their Council were held on the islets, where a feasting hall and other buildings were located. Being the southernmost island of the Inner Hebrides, Islay had assumed importance as a focal point in the important seaways between Scotland and Ireland and had been settled by both Norse and Gaelic peoples. From around the eleventh century an aggressively independent line of rulers or lords emerged, and by the fourteenth century Islay was central to a virtually independent Gaelic kingdom, the Lordship of the Western Isles, with its capital at Finlaggan. But in 1493 James IV of Scotland abolished the Lordship.

It is a strange to stand on these islets among the ruins of the buildings there and with a direct view to

Loch Finlaggan, Islay, a sacred lake for at least 7000 years.

Above: The standing stone by the shores of Loch Finlaggan.

Below: The startling view from the top of Cnoc Seanndda: the breasts of Jura's Earth Mother make it clear why it was a sacred spot from mesolithic times. The standing stone is visible in the field at lower right.

the Paps of Jura and to realize that this place had been viewed as sacred and important for some six millennia. Two of the most natural types of sacred sites – holy lake and sacred mountains – had gradually become monumentalized. The assemblage of natural features, sacred sightlines and monumental accretions together form a kind of fossil of a Stone Age mythic vision left in the wonderful landscape of the Inner Hebrides.

LOST HORIZONS

It is surely now clear that when one is in a prehistoric complex it is important to keep one's eyes – and mind – open in order to be alert to unexpected clues. But when one is looking for what is not immediately obvious it can sometimes mean that one has to look more closely at what is obvious. Sometimes the greatest secrets are the open ones.

The present writer gradually learned this lesson at the Avebury complex, which is about 32 kilometres (20 miles) north of Stonehenge. A skyline coincidence was involved, but this led to more substantial insights.

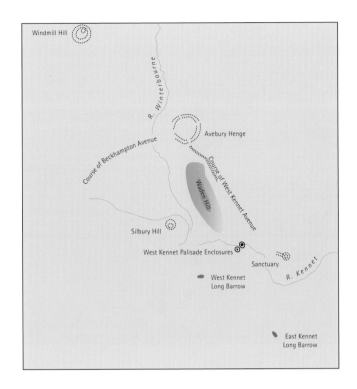

Simplified sketch map of some of the main features of the Avebury complex. Silbury Hill is visible from all the sites marked, but not from most of the courses of the stone avenues. Modern roads have been excluded.

The main complex stretches for a few miles across the Wiltshire countryside and contains the great Avebury henge and stone circle, the largest in the world; two avenues of stones connecting with the southern and western entrances of the henge (the extant Kennet Avenue and the no longer visible Beckhampton Avenue, recently confirmed by archaeological investigation); the remains of a timber and, later, stone multiple-ringed feature, the Sanctuary, originally linked to the henge by the Kennet Avenue; the great artificial mound of Silbury Hill, Europe's tallest prehistoric earthwork; various remnants of stone settings; and a number of long barrows, not all of which seem to have been associated with burial or other mortuary activities (Barrett 1994). The foundations of a great timber enclosure, probably a temple, were also uncovered. The

whole Avebury complex is overlooked from its northern edge by Windmill Hill, a natural eminence and a scene of decidedly ritual gatherings before any of the monuments were built, which process took over a thousand years, from c.3700 BC when some of the long chambered mounds, such as the West Kennet Long Barrow, were constructed, until c.2500 BC, when the henge and great circle were created and perhaps the last phase of Silbury Hill completed.

Considering the monuments as being separate places scattered over the countryside – the 'single site syndrome' – is not the way to see the complex. In actuality, the monuments are keyed in closely to the natural topography of the area. It is also a great error to think of the henge and great circle as the centre of the ritual landscape; this is an impression many visitors receive, for that is where the village, shops, museums and restaurants are located. In truth, it is Silbury Hill that is at the heart of the complex, and it took the writer a long time to really appreciate this simple fact. This mound is a fascinating monument. It was

The southwestern quadrant of Avebury henge. Visible are the outer bank, ditch and stones of the great circle that runs around the inner lip of the ditch. It is the bank and ditch that form the actual henge.

Silbury Hill (left) adjacent to Waden Hill (right), as viewed from West Kennet Long Barrow.

built in phases on a natural rise in the ground and stands 40 metres (130 feet) tall. Its summit is flat, like a platform, and a weathered ledge runs around the mound's otherwise smooth and regular sides, roughly 4.6 metres (15 feet) below the top. Originally thought to have been an extra large Bronze Age burial mound, excavation revealed no burial or central chamber, and its age was revised backwards into the neolithic period. In the centre of the mound, turves were found that had been turned when the structure was commenced and were still green after nearly five millennia. The blades of grass held the remnants of flying ants, indicating that work on Silbury had started one long-ago summer around the end of July or early in August. We have noted that this period is known as Lughnasa in the Pagan Celtic calendar and Lammas in the Christian one. The purpose of the mound is not known, nor why it should be placed alongside a natural ridge, Waden Hill, virtually the

same height as itself. To our way of thinking, if one is going to build a giant structure it ought to be placed in full view, preferably where its height would be enhanced, but Silbury is placed at a low spot and springs into visibility only from certain locations within the complex, shielded on the east as it is by Waden Hill.

It took the writer a considerable length of time to see the obvious fact that the profile of Silbury Hill shared a relationship with the skyline behind it. This

The megalithic façade of West Kennet long barrow, Avebury.

realization first occurred, quite suddenly, when the mound was viewed from West Kennet Long Barrow. The skyline to the north from that position is formed by Windmill Hill, and this intersected the profile of the mound at about the same height as the weathered ledge. This observation is possible only from the western tip of the long barrow, and it is significant that this part was an extension that had been added to the barrow – perhaps around the time Silbury was being built. An engineered sightline? It allowed a visual connection between one of the oldest monuments, West Kennet long barrow, and the ancestral Windmill Hill and associated these sites with the awesome 'new' monument of Silbury between. Observations of the great mound were made from the other key monumental sites in the heart of the complex, namely, East Kennet long barrow, the Sanctuary, Avebury henge and another long barrow to the west. Silbury was visible from all these and in each case the skyline passed behind the profile of the great mound somewhere between the flat summit and the weathered ledge. At Avebury henge, the viewing position was taken to be where the tallest stone had stood, a now-destroyed feature, which had been called the Obelisk and which had stood in the northern half of the great circle. Only the top segment of Silbury is visible, visually wedged between the distant horizon and the foreground slope of Waden Hill. A very tight, precise sightline, so precise, in fact, that just before harvest time the height of the cereal crop on Waden Hill blocks it. This must always have been the case, for it is known that cereals were grown there in neolithic times. This seems to relate to the fact that Silbury started to be built at harvest time, suggesting that it was connected with harvest celebrations and rituals – the forerunners of Lughnasa and Lammas – and perhaps the fecundity of the Earth in general.

It was clear that this top segment of Silbury Hill was

A telephoto view from the western tip of West Kennet Long Barrow to Silbury Hill. The horizon is formed by Windmill Hill, which intersects Silbury's profile at the same height as the eroded ledge on the great mound's sides.

Looking towards Silbury Hill from the position of the Obelisk within the henge. The very top of Silbury can be seen as a dark shape 'wedged' between foreground and background.

DOUBLE SUNRISE AT AVEBURY

Above: Looking eastwards at Lughnasa/Lammas from the summit of Silbury Hill. The first gleam of the sun is visible on the far horizon, which shows up as a fainter strip above the dark form of Waden Hill nearby, which makes up the lower part of the picture.

Below: Looking eastwards from the ledge on Silbury Hill. The sun appears to rise again a few minutes later over the ridge of Waden Hill. As the observer's viewing point is lowered from summit to ledge, part of the distant horizon dips behind the bulk of Waden Hill, allowing the sun to 'rise' for a second time.

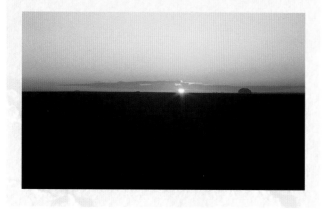

particularly significant, and further investigation revealed why. Looking eastwards from the top of Silbury around the times of Lughnasa and Beltane, when the sun rises from the same part of the horizon), the far skyline is visible just over the top of nearby Waden Hill. The sun can be seen rising from it. If the viewpoint is immediately moved lower down to the east-facing part of the Silbury ledge, the distant horizon appears to drop behind the bulk of Waden Hill's looming ridge and the sun is seen to rise, again, over this a few minutes later. So Silbury was made exactly tall enough to separate the near and far easterly skylines and so facilitate a symbolic 'double sunrise' at ceremonially important times of the year. What appears to be a further, even more dramatic piece of ritual showmanship can be experienced by an observer on Silbury at these times: a glow of light can be seen stretching away to the western horizon from the tip of Silbury's shadow cast by the rising sun. This is a refractive effect known as a 'glory' created in the dewdrops in the fields below. The psychological effect of this phenomenon is to make one feel as if Silbury Hill is blessing the crops and the land.

It appears, therefore, that Silbury Hill stands just where it does and to the height that it does in order to be able to facilitate the north–south visual link between West Kennet long barrow and Windmill Hill, the demands of the 'double sunrise' effect to the east and to enable the skyline association to be visible from the key monument sites all around. It is a staggering display of sacred geography. Interpretation is always a risky business, but it seems reasonable to see Silbury Hill in terms of acting as an intermediary between the fecundity of the Earth and the source of life, the sun – considered to be a goddess, Sunna, in early northern Europe. Perhaps the great mound symbolized the Earth Mother herself. These probable feminine associations are supported by other symbol-

The Silbury 'glory'. Looking west from the summit of Silbury Hill as the sun rises in the Beltane or Lughnasa periods (early May, early August), the shadow of the great mound has a glow of light emerging from it that reaches into the distance. This is caused by a refractive effect in the dewdrops in the fields. Neolithic ceremonial showmanship.

ism in the Avebury complex, such as the vulva-stone (see Part Three) and the little Kennet River, 600 paces south of Silbury. The Kennet issues from the Swallowhead spring, which is dry in winter and then runs towards the east, the direction of the sunrise. Its waters were thought special and life giving even as late as the seventeenth century (Goulstone 1985). Furthermore, the name 'kennet' is thought by some commentators possibly to be a neolithic survival (Burl 1979) and to relate to the female genital organ.

ROADS LESS TRAVELLED

There is a class of primarily British neolithic monument that is on a landscape scale in its own right, as well as being part, and often the focus, of ritual landscapes made up of other monuments. It is a type of linear earthwork called a 'cursus'. This curious name, which is Latin for 'racecourse', was given to the nearly 3-kilometre (2-mile) long feature just north of Stonehenge discovered by the antiquarian William Stukeley in 1723. Assuming that it dated from Roman times, he thought

the 'noble' earthwork was just that – a racetrack for chariots. Later in the eighteenth century a Roman origin was similarly ascribed to the Cleaven Dyke in Perthshire, Scotland, now also recognized as being a neolithic cursus. It was a long while after these antiquarian observations before the archaeological community began to get interested in monuments of this kind.

The first breakthroughs came in the 1930s with the advent of aerial photography, for most cursuses (the strictly correct plural form is actually cursûs) are very difficult to see at ground level and some show up at all only as crop marks viewed from the air. By about 1980 nearly fifty cursus monuments were known, and this

An airview of crop marks revealing the course of a cursus. This one is at Scorton, Yorkshire. It is straight and regular and runs for over a mile. In this picture its outlines can be followed off the top of the frame. (Crown Copyright/MOD)

The earthen avenue formed by parallel embankments and known as the Banqueting Hall. This is one of the numerous monuments on the Hill of Tara, Ireland. It is now thought it may be a preserved section of a neolithic cursus.

number has gradually increased so that by 1999 approximately one hundred possible cursuses had been identified in the British Isles. They occur in areas throughout the land, with notable concentrations in southern England, the Midlands, lowland Scotland and eastern mid-Wales. In addition, at least four possible cursuses have been identified in County Meath, Ireland: on the Hill of Tara (the earthwork known as the Banqueting Hall); near Newgrange; below the Loughcrew Hills on which over twenty chambered cairns are placed; and the 'Knockauns' at Teltown (Newman 1999). There are also groups of linear earthworks in northern France and Brittany that may come within the definition of the monument type (Kinnes 1999). Although it was a long-neglected class of monument, investigation of the cursus type of monument increased dramatically in the final two decades of the twentieth century, and this welcome expansion of interest continues at the time of writing.

The basic form of the cursus is easy enough to describe: it is a long earthen avenue usually defined by ditches and internal banks and almost always having closed ends, which can be square, rounded or slightly bowed. It may, therefore, be described as a very elongated enclosure. But there are a great many variations on this basic form. Some cursuses were outlined by pits or postholes rather than by ditches. Cursus lengths can vary from a few hundred yards to a mile or more, and cursuses are, therefore, often placed in two categories, 'major' and 'minor'. Major ones would include, among many others, the Stonehenge cursus already mentioned; the Dorset cursus, which is really two cursuses butted end-to-end and extending in all for about 10 kilometres (6 miles); the 1.6-kilometre (1-mile) long Drayton cursus in Oxfordshire; and a cursus running for 3 kilometres (2 miles) immediately to the west of Heathrow Airport, London. In a major cursus the long axis is generally about five times longer than its width, so in plan it looks like a narrow feature, although on the ground that width is still a broad area. Minor cursuses can shade into monuments defined as 'rectangular enclosures' or even 'cursus-like enclosures'. A cursus is usually fairly straight, sometimes exactingly so, or straight in sections, and it is this regularity that is a key identifying characteristic of the monument type. Nevertheless, there are cursuses with sinuous or crooked sections or with slightly curved sides.

Even though they represent the largest scale prehistoric monument in Europe, the purpose of cursuses is unknown. They are a true ancient mystery, and attempting interpretation is a nightmare. Excavation has been limited, and although some evidence of postholes, cremations, inner mounds and other signs of ritual activity has been detected in parts of some of them, cursuses seem in the main to have been rather empty features – at least as far as current investigation has found. But their vast scale and the amount of work that went into them must indicate that they were of great importance to neolithic peoples. Because they are linear, it has been widely assumed that they were associated with processional activities of some kind. One pattern associated with the siting of cursuses is that most of them are located close to a river, or the course of the cursus crosses that of a stream. It has been suggested, therefore, that there may have been a symbolic link between the flow of the river and processional movement within a cursus (Barclay and Hey 1999). Another suggestion is that cursuses were ritual paths. A variant on this idea is that cursuses marked where such a holy or ceremonial way had once existed – a monumentalization of a sacred axis (Johnston 1999). The problem with all these kinds of interpretation is that cursuses have ends. They are not through ways, they are enclosures, no matter how long they may be. The present writer feels that the focus on physical ceremonial activity might be misguided and that cursuses may have been areas delimited for the presence of spirits. Cursuses were important monuments, and nothing was more important to ancient peoples than a concern about spirits – spirits of nature, spirits of the dead – and cursuses occur in the company of mortuary monuments, many of which are likely to have been contemporary or earlier. The idea of ancestral spirits moving around the landscape is enshrined in at least some Eurasian shamanic traditions (see later), and we have already noted rock art in Scandinavia where footprints were carved as if a spirit was walking from a cemetery (see Part Two).

Another type of prehistoric monument in Britain, stone rows, pass through or link burial sites and could be a variant of the same idea as the earlier cursuses. It is possible that all these represent expressions at different times and places of a deep-rooted archaic idea regarding spirits walking abroad. It can be traced into historical times, with the belief that crossroads were where spirits assembled and that old roads had to be swept clear of spirits or that spirit traps had to be erected on them. Folklore in some parts of Europe tells of invisible ghost roads linking medieval cemeteries and some physical 'death roads' seem to embody similar ideas. It could even be that funeral paths and church ways, common in medieval times, were to some extent coloured by such ancient beliefs – there are some ritual aspects to their use that seem to indicate this.

The siting of cursuses offers only annoyingly variable clues that might contribute to their interpretation. The only really detectable pattern is the association with rivers mentioned earlier. It does seem that rivers were seen as significant and therefore presumably sacred, and this is reinforced by the fact that a particular type of pottery, Peterborough Ware, has been found in some cursuses as well as in river deposits or offerings. Because of the river connection, it follows that cursuses are frequently sited in low-lying areas, and this, combined with the fact that they are (now) low-key, often ploughed-out monuments, makes visits to their sites often somewhat undramatic. But this is not always the case, and a number of archaeologists consider that some cursuses do refer to their natural surroundings. The Stonehenge cursus, for example, aligns to a point on a distinctive ridge on the western horizon called Beacon Hill, a name that underlines its visibility (Pennick and Devereux 1989). Cleaven Dyke aligns to the Hill of Lethendy in the northwest for much of its length.

Archaeologist Roy Loveday has focused on the Dorchester-on-Thames cursus and has sifted the evidence that tells him it was probably a ritual or cult centre, perhaps the focus of pilgrimage (Loveday 1999).

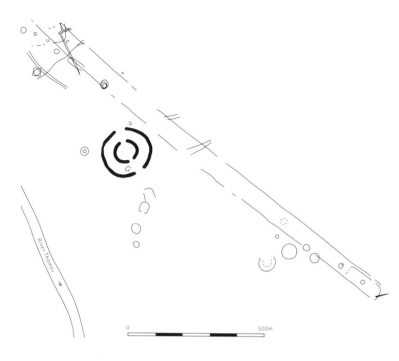

Groundplan of the Dorchester-on-Thames cursus, and surrounding monuments

Wittenham Clumps from the south

There is certainly a rich concentration of neolithic monuments surrounding the cursus, whose axis seems to have been respected for a thousand years. What was special about the site, then? Loveday raised his eyes to the skyline and there, in clear view from the cursus and its accompanying ritual landscape, are the prominent Sinoden Hills, rising dramatically from the flat flood-plain of the Thames. These hills are crowned by the Wittenham Clumps, a favourite subject for artists (notably Paul Nash). They are the kind of twin, rounded hills that, as we have seen time and again in this book, ancient people saw as breast forms, just as we can ourselves today, and that they inevitably regarded as a sign of the presence of the fertility or Earth-goddess. Loveday suspects that it was no different at Dorchester and that that may have been the reason this site became such a focus. Unlike the Paps of Anu or the Paps of Jura, there are no name clues to support this observation regarding the Sinoden Hills, and there are no extant pieces of lore that associate them with breasts, but there is a fragment that tells us that they were regarded in terms of body metaphor until recent centuries: Margaret Gelling notes an eighteenth-century name for them as 'Mother Dunche's Buttocks', a reference, apparently, to a local landowner (Gelling 1974).

Temples in the Landscape

Even in places and times when more sophisticated temples were constructed than those of the Stone Age era, they still had close ties with the natural landscape in some cultures. Their placing expressed deep symbolism and religious beliefs.

MINOAN AND GREEK TEMPLES

One of the first to bring to general attention the significance of the landscape settings of Minoan and

Greek temples has been the Yale scholar, Vincent Scully. The import of his pioneering work of the 1950s in Crete and Greece has still not been taken properly on board in some academic quarters, and in the preface to the 1979 edition of his classic work, *The Earth, The Temple, and the Gods*, Scully confessed to being 'exasperated' by what he termed the 'obdurate blindness' some scholars insisted on maintaining with regard to temple–landscape relationships. It is probably true to say, however, that with the growing scholarly interest in ancient sacred geographies in subsequent decades, his work is becoming more widely read. One younger scholar has nicely expressed this new appreciation:

> Landscape architect Vincent Scully visited the Minoan palaces, stood in those central courtyards and peered out into the countryside around him. By looking at the palace from this perspective, he was able in one visionary moment to sink deep shafts of understanding into the society and mind of the people who constructed them 4000 years earlier. (Favaloro 1988)

It can take people a long time to absorb visionary moments.

The first wave of Minoan palaces was built between c.2000 and c.1700 BC, after a 'Pre-Palace' period of several centuries in which the arrival on Crete of people with a knowledge of bronze-working led to the emergence of a more sophisticated material culture than the neolithic one that already existed on the island, namely the Minoan. These Old Palaces, as they are known, such as Knossos, Phaistos and Mallia, were where wealth, culture and religion were focused. Around 1700 BC a massive earthquake shattered the Old Palaces, but the Minoans rapidly built New Palaces on the ruins of the old ones, and it is primarily the

remains of New Palace architecture that visitors to Crete see today, although some parts of the Old Palaces have survived. Again, the palaces formed the centres of the cultural and spiritual life of the seemingly peaceable Minoans, and this continued until c.1450, when another devastating earthquake occurred – thought to be associated with the incredible natural catastrophe that consumed much of the island of Santorini (Thera) to the north of Crete. The Mycenaean Greeks took advantage of the subsequent confusion and established themselves on Crete. Only Knossos was rebuilt, and this became the seat of Mycenaean power. The culture of the island was given a new, more militaristic tone, and Minoan civilization as such collapsed. The Mycenaeans did absorb cultural and religious ideas from the Minoans, however, and these influences found their way to the Greek mainland.

We know little in detail about the high Minoan culture, and most of what is known has been deduced from the archaeological record left by the civilization, primarily at the palaces. This evidence indicates that

The famous 'horns of consecration' at Knossos, Crete

Among countless 'upraised arms' figurines, this one is of special inter-est. Known as the Poppy Goddess because of the poppy pods in her headband, the figurine was found in what seems to have been a Bronze Age 'opium den'. (Now in Heraklion Museum)

appears that they were placed on walls and other prominent parts of the palaces, and banks of them are visible in the background of the scene on the seal impression. Like an underlying rhythm, this horn-like shape recurs in various guises in the imagery we have retrieved from Minoan Crete. Figurines endlessly show goddesses or priestesses making a gesture with upraised arms. This shape is echoed by the fact that they are bare breasted or are holding snakes wriggling in a similar shape or are grasping double-bladed axes, the hallmark symbol of Minoan culture. This appears in the form of actual metal and stone artefacts, as depictions in figurines, pottery vessels and other sculpted items throughout the Minoan sphere of influ-ence, and in a highly stylized architectural mark known as the *labrys*. Bull's horns, breasts, gestures, double-bladed axes, the *labrys* – what was this basic shape all about? What did it mean?

The rites conducted at the palaces seem to have developed from the natural sacred places that had been used on Crete for untold generations. We see Minoan structures at peak sanctuaries and sacred caves, and, the corollary of that, the pillar crypts in the palaces appear to have been architectural mimicry of the caves

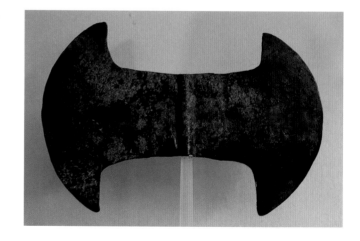

One of the large bronze double-bladed axes found at Knossos. (Now in Heraklion Museum)

there was a major goddess cult, and a Minoan seal impression shows the goddess, in the company of wild animals, being saluted on a mountain peak – the Woman of the Mountains, the Mistress of the Beasts. There was also a great emphasis on iconography developed from the bull, especially the bull's horns. There is the famous mural depicting a bull-leaping ritual or display at Knossos, and scattered through-out the archaeological remains of Crete are stone 'horns of consecration' of various sizes and forms. It and stalagmites, as was discussed in Part Two. It would seem that Minoan religion simply embellished and formalized a strand of sacred observance that went back into remotest antiquity on the island. It was Scully's insight that this link with the past was also expressed by the placing and orientation of the palaces. He saw that the horn-shape had been present from all time in the landscape: it was visible in the twin, saddle and cleft peaks of Cretan mountains, the sacred summits of the island where worship had taken place, the holy mountains on whose flanks were located the sacred caves, which, in turn, contained the stalactites and stalagmites that were the natural precursors of the Minoan pillar cult. It was evident to Scully that the palaces had been placed in relation to these sacred peaks and sometimes also secondary hill features with conical shapes or rounded forms suggestive of female breasts – an association we have seen was by no means confined solely to Crete.

Archaeology bore him out, as excavation has revealed that the sites of the palaces had been marked by cleared and sometimes paved areas perhaps nearly a century before palaces were actually built around them. When they were constructed, as Scully saw,

The central court at the Minoan palace of Phaistos aligns to the saddle-peaked Mount Ida (Psiloritis), here slightly shrouded in cloud.

Labrys carved on a pillar in the pillar crypt at Mallia.

they were often oriented towards the cleft or horn-like peaks. So at Knossos, the central court is directed southwards to Mount Juktas, whose peak is both conical and cleft, as Scully observes. At the southern end of the court the great 'horns of consecration' there frame the sacred peak. Similarly, the courtyard of Phaistos aligns to the saddle of Mount Ida (Psiloritis) and its great, sacred cave of Kamares. At Mallia the palace is located directly beneath the Dictaean massif, home of the birth-cave of Zeus. The Minoan town of Gournia in the east of the island straggles along a ridge in the bottom of valley. The small palace there aligns to a pair of hills distinctively shaped like breasts. Scully felt that at Gournia 'one has the inescapable impression that human beings were conceived of as children who lie upon the mother's body, enclosed by her arms and in the deep shadow of her breasts'. In the other direction, far away to the northwest, the split peak of Mount Dicte is visible.

Notable examples of similar temple-mountain relationships on the Greek mainland include the temples

The breast-like hills rising immediately to the southeast of Gournia and to which the palace in the Minoan town is aligned.

atop the sacred heights of the Acropolis in Athens and the temple of the Mysteries at Eleusis. From the Acropolis, on which was found an image of Gaia, the Earth-goddess, and remains of a Mycenaean citadel, the classical temples of the Parthenon and its companions look across to the horned saddle of Hymettos in the east, which Scully considered to be the prime sacred mountain of the Attic region. The early version of the Temple of Athena Polias, the goddess of Athens, on the Acropolis oriented directly to Hymettos. At

This design found on a Mycenaean vase manages to assemble the bulls' horns, the Horns of Consecration, and the double-bladed axe/labrys. [Arthur Evans 1901]

Eleusis the dramatic cleft peak of Mount Kerata (the name means 'horns') rises on the skyline, while the cross-axis of the Telesterion, the main temple of initiation at Eleusis, aligns to a saddle in a ridge on the island of Salamis, a short distance offshore.

In all, Scully studied 150 Greek and Cretan temple sites, and the basic relationships indicated in these examples were found to occur in some form or other at most of them. There were differences and variations, but this was in keeping with the idea of a deity that was certainly the norm during classical times and doubtless before: although the names of deities were common to the whole culture, they still manifested as deities of place. So while there was a universal concept of, say, Athena, there would be Athena of specific places. The architecture of a temple might be governed by underlying universal themes, but it, too, would nevertheless enter into an intimate dialogue with its local landscape. It was the landscape that ultimately shaped and focused the temple. Regarding the cleft or horn-shaped peaks, Scully felt that they:

> ....create a profile which is basically that of a pair of horns, but it may sometimes also suggest raised arms or wings, the female cleft, or even, at some sites, a pair of breasts.   (Scully 1979)

The landscape thus also shaped the Minoan mind and conjured its religious symbolism.

MAKING MOUNTAINS

They may have been far away in time and space from ancient Greece, but the temple builders of Mesoamerica and South America also responded to their landscapes in their architecture. They symbolically recreated the caves, the waters and, above all, the mountains in the already sanctified natural landscapes they inhabited.

The ceremonial core of the ancient city of Tiahuanaco, high in the Andes of modern Bolivia, contains the Akapana, a terraced pyramid surrounded by a moat. We saw in Part Two that this was in mimicry of the sacred Island of the Sun, the place of origin, in nearby Lake Titicaca. But there was more symbolism at work than this. The ceremonial complex associated with the Akapana was organized on a strong east–west axis, acknowledging the rising equinoctial sun over the three sacred peaks of Mount Illimani on the eastern horizon and its setting into Titicaca in the west. Only from the 17-metre (56-foot) high summit of the Akapana are both the mountains and the lake simultaneously visible. The terraced pyramid had originally been covered with green gravel brought from stream beds in the Quimsachata Mountains to the south. Archaeologist Alan Kolata realized that this substance symbolized both mountains and water and that the Akapana was itself a model mountain – a model sacred mountain. His investigations revealed that in its heyday rainwater collected on the monument's sunken summit would have cascaded down both internally through the pyramid's carefully engineered drainage system and externally over its terraces – exactly as water passes down a mountain. In exceptional downpours the process would have created a deep, roaring noise, like the thunder in the distant sacred mountains.

The Olmec, the earliest known civilization of prehistoric Mexico, was at the height of its power between c.1000 and c.600 BC. The Olmec's sacred mountain, their place of creation, was the mighty volcano of San Martin Pajapan, in the Tuxtla Mountains on the Gulf coast of Veracruz. It towers above surrounding peaks and dominates the area around the sacred lake of Catemaco. In 1897 a lifesize statue was found between two peaks on the volcano's crater. It depicted an Olmec ruler kneeling and grasping the trunk of the

The great, axial Street of the Dead in Teotihuacán, Mexico, aligns to the Pyramid of the Moon, which in turn is framed against Cerro Gordo, the sacred notched mountain of the Teotihuanicos.

World Tree. In La Venta, one of their major centres, the Olmec built a huge effigy of this volcano out of local clay. They fluted the sides of the mound to create a realistic image of a volcano. It was, in effect, the first of the Mesoamerican pyramids and was part of a ritual complex that was a built analogue of a natural sacred landscape.

Another early Mesoamerican civilization was the one that built the great ceremonial city of Teotihuacán in the Valley of Mexico around 2000 years ago. We know little about these people, but it is clear that they also were making mountains. We can tell this from their architecture. The main north–south axis of Teotihuacán is marked by a straight ceremonial way, now called the Street of the Dead. This aligns directly to the Pyramid of the Moon, whose shape echoes that of Cerro Gordo behind it, undoubtedly a holy mountain. Viewed from the top of this pyramid, the other, larger pyramid in the city, the Pyramid of the Sun, is seen with another mountain as its backdrop and echoes its overall shape (see frontispiece). The image of the mountain and the cave was important to the people of Teotihuacán, as we can tell from the carved symbols they left behind.

The Maya, who began to emerge as a recognizable culture in the last centuries BC and whose civilization reached its height between AD c.300 and c.900, similarly built pyramids in mimicry of sacred mountains and, indeed, referred to them in precisely that way. Mayan pyramids are related to plazas, which in Mayan symbolism represented lakes, for the Mayan word *nab* meant both plaza and a large sheet of water. The stepped pyramid standing in a plaza in a Mayan ceremonial city, therefore, represented the First True Mountain, the place of creation, rising out of the primordial waters (Freidel *et al.* 1993). The interiors of the Mayan stepped pyramids were thought of as symbolic caves, portals to the underworld, as were temples on top of the pyramids (Brady and Ashmore 1999).

The Castillo, Chichén Itzá. This stepped pyramid, with its corners directed towards the rising and setting positions of the sun at its solstices, is a temple-mountain, specifically, the Creation Mountain. The great plaza in which it stands symbolizes the primordial Sea of Creation.

The Aztecs, who were at the peak of their power when the Spaniards arrived, continued this most ancient Mesoamerican tradition of making artificial sacred mountains. Their capital city was Tenochtitlán, which was built on an island in the swampy Lake Texcoco in the Valley of Mexico and is now beneath modern Mexico City. It had a sacred precinct at its heart containing an awesome temple complex. Now partially excavated, its ruins are visible next to Mexico City's central square. A great pyramid developed in this precinct had two shrines on its summit, one dedicated to the rain-god, Tlaloc, the other to the war-god, Huitzilopochtli. Tlaloc was worshipped and entreated on mountain tops. He was associated with mountains because they produce the rains, and in the Aztec mind mountains were, in effect, disguised water containers. The great pyramid of Tenochtitlán, Templo Mayor, was a representation of *atl-tepetl*, 'water mountain'. Specifically, Aztec scholar Richard Townsend has

pointed out, the pyramid and its shrines were models of Mount Tlaloc and the hill of Tetzcotzingo, both a fairly short distance to the east of Mexico City and, therefore, in Aztec times, Tenochtitlán. As was noted earlier in this book, these peaks have petroglyphs, the remains of temple enclosures and ceremonial ways, rock-cut baths and other features on them showing them to have been the centres of important ceremonies. Indeed, rituals in the temple precinct in Tenochtitlán were conducted in connection with observances taking place concurrently on Mount Tlaloc (Townsend 1993).

THE PURE LANDS

The early Buddhists also had their sacred geographies. We have already made passing note that Himalayan landscapes were conceived of in sacred geographical terms, with simulacra – the likeness to human or animal forms – figuring prominently as part of that. As Toni Huber has put it: 'A pilgrim who appears to be just staring at a group of boulders may be in the process of a sophisticated landscape interpretation exercise' (Huber 1994). Elisabeth Stutchbury writes:

> The landscape of Karzha [Lahul, Himachal Pradesh] is considered to be both empowered and empowering. We might interpret this with the suggestion that there is a 'sacred' geography which somehow interpenetrates with the mundane geographical features of the landscape and that furthermore the process of sanctification is understood to be intrinsically linked to the meditational powers of yogic practitioners ...
>
> The yogins of Karzha, through the tantric practices of Tibetan Buddhism ... have transformed ordinary geographical features, such as rivers, caves, rocks and mountains, the macrocosm, into 'sacred' places which constitute a 'sacred' geography conceptualized as a mandala.   Stutchbury 1994)

In short, a mindscape has been projected on to the physical landscape; the heavenly pure lands of Buddhist theology are conjured on the mundane Earth.

There was no single, hard-and-fast concept of sacred geography in early Buddhism, and so it takes various forms in different places. Gina Barnes has, however, particularly noted one significant aspect: the use of large-scale outdoor rock carvings on cliff walls or mountain boulders from Afghanistan, across northern China and into Korea. These rock-cut sculptures have 'forever changed the visible landscape at that point from a natural to an anthropogenic one with specific symbolic content' (Barnes 1999). She remarks that the larger examples of these sculptings, such as a cliff sculpture at Bamiyan, Afghanistan, can be seen from some miles distant. Whole areas were sometimes rendered sacred by concentrations of such carvings located in intervisible positions, thus making the landscape in between them holy as well. Barnes has studied two specific Buddhist landscapes in eastern Asia, one at Haitangshan in northeastern China and the other in Namsan in southeastern Korea. Both consist of complexes of temples built in mountainous terrain and accompanied by numbers of outdoor Buddhist sculptures. She sees both examples as resulting from a mix of Buddhist cosmology concerning axial World Mountains and Chinese folk beliefs regarding sacred mountains.

The first sacred spot or locus on Haitangshan near Fuxin, Lianing province, was a cave used by a tantric Buddhist monk. From this seed developed a whole Buddhist geography on the mountainside. Legend has it that, guided by this monk and other locals and using various forms of divination, including *feng shui* and the seeking of rocks of certain shapes, representatives of a prince early in the Qing Dynasty (AD 1644–1912) determined the location of what was to be the second largest temple in the area. This was the Pu'an Temple, now defunct. Around this temple are boulders carved with images of buddhas, bodhisattvas and other guardian deities and holy warriors. They are interspersed with unadorned rocks whose shapes suggest animals or objects – so there is Toad Rock, Mountain Eagle Rock and Coiled Dragon Rock, among many others. The complex as a whole, which evolved over two centuries, covers several acres of the mountain's slopes and involves twenty-six large buildings, 8 kilometres (5 miles) of preaching paths and 200 sculpted boulders.

A much larger sacred landscape is centred on the sacred peaks of Namsan, on the southern border of the Kyongju Basin. Namsan is a massif with many valleys and slopes. It was co-opted by Buddhism in the sixth century AD, but it was sacred before then. Shamans conducted rain dances on parts of the mountain, and megalithic monuments, dolmens, dating to the first millennium BC, have been found. There is evidence that certain places on Namsan were used for making offerings to nature spirits, so it is perhaps not surprising that the Buddhists believed that Namsan harboured many buddhas and bodhisattvas. Barnes believes that one reason the mountain attracted spiritual attention over such a long period were the many granite rocks scattered over it 'resembling animals and objects':

> Such figurative rocks abound particularly in the Yongjang valley, where they bear such names as Fierce Tiger, Lion, Big Bear, Old Man, Boar, Cat, Python and the natural outcome of all these beings, Dung Rock. (Barnes 1999)

The seeking of particular rocks was part of the locational divination used at Haitangshan, and this factor was unquestionably more widespread than Buddhism throughout the ancient world, as we have commented at points throughout this book. Namsan harbours more than a hundred temples, most of them now archaeological sites, sixty-three pagodas and about ninety rock sculptings, ranging from sculptures of buddhas in standing or seated positions to high- and low-relief carvings on boulders. The largest sculpted boulder is the 9-metre (30-foot) tall Buddha Rock in T'ap valley.

Of Shamans and Kings

Societies in which shamanism or its more structured expression, sacral kingship, was a major factor also projected mindscapes on to the physical landscape.

LANDSCAPES FIT FOR A KING

The landscape of ancient Egypt was particularly well suited for the development of a symbolic or sacred geography. The Nile running through the desert to the Mediterranean had created a 'ribbon oasis', a fertile floodplain where a civilization could live and prosper. But the edge between the fertile land – *Kmt*, the Black Land – and the ever-present desert – *Dsrt*, the Red Land – was then as now sudden and dramatic. The desert, rising to hills and cliffs and distant ranges, was the wild, unpredictable realm, visible to east and west, but it was in the western desert that the sun died each night, and so it was conceptualized primarily as the realm of the dead by the ancient Egyptians. The maintenance of order was the chief organizing principle of Egyptian life, and, scholar Janet Richards asserts, this 'was most exemplified in the development, meaning and use of explicitly sacred landscapes'. This attitude is documented in indigenous texts from the third millennium BC onwards.

The Egyptians did not have a concept or word for 'landscape'; rather, they recognized natural features and absorbed them into their main religious themes. An example is the prominent mountain peak opposite

The Theban mountain, the Mistress of the West, with its natural pyramidical peak, rises over the great necropolis of the Valley of the Kings.

Luxor, the former Thebes, which dominates the Valley of the Kings. This was known by several names, including the Mistress of the West. It is shown in Egyptian papyrus texts laden with symbolism associated with the cow-goddess, Hathor. The Theban peak was the proto-pyramid and was seen, like the later monuments modelled on it, as the primeval mound emerging from the waters of the first inundation – a creation concept not unlike that of the ancient Maya, no doubt due to its archetypal nature. This absorbing of natural elements into their cosmological schemes was one way the Egyptians could order the chaos of the wilderness. Another was to create architectural sacred landscapes that referenced the natural environment and the cosmological principles with which its perception was coloured. Before the New Kingdom period, Richards notes, much energy was devoted to 'the creation of potent ideational landscapes in the low desert', and attention was directed westwards to 'the taming of the waterless, unpredictable Sahara'. Sacred places that developed in the desert were 'for the most part mortuary landscapes, organized according

to the beliefs and practices relating to the disposal of the dead ... these landscapes were functionally equivalent to temples' (Richards 1999).

Richards has concluded that certain desert places were chosen and maintained as such 'conceptual landscapes' on the basis of topographical features. One of the examples she presents is Abydos, a huge complex of temples, cemeteries and royal installations located on the west of the Nile in a semicircular sweep of low desert stretching from the edge of the fertile floodplain back to a great bay of the cliffs, where it rises as a steep escarpment. A shallow *wadi* creates an opening in this and the line of cliffs and also provides a natural ceremonial way. This gap was seen as a gate to the otherworld. 'In c.3100 BC the first kings of politically unified Egypt laid claim to control of this otherworldy "gate", establishing their tombs at the southern end of an existing elite cemetery,' she notes.

The tombs had 'back doors' oriented to the gap in the cliffs, towards the gate to the otherworld. The kings saw the majestic and theatrical setting as ideal for enacting 'politico-ritual events' as Richards puts

The strange Osireion at Abydos, said to have been built by Seti I, located behind the Temple of Seti. The massive granite structure of this curious building only half emerges from the sands and rising water table today.

it. Their presence both in life and in death made them the symbolical gatekeepers of the realm of the dead. The complex was used in this way for seven centuries, before royal mortuary complexes were switched to Saqqara. But use of the sacred landscape nevertheless persisted for thousands years.

To take another, very different example of a royal landscape, we can go to pagan Celtic Ireland. It was focused on Navan Fort, the ancient Emain Macha, near Armagh in Northern Ireland. The site is a low hill that nevertheless commands wide views and has an earthwork enclosure on its summit dating to c.700 BC. Bronze Age earthworks had also been made on the site. It was on this hill that archaeologists uncovered the foundations of a great timber building dating to c.100 BC, at the centre of which was a massive post, as described in Part Two. It is recorded in the ancient Celtic literature as having been the royal seat of Ulster, the stronghold of King Conchobar mac Nessa. Two ancient foundation legends are associated with the site. One states that a great warrior queen, the ruler of the whole of Ireland, had prisoners of war build the stronghold, working to a plan she had scratched out on the ground with a brooch pin. Another tells of the arrival at Emain of the goddess Macha, who had to outrun the king's horses in order to save the life of her mortal husband. While successfully accomplishing this, she gave birth to twins (*emain* is Old Irish for 'twin'). The ancient text, the *Ulster Cycle*, also associated the great hero Cú Chulainn with the place, and he was subject to taboos related to dogs (he would die if he was ever tricked into eating dog meat), and his name actually means 'Culann's Hound'. It is at least interesting, therefore, that a dog's skull was found in the great timber building. Archaeological investigation has revealed that the landscape around the hill was a ritually symbolic one. To the west of the hill is the King's Stables, an artificial pool that was dug out in the Bronze Age. It contained

deposits of animal bones, principally those of red deer and of ... dogs. The front of a human skull was also found, severed from the back part as if to create a gruesome mask. To the east of the hill lies Lough na Shade, and this, too, was a ritual lake, containing four bronze trumpets along with human skulls and animal bones. It seems as if the whole site was a series of pagan Celtic developments on a ritual landscape that had been created in Bronze Age times.

PARALLEL WORLDS

In Mongolia Caroline Humphrey found that shamanic and chiefly landscapes co-existed and that relating to which was which in the physical topography depended on the criteria that were used. In Mongolian culture in general it was interaction with the landscape rather than contemplation of it that was paramount. The land possessed powers greater than the human.

> The Mongols do not take over any terrain in the vicinity and transform it into something that is their own. Instead, they move within a space and environment where some kind of pastoral life is possible and 'in-habit' it. That is to say, they let it pervade them and their herds, influencing where they settle, when they move and what kind of animals they keep. (Humphrey 1995)

Common to all Mongolian attitudes of the landscape is the concept that the 'landscape seethes with entities'; these can be conceived of as generalized forces in some instances and as specific, localized spirits in others. There is a general consensus that the land should not be marked, interfered with or polluted. So one takes water from a river in order to wash rather than washing directly in the river itself. As might be expected with a nomadic culture, it lives lightly on the land.

Although shamans and chieftains could sometimes take over each other's functions to some degree, there was usually a tension between them, and in some instances chiefs suppressed shamanism. Typically, where the structure of society was weakening, the people would turn more to shamanism.

Chiefly landscapes are based on the idea that the chief is the centre, and when a group moves along its annual cyclical journey, the centre is established anew each time the people halt for a while and set up camp. The journeying between stopping places is considered to occur outside the normal frame of things, and it is conducted in accord with astrological determinants and special clothes are worn. In a conceptual sense there is no movement in the chiefly tradition: it is based on vertical concepts rather than horizontal ones, with linkage to the sky, thought of as being the most powerful element of the environment. This verticality can be expressed in physically real events, such as a column of smoke rising from a fire. Because there is conceptually no movement, landscape features tend to be named purely with recurring descriptive terms, so there are many Red Mountains, Black Springs, Rich Valleys and the like. The chiefly landscape is populated with spirits, but these are referred to in terms of being 'masters' or 'rulers'. Metaphors for thinking about or describing the landscape derive from bodily imagery, so that a feature is considered to have a front, a back, cheeks, brows, thighs and so on. Mountains express the idea of vertical axis and are considered to be the site in chiefly landscapes where the power of the land can be addressed by the chief, the agent of those forces in the social world. (These 'mountains' can sometimes be very modest hillocks or rises in the ground, but this does not affect the symbolism.) The main kind of chiefly altar is a mountain top cairn of stones built around a pole. It is ritually renewed by the addition of fresh rocks, flags or tree branches. Circumambulation takes place during ceremonies of 'circular beckoning' to the forces or spirits of the environment. Chiefly traditions have been considerably modified and standardized by Buddhist influences, Humphrey reports. There were incursions of Buddhism into Mongolia at various times, and it finally penetrated almost the whole steppe region. It allied itself with the chiefly form of sacred geography, and 'lamas became in effect priests for political leaders', Humphrey notes.

Mongolian shamanic landscapes are based on wider, more Earth-centred and land-based conceptions than chiefly ones. They are more 'horizontal' than 'vertical', so to speak. Rituals are conducted at caves and other types of natural site, and certain rocks, cliffs and other features were considered to be inhabited by spirits. The Buddhist lamas loathed shamans, and they viewed such spirit places as power-points to be obliterated or converted to Buddhism. Unlike chiefly landscapes, movement is recognized in the Mongolian shaman's worldview, so in addition to localized spots containing spirits, a whole length of land could be viewed as being inhabited by a spirit. Further, whereas chiefly spirits are a given factor of the landscape, spirits in the shamanic worldview belonged originally to remarkable persons or people who died in strange ways and who then take on the role as the spirit of a place. This is especially the case with a shaman's spirit after death: it is believed to melt into landscape features like cliffs, or it can guard an area selected by him while alive by moving around it using spectral tracks. The means by which a living shaman in trance was able to reach the otherworld also involved 'ways' or 'paths' through the landscape that were invisible to ordinary people. This idea of shamans having invisible paths through the physical landscape appears to be universal and is found in various forms in many different traditions around the world.

TRANCE LANDSCAPES: MAPPING THE INVISIBLE

Shamanic sacred landscapes were marked directly on the ground in various ways and usually ignored the actual physical terrain. This is because, no matter how stylized and structured they may have become in some cultures, their origins lie in the experiences of altered states of consciousness, and in that sense they are different in nature from the other kinds of sacred landscape we have been considering. They represent the direct mapping of mindscapes. (Shamanic rock art imagery is a close cousin, if smaller in scale.) There are three basic types of these landscapes: ground markings that depict geometric, non-representational lines; terrestrial effigy figures; and straight line markings, paths or "roads". These forms of imagery can occur in isolation, but at some locations all of them can be found. They can be marked on the ground in a variety of ways depending on the local circumstances: by scouring into the ground, which is

common on desert surfaces and often referred to as *intaglios*; by laying out the imagery with small rocks and boulders either laid on the ground or pressed into its surface and technically referred to as 'petroforms' or 'boulder mosaics'; or by means of earthworks.

Landscapes of these kinds are relatively well preserved in the Americas. Probably the best known examples are the concentrations of desert intaglios on the tablelands or pampas around the Nazca area of Peru: the 'Nazca lines'. The most famous of the markings in this Andean area are the unerring straight 'lines', but there are also abstract, geometric markings and images of animals and birds, properly called 'geoglyphs'. Various dates are hypothesized for the markings, but the majority of them seem to have been produced at some point between c.200 BC and AD c.800. Similar markings occur in several other areas of the Andes, notably the straight ritual paths of the Bolivian altiplano, which are longer than any at Nazca. There are straight causeways in the lowland areas of South America that have had little archaeological investigation carried out on them, and there are ethnological rumours of 'songline'-type paths in the Amazon.

All these South American peoples have long traditions of using plant hallucinogens for shamanistic purposes, and they are continued in the Amazon. Thousand-year-old paths 'tending to straightness' lead to burial grounds over mountainous rainforest country in Costa Rica. There are several examples of the same kind of imposed landscapes in Mesoamaerica, the prime one being the straight causeways laid through the rainforests of their domain by the ancient Maya. The modern Maya refer to them as *sacbeob*, 'white ways'. The Maya were and are a shamanistic people, but their shamanism had developed into a structured, hierarchical expression with organized priesthoods during the efflorescence of the classic

Nazca, Peru. Mysterious, straight line markings converge towards or cross the Pan-American Highway. The ancient desert markings are as straight as the modern road. (Gary Urton)

In the present-day United States engineered straight roads linked Anasazi great kiva sites across the San Juan Basin, which is better known today as the Four Corners region, where the modern states of New Mexico, Arizona, Utah and Colorado meet. These probably fit into a vaguely similar category as the Mayan *sacbeob*. These features are between 800 and 1000 years old. Along with thousands of petroglyphs, there are around fifty ground markings at Sears Point in the Gila River valley in southwestern Arizona. They range from meandering patterns to straight lines and

The course of an ancient Mayan causeway or sacbe leading to the 'arch' at Kabàh, Yucatán, Mexico.

Mayan culture. The *sacbeob* were principally used as ceremonial causeways, but their unerring straightness harks back to simpler, yet deeper beginnings. The *sacbeob* also had communication purposes, as well as obscure religious associations, indicated by the altars and other architectural devices that occur on them. There are traditions, still extant within the Mayan sphere, that there were also invisible, mythical *sacbeob* running underground and through the air. Some of the physical causeways may have involved astronomical alignments and even mapped out large-scale celestial configurations on the ground (Folan 1991). As well as state-level ceremonial *sacbeob*, there were smaller versions belonging to family groups, and there were even individual ones (Folan personal communication). In northern Mexico the (probably Toltec) citadel of La Quemada had similar kinds of straight causeways radiating out around it.

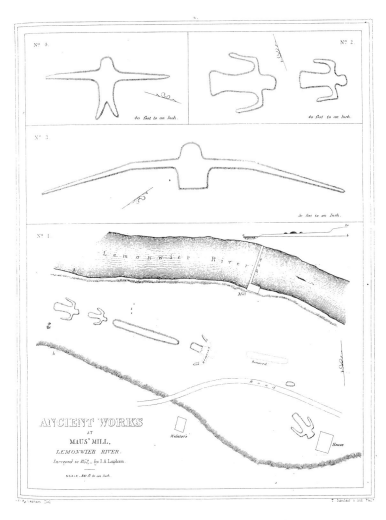

Examples of some effigy mound groundplans, in Wisconsin. (From nineteenth-century surveys by I. A. Lapham.)

include both *intaglios* and petroforms. This area was associated with *Datura*-based shamanism. In the Death Valley–Chocolate Mountains region of southern California there are large-scale petroform designs, principally of the meandering kind and also with enclosures and grids. Shamans' 'hearths' (vision-questing sites) have been detected among the markings (Werlhof 1987). Further north, in the Californian Sierras, the Miwok Indians left long tracks of 'airline straightness' through the rugged terrain. In north-midwestern parts of the United Sates, along the Mississippi Valley and especially in the states of Iowa, Wisconsin and Ohio there was a profusion of effigy mounds, built by the Mississippian Indians and the earlier Hopewell culture, a consortium of Indian peoples who shared a shamanistic religious system. Surviving mounds range from huge earthworks of careful geometric design and large effigy mounds, like the famed Serpent Mound in Ohio or Bear Mound in Iowa, to relatively small mounds depicting a variety of creatures, such as lizards, birds and panthers, as well as geometric forms. Some of the mounds, but by no means all, were used for burial.

In southern Manitoba, Canada, there are a number of petroform sacred landscapes to be found at various locations in the forested wilderness of Whiteshell Provincial Park. The two main ones are Tie Creek and Bannock Point. Of these, Tie Creek is the better preserved, because it is the more remote and access is allowed only with a guide approved by the local

An ancient 'turtle' arrangement of rocks at Bannock Point.

WHERE GOD SITS

Some of the boulder mosaic or petroform patterns and figures at Tie Creek and Bannock Point, Whiteshell Park, Manitoba. The areas of the ground designs are referred to collectively as 'where god sits' by today's Indians.

Left: A mysterious design at the edge of a tablerock area, Tie Creek.

A stone 'bear track' near the forest fringe of a tablerock area at Bannock Point.

Anishinabe (Ojibway) people. The petroform locations are broad areas of exposed tablerock within the forest, on which abstract and figurative designs, large and small, have been laid out by an unknown people long ago using small rocks. The antiquity of some of the features is obvious because of the dense growth of lichen around the rocks, but their exact age is uncertain. Archaeologists have dated an ancient campsite found among the ground markings to AD c.500. The lore of the present-day Anishinabe states that the designs were laid out by the First People, and there are various stories about the meaning of the petroforms. There is no way of knowing if these legends enshrine any fragments of actual, original information or whether they are simply the notions of a later people who moved to the area. The ground designs include large-scale abstract and geometric patterns and enclosures as well as smaller depictions of turtles, snakes and even giant wolf and bear paw marks made from rocks.

The meanings of all these markings throughout the Americas has to lie within the ancient Native American mind, the religious and spiritual beliefs that held sway in the Americas in remote antiquity. All the areas of sacred geography occur in territories that were once, or are still, occupied by shamanistic people, so reinforcing the basic source of the markings, although different kinds of marking related to different aspects of shamanic activity. The meanders, wandering lines and, probably, the enclosures seem to have represented magical symbolic landscapes used in contests between rival shamans. Ethnological information reveals that shamans could 'raise' a power mountain by drawing a line on the ground, creating an insuperable barrier for another shaman to cross (Hoskinson 1992). In addition, a shaman might draw a line or enclosure around himself, representing a magical circle of mountains. The effigy mound and geoglyphs probably related to

'power animals', the spirit familiars used by shamans when they went on their trance journeys to the otherworld and also, in some contexts, totemic creatures. The geometric patterns and shapes in all the ground markings probably related to the entoptic patterns encountered during trance, and they were invested with various cultural meanings, as was the case with some forms of rock art (see Part Two). The origins of the obsession with straight lines also probably lies in entoptic patterns, perhaps especially as an archaic version of the 'tunnel' entoptic form commonly reported in modern out-of-body and near-death experiences (Dobkin de Rios 1977; Devereux 1992, 2000) The use of a line to express this 'spirit flight' sensation is known in rock art, and the ground markings are, essentially, simply larger, horizontal versions of that kind of iconography. The more engineered and structured features, such as ceremonial causeways, were simply the development on these conceptual foundations by more complex, state-scale societies. Even some of the desert lines, like those at Nazca, were walked intensively for unknown, ritualistic purposes, but the Kogi of Colombia say they have to walk their paths, some of which are considered to be physical traces of spirit routes taken by their shamans in the otherworld dimension, because of a religious imperative.

There is much still to learn about these enigmatic landscapes that, like the cursuses in Britain, have been ignored for too long by archaeology. One key reason for this is that they are too rarely perceived as a range of related features. They are disappearing from the land because of the depredations of time and human activity, so their proper appraisal is an urgent matter. It would be a grave loss if they were allowed to slip from our sight, for they probably represent the deepest, most mysterious and telling of the archaeological legacies left to us by ancient peoples.

epilogue

The sacred place in all its ancient forms, whether natural or constructed, is the outcome, the trace, of the human soul's journey through the natural world and perhaps of deep reflexes between mind and nature that we still do not understand and cannot articulate. By returning to the sacred places of antiquity and trying to recognize that the landscape was to our ancestors full of mythic imagery, memory, spirits and powers, we reach back to deep springs of consciousness. Perhaps that effort can enable us to rekindle our own appreciation of the spiritual power of the natural world. It was the land, after all, that first caught our eye and whispered in our ear to tell us about sacred place; all our religions and places of worship came from that early communication. The idea of the holy was inherent in the landscape from all time and it was the landscape that made it stir within our heart and mind.

Holy Hill, Sacred Circle
Swinside stone circle, Cumbria, England.
(John Glover)

bibliography

Although this is a reasonably comprehensive bibliography, it is not complete. It does, however, include references made in the text.

Alcock, S. and Osborne, R. (eds.), *Placing the Gods - Sanctuaries and Sacred Space in Ancient Greece*, Oxford: Clarendon Press, 1994

Allen, N., 'The Thulung Myth of the Bhume Sites and some Indo-Tibetan Comparisons', in Fürer-Haimendorf, *op. cit.*, 1981

Alves, L.B., 'Rock Art and "Enchanted Moors": the Significance of Rock Carvings in the Folklore of Northwest Iberia', paper read at *A Permeability of Boundaries?* conference, University of Southampton, December 1999

Ashmore, W. and Knapp, A. (eds.), *Archaeologies of Landscape*, Oxford: Blackwell, 1999

Bäckman, L. and Hultkrantz, A. (eds.), *Saami Pre-Christian Religion*, Stockholm: Almqvist & Wiskell International, 1983

Bahn, P., 'Palaeolithic Art', in Fagan, *op. cit.*, 1996

Bahn, P. (ed.), *Wonderful Things*, London: Weidenfeld & Nicolson, 1999

Barclay, A. and Harding, J. (eds.), *Pathways and Ceremonies*, Oxford: Oxbow Books, 1999

Barclay, A. and Hey, G., 'Cattle, cursus monuments and the river: the development of ritual and domestic landscapes in the Upper Thames Valley', in Barclay and Harding, *op. cit.*, 1999

Barham, L., Priestley, P. and Targett, A., *In Search of Cheddar Man*, Stroud: Tempus, 1999

Barnes, G., 'Buddhist Landscapes of East Asia', in Ashmore and Knapp, *op. cit.*, 1999

Barrett, J.C., *Fragments of Antiquity*, Oxford: Blackwell, 1994

Basso, K., 'Wisdom Sits in Places: Notes on a Western Apache Landscape', in Feld and Basso, *op. cit.*, 1996a

Basso, K., *Wisdom Sits in Places*, Albuquerque: University of New Mexico Press, 1996b

Beckensall, S., *Prehistoric Rock Motifs of Northumberland*, vol. 2, Hexham: private, 1992

Bender, B. (ed.), *Landscape: Politics and Perspectives*, Providence/Oxford: Berg, 1993

Bergh, S., *Landscape of the Monuments*, Stockholm: University of Stockholm, 1995

Berrin, K. and Pasztory, E. (eds.), *Teotihuacán*, London: Thames and Hudson, 1993

Birge, D., 'Trees in the Landscape of Pausanias' Periegesis', in Alcock and Osborne, *op. cit.*, 1994

Blair, J., *Anglo-Saxon Oxfordshire*, Stroud: Sutton Publishing, 1994

Blofeld, J., *The Wheel of Life*, (1959), London: Rider, 1972

Bloom, J. Harvey, *Folk Lore, Old Customs and Superstitions in Shakespeare Land*, East Ardsley: EP Publishing, 1976 (first published 1930)

Boyd, C., 'Pictographic evidence of peyotism in the Lower Pecos, Texas Archaic', in Chippindale and Taçon, *op. cit.*, 1998

Brady, J. and Ashmore, W., 'Mountains, Caves, Water: Ideational Landscapes of the Ancient Maya', in Ashmore and Knapp, *op. cit.*, 1999

Bradley, R., 'Deaths and Entrances: A Contextual Analysis of Megalithic Art', *Current Anthropology*, vol. 30, no. 1, February 1989

Bradley, R., Foreword to Beckensall, *op. cit.*, 1992

Bradley, R., *Altering the Earth*, Edinburgh: Society of Antiquaries of Scotland, 1993

Bradley, R., 'Symbols and signposts - understanding the prehistoric petroglyphs of the British Isles', in Renfrew, *op. cit.*, 1994

Bradley, R., 'Daggers drawn: depictions of Bronze Age weapons in Atlantic Europe', in Chippindale and Taçon, *op. cit.*, 1998

Bradley, R., *An Archaeology of Natural Places*, London: Routledge, 2000

Brecon Beacons National Park Committee, *Field Monuments in the National Park*, 1983

Brennan, M., *The Stars and the Stones*, London: Thames and Hudson, 1983

Burl, A., *The Stone Circles of the British Isles*, New Haven: Yale University Press, 1976

Burl, A., *Prehistoric Avebury*, New Haven: Yale University Press, 1979

Burl, A., *Megalithic Brittany*, London: Thames and Hudson, 1985

Burl, A., *From Carnac to Callanish*, New Haven: Yale University Press, 1993

Butter, R., *Kilmartin - Scotland's Richest Prehistoric Landscape*, Kilmartin: Kilmartin House Trust, 1999

Cadogan, G., *Palaces of Minoan Crete*, London: Methuen, 1976

Campbell, J. (ed.), *Spirit and Nature*, Princeton: Bollingen edition, Princeton University Press, 1954

Carmichael, D., 'Places of Power: Mescalero Apache sacred sites and sensitive areas', in Carmichael *et al.*, *op. cit.*, 1994

Carmichael, D., Hubert, J., Reeves, B. and Schanche, A. (eds.), *Sacred Sites, Sacred Places*, London: Routledge, 1994

Carr, I., 'In the Wake of Dead Leys', *The Ley Hunter*, no. 131, 1998

Casey, E., 'How to get from Space to Place in a Fairly Short Stretch of Time: Phenomenological Prolegomena', in Feld and Basso, *op. cit.*, 1996

Channel Four Television, *The Time Team Reports*, London, 1995

Chauvet, J.-M., Deschamps, É.B. and Hillaire, C., *Dawn of Art: The Chauvet Cave*, New York: Harry N. Abrams, 1996 (first published 1995)

Chippindale, C. and Taçon, P.S.C., 'The many ways of dating Arnhem Land rock art, north Australia', in Chippindale and Taçon, *op. cit.*, 1998

Chippindale, C. and Taçon, P.S.C. (eds.), *The Archaeology of Rock Art*, Cambridge: Cambridge University Press, 1998

Clarke, D., 'The Hag's House', *The Ley Hunter*, no. 120, 1994

Clottes, J., 'The "Three Cs": fresh avenues towards European palaeolithic art', in Chippindale and Taçon, *op. cit.*, 1998

Cooper, R., 'Some Oxfordshire Leys', *The Ley Hunter*, no. 86., 1979

Corbin, H., *Spiritual Body and Celestial Earth*, London: I.B. Taurus, 1990 (first published 1976)

Cornelius, G. and Devereux, P., *The Secret Language of the Stars and Planets*, London: Pavilion, 1996

Cotterell, A., *The Bull of Minos*, London: Pan Books, 1963 (first published 1953)

Cotterell, A., *The Minoan World*, London: Michael Joseph, 1979

Critchlow, K., *Time Stands Still*, London: Gordon Fraser, 1979

Crumley, C., 'Sacred Landscapes: Constructed and Conceptualized', in Ashmore and Knapp, *op. cit.*, 1999

Davidson, H.R. Ellis, *Pagan Scandinavia*, London: Thames and Hudson, 1967

Dayton, L., 'Rock art evokes beastly echoes of the past', *New Scientist*, 28 November 1992

Deacon, J., 'The power of place in understanding southern San rock engravings',

World Archaeology, vol. 20, no. 1, 1988

Devereux, P., 'Three-dimensional aspects of apparent relationships between selected natural and artificial features within the topography of the Avebury Complex', *Antiquity*, vol. 65, no. 249, December 1991

Devereux, P., *Symbolic Landscapes*, Glastonbury: Gothic Image, 1992

Devereux, P., *Shamanism and the Mystery Lines*, London: Quantum, 1992b

Devereux, P., *Re-Visioning the Earth*, New York: Fireside/Simon and Schuster, 1996

Devereux, P., *The Long Trip*, New York: Penguin Arkana, 1997

Devereux, P., *The Illustrated Encyclopedia of Ancient Earth Mysteries*, London: Cassell, 2000

Devereux, P. and Jahn, R.G., 'Preliminary investigations and cognitive considerations of the acoustical resonances of selected archaeological sites', *Antiquity*, vol. 70, no. 269, September 1996

Dobkin de Rios, M., 'Plant Hallucinogens, Out-of-Body Experiences and New World Monumental Earthworks' in Du Toit, *op. cit.*, 1977

Donohue, V.A., 'The Goddess of the Theban Mountain', *Antiquity*, vol. 66, no. 253, December 1992

Dowson, T., *Rock Engravings of Southern Africa*, Johannesburg: Witwatersrand University Press, 1992

Dronfield, J., 'Migraine, Light and Hallucinogens: The Neurocognitive Basis of Irish Megalithic Art', *Oxford Journal of Archaeology*, vol. 14, no. 3, 1995

Du Toit, B. (ed.), *Drugs, Rituals and Altered States of Consciousness*, Rotterdam: A.A. Balkema, 1977

Dyer, J., *The Penguin Guide to Prehistoric England and Wales*, London: Allen Lane, 1981

Eck, D., 'India's Tirthas: "Crossings" in Sacred Geography', *History of Religions*, vol. 20, no. 4, 1981

Eliade, M., *Shamanism: Archaic Techniques of Ecstasy*, Princeton: Bollingen edition, Princeton University Press, 1964 (first published 1951)

Eliade, M., *Yoga*, London: Penguin Arkana, 1988 (first published 1958)

Eliade, M., *The Myth of the Eternal Return*, Harmondsworth: Arkana, 1989 (first published 1954)

Eliade, M., 'The World, the City, the House', in Twiss and Conser, *op. cit.*, 1992 (first published 1976)

Evans, A.J., *The Mycenaean Tree and Pillar Cult*, London: Macmillan, 1901

Fagan, B., *The Oxford Companion to Archaeology*, Oxford: Oxford University Press, 1996

Favaloro, C., 'Cretan Geomancy', *The Ley Hunter*, no. 105, 1988

Feld, S., 'Waterfalls of Song', in Feld and Basso, *op. cit.*, 1996

Feld, S. and Basso, K. (eds.), *Senses of Place*, Santa Fe: School of American Research Press, 1996

Fergusson, J., *Rude Stone Monuments in All Countries*, London: John Murray, 1872

Fjellström, P., 'Sacrifices, burial gifts and buried treasures: function and material', in Bäckman and Hultkrantz, *op. cit.*, 1983

Flood, G. (ed.), *Mapping Invisible Worlds*, Edinburgh: Edinburgh University Press, 1993

Folan, W., 'Sacbes of the northern Maya', in Trombold, *op. cit.*, 1991

Frankel, D., 'Australian Rock Art', in Fagan, *op. cit.*, 1996

Fraser, D., 'Land and Society in Neolithic Orkney', B.A.R. no. 117, Part 2, 1983

Freidel, D., Schele, L. and Parker J., *Maya Cosmos*, New York: William Morrow, 1993

Friar, S., *The Batsford Companion to Local History*, London: Batsford, 1991

Fürer-Haimendorf, C. von (ed.), *Asian Highland Societies in Anthropological Perspective*, New Delhi: Sterling Publishers, 1981

Furst, P., *Hallucinogens and Culture*, Novato: Chandler and Sharp, 1976

Garwood, P., Jennings, D., Skeates, R. and Toms, J. (eds.), *Sacred and Profane*, Oxford: Oxford University Committee for Archaeology, 1991

Gelling, M., *The Place-Names of Berkshire*, Nottingham: English Place-Name Society, 1974

Gibson, A., 'Stonehenge and Timber Circles', 3rd Stone, no. 34, April-June 1999

Goulstone, J., *The Summer Solstice Games*, private, 1985

Green, M.J., *Dictionary of Celtic Myth and Legend*, London: Thames and Hudson, 1992

Green, M.J., 'On the Road', *British Archaeology*, no. 52, April 2000

Greenhalgh, M. and McGraw, V. (eds.), *Art in Society*, London: Duckworth, 1978

Guchte, M. van de, 'The Inca Cognition of Landscape', in Ashmore and Knapp, *op. cit.*, 1999

Hadingham, E., *Ancient Carvings in Britain: A Mystery*, London: Garnstone Press, 1974

Hall, R., *An Archaeology of the Soul*, Urbana: University of Illinois Press, 1997

Halpern, D. (ed.), *On Nature*, San Francisco: North Point Press, 1987 (first published 1986)

Harbison, P., *Pre-Christian Ireland*, London: Thames and Hudson, 1988

Harner, M., *The Jivaro - People of the Sacred Waterfalls*, Berkeley: University of California Press, 1984 (first published 1972)

Hartley, R. and Wolley Vawser, A., 'Spatial behaviour and learning in the prehistoric environment of the Colorado River drainage (southeastern Utah), western North America', in Chippindale and Taçon, *op. cit.*, 1998

Herdick, R., 'Remarks on the Orientation of the Large Stupas in the Kathmandu Valley: A Discussion of Principles of Lunar Ordering', in Ramble and Brauen, *op. cit.*, 1993

Hirsch, E. and O'Hanlon, M. (eds.), *The Anthropology of Landscape*, Oxford: Clarendon Press, 1995

Hooke, D., *Anglo-Saxon England*, London: Leicester University Press, 1998

Hoskinson, T., 'Saguaro Wine, Ground Figures and Power Mountains: Investigations at Sears Point, Arizona', in Williamson and Farrer, *op. cit.*, 1992

Huber, T., 'Putting the *gnas* back into *gnas-kor*: Rethinking Tibetan Buddhist Pilgrimage Practice', *The Tibet Journal*, vol. 19, no. 2, 1994

Hubert, J., 'Sacred beliefs and beliefs of sacredness', in Carmichael et al., *op. cit.*, 1994

Humphrey, C., 'Chiefly and Shamanist Landscapes in Mongolia', in Hirsch and O'Hanlon, *op. cit.*, 1995

Johnston, R., 'An empty path? Processions, memories and the Dorset Cursus', in Barclay and Harding, *op. cit.*, 1999

Joussaume, R., *Dolmens for the Dead*, London: Batsford, 1987 (first published 1985)

Jung, C., 'The Spirit of Psychology', in Campbell, *op. cit.*, 1954

Kahn, M., 'Your Place and Mine: Sharing Emotional Landscapes in Wamira, Papua New Guinea', in Feld and Basso, *op. cit.*, 1996

Kaplan, R., 'The Sacred Mushrooms in Scandinavia', *Man*, no. 10, 1975

Kelly, J., *An Archaeological Guide to Mexico's Yucatán Peninsula*, Norman: University of Oklahoma Press, 1993

Kerenyi, C., *Eleusis*, Princeton: Princeton University Press, 1967

Kinnes, I., 'Longtemps ignoreés: Passy-Rots, linear monuments in northern France', in Barclay and Harding, *op. cit.*, 1999

Kitigawa, J., 'Three Types of Pilgrimage in Japan', in Twiss and Conser, *op. cit.*, 1992

Kjellström, R., 'Piles of bones, cult-places or something else?', in Bäckman and Hultkrantz, *op. cit.*, 1983

Kolata, A., *Valley of the Spirits*, New York: John Wiley, 1996

Law, B.C., *Geography of Early Buddhism*, New Delhi: Oriental Books Reprints, 1979 (first published 1932)

Levy-Bruhl, L., *Primitive Mythology*, St Lucia: University of Queensland Press, 1983 (first published 1935)

Lewis-Williams, J.D., 'Upper palaeolithic art in the 1990s: a southern African perspective', *South African Journal of Science*, vol. 87, September 1991

Lewis-Williams, J.D., 'Rock Art and Ritual: Southern Africa and Beyond', *Complutum*, no. 5, 1994

Lewis-Williams, J.D. and Dowson, T., 'The Signs of All Times', *Current Anthropology*, vol. 29, no. 2, April 1988

Lewis-Williams, J.D. and Dowson, T., *Images of Power*, Johannesburg: Southern Book Publishers, 1989

Lewis-Williams, J.D. and Dowson T., 'Through the Veil: San Rock Paintings and the Rock Face', *South African Archaeological Bulletin*, 45, 1990

Loveday, R., 'Dorchester-on-Thames - ritual complex or ritual landscape?', in Barclay and Harding, *op. cit.* 1999

Malone, C., *Avebury*, London: Batsford, 1989

Malville, J. McKim, 'Astronomy at Vijayanagara: Sacred Geography Confronts the Cosmos', in Singh, *op. cit.*, 1993

Marshack, A., *The Roots of Civilization*, New York: McGraw-Hill, 1972

Matunga, H., 'Waahi tapu: Maori sacred sites', in Carmichael et al., *op. cit.*, 1994

McCafferty, G., 'The Sacred Cenote of Chichén Itzá', in Bahn, *op. cit.*, 1999

McKenna, P. and Truell, M., *Small Site Architecture of Chaco Canyon*, New Mexico, Santa Fe: US Park Service, US Department of the Interior, 1986

Meaden, T., *The Stonehenge Solution*, London: Souvenir Press, 1992

Mercer, H., *The Hill-Caves of Yucatán*, Norman: University of Oklahoma Press, 1975 (first published 1896)

Michell, J., *The Old Stones of Land's End*, London: Garnstone Press, 1974

Michell, J., *Simulacra*, London: Thames and Hudson, 1979

Miller, M and Taube, K., *The Gods and Symbols of Ancient Mexico and the Maya*, London: Thames and Hudson, 1993

Millon, R., 'The Place Where Time Began: An Archaeologist's Interpretation of What Happened in Teotihuacán History', in Berrin and Pasztory, *op. cit.*, 1993

Mohen, J.-P., *The World of Megaliths*, London: Cassell, 1989

Mohs, G., 'Stolo sacred ground', in Carmichael et al., *op. cit.*, 1994

Moore, T., 'Animus mundi, or the bull at the center of the world', Spring, 14, 1987

Mountford, C., *Winbaraku and the Myth of Jarapiri*, Adelaide: Rigby, 1968

Mulk, I.-M., 'Sacrificial places and their meaning in Saami society', in Carmichael et al., *op. cit.*, 1994

Mumah, M., 'Sacred sites in the Bamenda Grassfields of Cameroon: a study of sacred sites of the Nso' Fondom', in Carmichael et al., *op. cit.*, 1994

Mylonas, G., *Eleusis and the Eleusian Mysteries*, Princeton: Princeton University Press, 1972 (first published 1961)

Nash, G., 'The landscape brought within: a re-evaluation of the rock painting site at Tumlehed, Torslanda, West Sweden', *The Ley Hunter*, no. 129, 1998

Neihardt, J., *Black Elk Speaks*, New York: Pocket Books, 1972 (first published 1932)

Newman, C., 'Notes on four cursus-like monuments in County Meath, Ireland', in Barclay and Harding, *op. cit.*, 1999

O'Keefe, J. and Nadel, L., *The Hippocampus as a Cognitive Map*, Oxford: Clarendon Press, 1978

O'Kelly, C., *Concise Guide to Newgrange*, Cork: private, 1996

Otto, R., *The Idea of the Holy*, Oxford: Oxford University Press, 1924

Ouzman, S., 'Towards a mindscape of land-scape: rock art as expression of world-understanding', in Chippindale and Taçon, *op. cit.*, 1998

Ovsyannikov, O. and Terebikhin, N., 'Sacred space in the culture of the Arctic regions', in Carmichael et al., *op. cit.*, 1994

Panagiotakis, G., *The Dictaean Cave*, Lasithi: private, 1988

Patterson, A., *Rock Art Symbols of the Greater Southwest*, Boulder: Johnson Books, 1992

Patton, M., 'On Entoptic Images in Context: Art, Monuments and Society in Neolithic Brittany', *Current Anthropology*, vol. 31, no. 5, December 1990

Patton, M., *Statements in Stone*, London: Routledge, 1993

Peatfield, A., 'After the "Big Bang" - What? Or: Minoan Symbols and Shrines beyond Palatial Collapse', in Alcock and Osborne, *op. cit.*, 1994

Pennick, N., *Celtic Sacred Landscapes*, London: Thames and Hudson, 1996

Pennick, N. and Devereux, P., *Lines on the Landscape*, London: Robert Hale, 1989

Radimilahy, C., 'Sacred sites in Madagascar', in Carmichael et al., *op. cit.*, 1994

Rajnovich, G., *Reading Rock Art*, Toronto: Natural Heritage/Natural History Inc., 1994

Ramble, C. and Brauen, M. (eds.), *Anthropology of Tibet and the Himalaya*, Zurich: Ethnological Museum of the University of Zurich, 1993

Ray, H.P., 'Kanheri: the archaeology of an early Buddhist pilgrimage centre in west-ern India', *World Archaeology*, vol. 26, no. 1, June 1994

RCAHMS, Kilmartin - *Prehistoric and Early Historic Monuments*, Edinburgh, 1999

Reichel-Dolmatoff, G., 'Drug-induced Optical Sensations and their Relationship to Applied Art among some Colombian Indians', in Greenhalgh and McGraw, *op. cit.*, 1978

Renfrew, C., 'Investigations in Orkney', *Reports of the Research Committee of the Society of Antiquaries*, no. 38, 1979

Renfrew, C., *The Ancient Mind- - Elements of Cognitive Archaeology*, Cambridge: Cambridge University Press, 1994

Richards, C., 'Monuments as landscape: creating the centre of the world in late Neolithic Orkney', *World Archaeology*, vol. 28, no. 2, October 1996

Richards, J., 'Conceptual Landscapes in the Egyptian Nile Valley', in Ashmore and Knapp, *op. cit.*, 1999

Ross, A., *The Pagan Celts*, London: Batsford, 1986 (first published 1970)

Sack, R.D., 'Magic and Space', *Annals, Association of American Geographers*, vol. 66, no. 2, June 1976

Sales, K., 'Ascent to the sky: A shamanic initiatory engraving from the Burrup Peninsula, northwest Western Australia', *Archaeol. Oceania*, no. 27, 1992

Sanmiguel, I., 'A ceremony in the "cave of idolatry": an eighteenth-century docu-ment from the Diocesan Historic Archive, Chiapas, Mexico' in Carmichael et al., *op. cit.*, 1994

Saunders, N., 'At the mouth of the obsidian cave: deity and place in Aztec religion', in Carmichael et al., *op. cit.*, 1994

Schaafsma, P., *Indian Rock Art of the Southwest*, Santa Fe/Albuquerque: School of American Research/ University of New Mexico Press, 1980

Schaafsma, P., 'North American Rock Art', in Fagan, *op. cit.*, 1996

Scully, V., *The Earth, the Temple and the Gods*, New Haven: Yale University Press, 1979 (first published 1962)

Sherratt, A., 'Sacred and Profane Substances: The Ritual Use of Narcotics in

Later Neolithic Europe', in Garwood et al., *op. cit.*, 1991

Silko, L., 'Landscape, History and the Pueblo Imagination', in Halpern, *op. cit.*, 1987

Singh, R.P.B. (ed.), *The Spirit and Power of Place*, Varanasi: National Geographic Society of India/Benares Hindu University, 1993

Smith, J., 'The Experience of the Holy and the Idea of God', in Twiss and Conser, *op. cit.*, 1992

Sognnes, K., 'Symbols in a changing world: rock art and the transition from hunting to farming in mid-Norway', in Chippindale and Taçon, *op. cit.*, 1998

Stone, A.J., *Images from the Underworld*, Austin: University of Texas Press, 1995

Straffon, C., *The Earth Mysteries Guide to Mid-Cornwall and the Lizard*, Penzance: Meyn Mamvro Publications, 1994

Stutchbury, E., 'Perceptions of Landscape in Karzha: "Sacred" Geography and the Tibetan System of "Geomancy"', *The Tibet Journal*, vol. 19, no. 4, 1994

Thackeray, F. and Knox-Shaw, P., 'Astronomical and Entoptic Phenomena', *MNASSA*, vol. 51, 1992

Theodoratus, D. and Lapena, F., 'Wintu sacred geography of northern California', in Carmichael *et al.*, *op. cit.*, 1994

Thom, A., *Megalithic Sites in Britain*, Oxford: Clarendon Press, 1967

Thomas, J., *Time, Culture and Identity*, London: Routledge, 1996

Thompson, J.E.S., *The Rise and Fall of Maya Civilization*, Norman: University of Oklahoma Press, 1964

Thompson, J.E.S., in the Introduction to Mercer, *op. cit.*, 1975

Tilley, C. (ed.), *Interpretative Archaeology*, Providence/Oxford: Berg, 1993a

Tilley, C., 'Art, Architecture, Landscape [Neolithic Sweden]', in Bender, *op. cit.*, 1993b

Tilley, C., *A Phenomenology of Landscape*, Providence/Oxford: Berg, 1994

Tilley, C., 'The powers of rocks: topography and monument construction on Bodmin Moor', in *World Archaeology*, vol. 28, no. 2, October 1996

Toren, C., 'Seeing the Ancestral Sites: Transformations in Fijian Notions of the Land', in Hirsch and O'Hanlon, *op. cit.*, 1995

Townsend, R. (ed.), *The Ancient Americas - Art from Sacred Landscapes*, Chicago: Art Institute of Chicago, 1992

Townsend, R., *The Aztecs*, London: Thames and Hudson, 1993 (first published 1992)

Trombold, C. (ed.), *Ancient Road Networks and Settlement Hierarchies in the New World*, Cambridge: Cambridge University Press, 1991

Tuan, Y.-F., *Passing Strange and Wonderful*, New York: Kodansha International, 1995 (first published 1993)

Twiss, S. and Conser, W. (eds.), *Experience of the Sacred*, Hanover, NH: Brown University Press, 1992

Tyler, H., *Pueblo Gods and Myths*, Norman: University of Oklahoma Press, 1964

Vorren, Ø., 'Circular sacrificial sites and their function', in Bäckman and Hultkrantz, *op. cit.*, 1983

Walderhaug, E., 'Changing art in a changing society: the hunters' rock art of western Norway', in Chippindale and Taçon, *op. cit.*, 1998

Walker, J., *Lakota Belief and Ritual*, Lincoln: University of Nebraska Press, 1991 (first published 1980)

Walter, D., *Closed Mouths and Empty Voices: Categories of Shamanic Experience and the Presence of Place in the Nepal Himalayas*, University of London: unpublished dissertation, 1995

Walter, E.V., *Placeways*, Chapel Hill: University of North Carolina Press, 1988

Wandibba, S., 'Bukusu sacred sites', in Carmichael *et al.*, *op. cit.*, 1994

Weatherhill, C., *Cornovia - Ancient Sites of Cornwall and Scilly*, Newmill: Alison Hodge, 1985

Werbner, R., *Ritual Passage, Sacred Journey*, Washington, D.C.: Smithsonian Institution Press, 1989

Werlhof, J. von, *Spirits of the Earth*, El Centro: Imperial Valley College Museum, 1987

Whitley, D., 'By the Hunter, for the Gatherer: Art, Social Relations and Subsistence Change in the Prehistoric Great Basin', *World Archaeology*, vol. 25, no. 3, February 1994

Whitley, D., *A Guide to Rock Art Sites*, Missoula: Mountain Press, 1996

Whitley, D., 'Finding rain in the desert: landscape, gender and far western North American rock art', in Chippindale and Taçon, *op. cit.*, 1998

Whitley, D., Dorn, R.I., Simon, J.M., Rechtman, R. and Whitley, T.K., 'Sally's Rockshelter and the Archaeology of the Vision Quest', *Cambridge Archaeological Journal*, vol. 9, no. 2, 1999

Williamson, R. and Farrer, C. (eds.), *Earth and Sky*, Albuquerque: University of New Mexico Press, 1992

Woodley, H., 'Prehistoric Sites in their Landscape Context', *The Ley Hunter*, no. 108, 1989

Woodward, A., *Memories of Brailes*, Shipston-on-Stour: Peter Drinkwater, 1988

Zachrisson, I., 'New archaeological finds from the territory of the Southern Saami', in Bäckman and Hultkrantz, *op. cit.*, 1983

index